D1195317

ORNAMENT

A MODERN PERSPECTIVE

JAMES TRILLING

A SAMUEL AND ALTHEA STROUM BOOK

University of Washington Press   Seattle & London

ORNAMENT

A MODERN PERSPECTIVE

This book is published with the assistance of a grant from the Stroum Book Fund,
established through the generosity of Samuel and Althea Stroum.

Library of Congress Cataloging-in-Publication Data

Trilling, James

Ornament : a modern perspective / James Trilling.

p. cm.—(Samuel and Althea Stroum lectures in Jewish studies)

Includes bibliographical references and index.

ISBN 0-295-98148-2 (alk. paper)

1. Decoration and ornament. 2. Modernism (Art) I. Title.

NK1175 .T55   2002

745.4'09'04—dc21   2001027508

The paper used in this publication is acid-free and recycled from 10 percent post-consumer and at least 50 percent pre-consumer waste. It meets the minimum requirements of American National Standard for Information Sciences—Permanence of Paper for Printed Library Materials, ANSI Z39.48–1984.

No architecture is so haughty as that which is simple;

which refuses to address the eye, except in a few clear and forceful lines;

which implies, in offering so little to our regards, that all it has offered is

perfect; and disdains, either by the complexity or the attractiveness of

its features, to embarrass our investigation, or betray us into delight.

JOHN RUSKIN, *The Stones of Venice*

You see, but you do not observe.

ARTHUR CONAN DOYLE, "A Scandal in Bohemia"

CONTENTS

ILLUSTRATIONS

PREFACE

LESS THAN A hundred years ago, anyone who cared about art cared about ornament. Today we scarcely know what it is. We have no shared definition, no sense of its history, its uses, how to look at it, least of all how to make it. Ornament is not *adornment*, a far broader term for everything that beautifies, from hairstyles to trees in a park. It is not *ornaments*, trinkets you put on the mantelpiece. Ornament is a specific word for a specific thing, yet it cuts across all the arts. It is the art we add to art: shapes and patterns worked into an object or building for the pleasure of outline, color, or fantasy. Often ornament is so familiar as to work subliminally, a kind of visual background music. Sometimes, unpredictably, it claims our full attention.

Ornament has been in disrepute for almost a century. I wrote this book to revive it. If I succeed, you will never look at a bolt of cloth—or a cathedral—in quite the same way again. For this to happen, the book must speak to architects and builders, and the people they build for; to designers and the people they design for; to masters and amateurs in every craft, from ceramics to knitting to blacksmithing; to collectors and dealers; to scholars, teachers, and students in the history of all the arts. It must speak to everyone who furnishes a home with care, goes to museums for pleasure, or spares a glance for the beauty or ugliness of a neighborhood.

I do not know if any book can hold so many interests, but it is vitally important to try. The world we live in is no longer the world that put a ban on ornament. Ornament is creeping back into our artistic lives, but in a haphazard, tentative, even furtive way. In the nineteenth century, books on ornament were everywhere. Anyone with an interest knew where to turn for guidance. Today there is no such thing as a general book on ornament that assumes no previous knowledge of the subject. There are historical, technical, and theoretical books, some of them very good, but they take too much for granted to win over a society as mistrustful of ornament as ours has been.[1] Even the knowledge of specialists lacks a larger focus. There are styles of art in which ornament predominates (Hiberno-Saxon, Islamic, and early Chinese, for example) and people who study them, but there is no modern tradition of *ornament studies*.

If we decide to have ornament again, no doubt we will have it. The only question is what kind. Ornament is almost never "original"; the skill lies in turning a recognized form into something different—familiar but also unique. To create an ornamental style one must have models, familiar forms passed down from generation to generation or borrowed from an earlier time or a foreign culture. Since our tradition of ornament has been interrupted, some of the most interesting models may be difficult to find—perhaps hidden away in books or museums off the beaten track. The "classic" literature on ornament is only a hundred years old, give or take a few decades, but its assumptions about art and society might as well have come from another world. Relying on the great studies and handbooks of the nineteenth century would be like traveling in a foreign country with a hundred-year-old guidebook telling how to get around, what to see, where to eat: a fascinating historical exercise but a disaster from a practical standpoint.

Reinventing ornament piecemeal will result in a style or styles of our own (there is nothing wrong with having several), but the process will be slow and wasteful. Doubly so, because taste as well as knowledge can become rusty with disuse. People who have been taught that ornament is beneath contempt are unlikely to develop an "eye" for it overnight. Nevertheless, many have a better eye for ornament than they realize, because the ban was never completely effective. It may not occur to us that when we pick out a rug, necktie, wallpaper, knitting pattern, or set of china, we are favoring one style of ornament over another. To make the best choices, not only as consumers but as designers and makers, we need only sharpen our everyday sense of style, so that we know *why* we like some things and not others, and combine it with the widest possible awareness of past and foreign styles.

This book is part visual guide and part cultural history. It explains how ornament works, and why it has to be explained. It is not a survey of styles, an anthology of patterns, or a detailed history of ornament. I have tried to illustrate a broad range of objects, but the choice was often limited. The pictures follow the argument, not vice versa. The resulting omissions or near-omissions would be inexcusable in a survey: Chinese ornament, for instance, and one of the most fertile European styles, the Gothic, not to mention my personal favorite, the Mycenean style with its unique blend of harshness and refinement (a particularly sad omission because so few specimens are on view outside Greece). In contrast, the European rococo is overrepresented. One reason is its complexity: if you can understand rococo ornament, you can understand any ornament. Another reason is the hostility it continues to provoke, a response that contributed in no small way to the modern prejudice against ornament itself. Both for the style's own sake and for a better understanding of its historical role, I thought it worth a slight imbalance to set the record straight.

Most of my examples come from Europe and western Asia. This is what I know best. It is also the material that best illustrates the wonderful adaptability of ornament. Like the history of the region itself, the history of its ornament is both continuous and fragmented, a kaleidoscope of unique but related civilizations. But unity-in-diversity is only part of the picture. Similar patterns can arise in very different cultures. Is this chance, human nature, or the legacy of connections hitherto unguessed? These questions are never far beneath the surface. Small wonder that until quite recently, art historians wishing to confront the central issues of historical change, cultural identity, and the nature of style and meaning often chose to approach them through ornament.

The first half of the book is an introduction to ornament: what it is, how to look at it, how styles evolve, how to "read" ornament for symbolic meanings (and how *not* to). The second half is about recent attitudes toward ornament, especially the reasons why it fell into disrepute. Most people think that machinery and mass production killed ornament, and that around the turn of the century European and American architects, designers, and critics nailed the coffin shut by declaring that less is more, form should follow function, and ornament is a crime. This explanation has the virtue of neatness and the strength of historical inevitability, but it is simplistic. On the one hand, cosmophobia—fear of ornament or, more loosely, prejudice against it—was already strong *before* the Industrial Revolution.[2] Mass production was only the last straw. On the other hand, the modern movement never really rejected ornament. Its founders created a new ornamental style which they could pretend was a rejection of ornament. They succeeded so well that for generations we have accepted the pretense as the truth.

To understand the rejection of ornament, imagined and real, we must look deep into the old fear of art as deception and corruption. When I began the search I had no idea it would encompass, among many other elements, the wars between Greece and Persia in the fifth century B.C., pagan and Christian myths of transformation, evolutionary theory before Darwin, Protestant sects in England, and the role of "primitive" societies in the development of modern social thought. Scholars will find familiar texts and ideas thrown together in unfamiliar ways. Beginners looking for a summary of what "happened" may feel bombarded with material on a succession of unrelated topics. I hope that even casual readers will follow the investigation to its end. It is worth the effort. The prejudice against ornament is cultural and religious, political and economic. To understand why and how these currents converged is more than a preparation for a new look at ornament. It is a lesson in how the past continues to shape the present. I have tried to preserve the sense of adventure I felt as I moved further and further into new territory. It is not an easy journey, but if it were, it would not be an adventure.

Anyone who turns to the nineteenth-century literature of ornament, or the twentieth-century literature of cosmophobia, will see that it is ideologically loaded. *What is right? What is moral? Honest? Progressive?* Although answers to these questions vary, all have the certainty of dogma. We need not fall into the same trap. Ornament has many uses, but they are subordinate to its one great purpose: to give pleasure. The question we should be asking is simply: *What gives the most pleasure, and how can we best achieve it?*

Others have asked this disingenuously, as a prelude to telling people what *should* give them pleasure. Since no one is completely without bias, let me put my ideological cards, such as they are, on the table. I am "for" ornament, and therefore "against" any system that exalts ideology over taste. Every age has its own moral agenda, but an introductory book needs a better foundation than the polemics of the moment. It must stand outside cultural fashion, or fashion will sweep it away. Nothing dulls so quickly as a cutting edge.

Far too often, moral judgments on art are a substitute for the skill and confidence to judge aesthetically. There is good ornament and bad ornament; the only way to tell the difference is to look hard at as many kinds as possible, asking each time which ones you like best, and why. I have my own preferences, and I see no point in either hiding them or presenting them as universal truths. There is only one kind of ornament I reject on principle, regardless of how it looks. That is ornament which spoils the usefulness of an object *made for use*. Think of an otherwise well-designed knife, not a display piece, whose decorated handle makes it uncomfortable or dangerous to hold.

In subtitling my book "A Modern Perspective," I have in mind both possible meanings of the word *modern: up-to-date* and *modernist.* The first is self-explanatory, but the second appears paradoxical. How can an introduction to ornament be modernist, when modernism was the sworn enemy of ornament? I have already hinted that the modernist response to ornament was more complex and less antagonistic than most people recognize, but this is not the only answer. I am also using the terms *modern* and *modernist* in specific contrast to *postmodern* and *postmodernist.* Whatever obstacles a modernist work of art may place in our path, its emphasis will be overwhelmingly on personal expression and engagement. Much of its difficulty will be the difficulty of engaging the artist's vision directly, with little or no help from conventions of style and content. The artist expects us to learn a new visual language, and in the process to explore the relation between perception and conception—in effect, to reexperience art from the ground up. Although it has its playful aspects, modernism as a whole is serious business.

The great exception is the branch of modernism called dadaism, with its agenda of disengagement, mockery, and irony. Postmodernism carries the dadaist agenda into the twenty-first century. Where modernism is the apotheosis of individual vision, postmodernism literally makes a joke of that vision. Thus, although postmodernism is often hailed as the savior of ornament from its modernist exile, irony has undercut the movement's promising eclecticism, and kept a true postmodern ornament from flowering. Against all expectations, it is modernism, sometimes whimsical but rarely ironic, and passionately visual despite its intellectualism, that preserves the spirit of ornament. Only very recently have efforts to fuse modern and postmodern aesthetics moved beyond superficiality. My epilogue presents one example of this fusion. The potential benefit to ornament is vast. The prognosis, still inconclusive on a cultural scale, is hopeful.[3]

Acknowledgments

I COULD NOT have written this book without a great deal of help. Whether it came in casual talk or formal consultation, it was equally necessary and equally welcome. I would like to thank the following: Edward Ahearn, the American Museum of Natural History, Leonard Andrade, Phil Beauchemin, Maggie Bickford, Carol Bier, Sarah Brett-Smith, David Brussat, Sheila Canby, the late Albert Cook, Anne Fausto-Sterling, Catherine Gill, David Gillerman, Mattiebelle Gittinger, Oleg Grabar, Charles Hartman, John Hollander, Renata Holod, Richard Hurley, Herbert Kessler, Deborah Klimburg-Salter, Franny Cohen Koch and Stephen Koch, David Konstan, David Lattimore, Joy C. Levy and the late Marion J. Levy Jr., Stephanie Merrim, Fritz Mote, Jeffrey Muller, Karen Newman, Maureen O'Brian, Cathleen Phillips, David Pingree, Melissa Rinne, the late Naomi Schor, Natasha Staller, Fritz Stern, Joseph Trapp, the late Diana Trilling, the Victoria and Albert Museum, Arthur Vidich, Arthur Waldron, Al Weisberg, and Jeffrey Wishik. I have tried to list everyone whose knowledge guided, ideas inspired, or enthusiasm encouraged me, but in such a diverse project a few names are bound to have slipped through the net. Those whom I inadvertently left out, please accept my apologies with my thanks.

Some of you have given me assistance above and beyond the call of duty. Susan Hay and Pam Parmal, of the Department of Costumes and Textiles at the Rhode Island School of Design Museum of Art, helped at every stage with their knowledge and cheerful willingness to make the resources of the collection available to me at a moment's notice.

When a portion of this book appeared in *Common Knowledge*, the editors, Jeffrey

Perl and Robert Nelsen, did far more than see a manuscript through the press. Selecting, condensing, and recombining, they created what would have seemed a new piece of work, were it not so completely my own. It was a master class in editing, and I have done my best to apply their lesson to the manuscript as a whole.

Few privileges are more often wasted than a general education, and mine was no expection. Two people gave the priceless gift of a second chance, and with it a new perspective on Western history. Charles Gillispie of Princeton University read the second half of the manuscript and did his best to weed out the most glaring scientific errors. In the process he showed me the glory—no other word will do—of early modern science, and made the Enlightenment a reality for me at last. Whatever misconceptions remain are mine alone. Robert Macieski, former curator of the Slater Mill Historic Site in Pawtucket, Rhode Island, opened my eyes to the history of labor, whose shaping role in our cultural (as distinct from social and economic) lives I had never suspected. His instruction will always be a part of me, though he may not agree with the use I made of it.

One stranger deserves the same special thanks as those who worked closely with me. This is the late Patrick O'Brian, author of the Aubrey and Maturin novels, which were almost my only recreational reading for the two hardest years of the project. On page 43 of *The Truelove* it was my great good fortune to meet a relative on the deck of the *Surprise*, Captain Aubrey's beloved frigate. This chance encounter had the quality of a blessing, a tremendous lift to my morale when I least expected and most needed it.

Naomi Pascal, Julidta Tarver, Marilyn Trueblood, and Xavier Callahan, of the University of Washington Press, encouraged me with their insights and their sustained enthusiasm for the project. Leila Charbonneau, the copyeditor, tracked down errors and inconsistencies in the manuscript with a diligence I would not have believed possible. The readers' reports were exceptionally learned and constructive.

My wife, Dore J. Levy, watched a straightforward history of ornament evolve into a ten-year exploration of almost everything else. Never knowing where the search might lead, or how it might end (there must have been times when it seemed unlikely to end at all), she not only kept her patience but contrived to keep a step or two ahead of me, waiting at every difficult turn with insight, common sense, and the kind of humor that cuts even the biggest problems down to size. My debt of thanks to her is beyond words. My daughters, Gabriel and Julian Trilling, have lived with "the ornament book" for as long as they can remember. Their love and unflagging encouragement were instrumental in helping me finish it.

This book is dedicated to the memory of Jeannette Mirsky (1903–1987), world traveler and world-class eccentric, collector and connoisseur of ornament, historian of exploration and industry, who combined the rigor of traditional scholarship with an ever youthful delight in new discoveries and unlikely connections. A lifelong independent scholar, she encouraged me by example as I prepared to embark on a similar career. Her other accomplishments include introducing me to my wife.

JAMES TRILLING

Providence, Rhode Island

ORNAMENT

A MODERN PERSPECTIVE

Introduction

MODERNISM DID TO art what monoculture did to farming. A change of climate sends us scurrying, unprepared, for resources that were ready to hand a hundred years ago. Ornament is one of those resources. Its rediscovery offers more than a new infusion of decorative forms, or a rethinking of architecture and design to accommodate them. Style is identity. Ornament has always been a powerful tool of ethnic and cultural self-definition. Modernism, in contrast, is cosmopolitan. Rejecting the past, it set itself above traditional identities. The widely proclaimed twilight of modernism coincides with a worldwide political and social fragmentation. Not just the ideal of internationalism but the reality of an inclusive, secular nation-state is under siege. But there is more to self-definition than self-imposed insularity. If we are entering a new era of particularized values and allegiances, let it be with open eyes as well as open minds. Ornament can be a bridge between cultures, and between "elite" and "popular" strains in the same culture. To grasp a culture's ornament, from within or without, is to grasp its heritage, its uniqueness, and its joy.

There is no mystery about ornament, but there are many misconceptions. The most potent of them originate in the distrust and fear of artifice. Everything designed by human minds and made by human hands is artificial, but ornament has come to stand for artifice in the worst sense, something not only contrived but inauthentic. "The world is still deceived with ornament," muses Bassanio in Act III of *The Merchant of Venice*, as he contemplates the three caskets which will decide his fate. Today, ornament may provoke a rush of dazzled pleasure, as fireworks do, but the thrill is insubstantial, and our sophistication scorns a pleasure that so obviously has no purpose but pleasure. To enjoy it in passing is frivolous; to respect it as art is to be seduced by a falsehood. Ornament still deceives, or would if we let it.

We do not let it. For almost a century, "advanced" architects, designers, and critics have insisted, with the passion of faith and the force of law, that ornament must not give pleasure. Under the laws of modernist aesthetics, ornament bears damning witness against itself. If we take it away, physically or in imagination, the shape and function of the object are intact. Ornament is unnecessary. In every corner of our created world, the modernist rejection of ornament has taught the beauty of the necessary: of undisguised materials, unconcealed techniques, and functional form.

Yet enough ornament survived the purge to bring both delight and a certain disorientation, if we take the trouble to look at it. New York, for example, is a city of ornament. I grew up there, in and among early twentieth-century buildings on the Upper West Side, far from the sleek glamour of Midtown. I never liked New York, perhaps because what other people meant by it, the city they found so exhilarating, was not the old city I lived in. Only after years spent elsewhere did I realize how much I was a product of my early surroundings. The past was built into me, and I thought of it as home.

I absorbed the past at a time when the past was supposed to be nothing and the future was supposed to be everything. Born in 1948, I was part of the generation whose childhood science lessons seemed always to culminate in a vision of the world made peaceful and prosperous by atomic energy. That dream is gone, and many others with it, but against all odds I have kept the optimism of those years, and the romance of "big" technology has never faded for me. I loved science fiction as a child, and I still do. At air shows, the screech of an afterburner thrills me like the climax of a symphony, and I am one of those who believe that the Apollo spacecraft stands to our age as the great cathedrals of the Middle Ages stood to theirs: the work of many minds and hands, embodying not just the conscious aspirations of a people, but a vision beyond goals or words.

Unlike some of my generation, who fell wholly under the spell of the new, I find no cause in that vision to reject or mock the past. By setting our sights on the future we lose the present, and the past becomes our only home. The past alone does not change, though the ways we see it and use it are always changing. It is like an old building that we renovate to suit our needs, even as it shapes our perception of those needs. Only the least imaginative would simply call it obsolete, and abandon it. In recent years, the need to reconcile past and present, or at least to let them coexist, has struck me on every visit to New York. The smooth, glistening facades of the last half century stand out against the lush textures of the older city, but the combination has an energy beyond simple contrast. Reflected in huge expanses of tinted glass, premodernist buildings have a ghostly second life, while the newer structures borrow the ornament they were meant to eclipse.

Ornament is visual texture, a constant shift of focus from the building as a whole to features deliberately accentuated, and so on down to the smallest detail, some bit of carving that holds the eye as we enter or walk past. Ornament against a background of rectilinear glass, metal, and concrete is just as dramatic as a skyscraper against a background of carved moldings, capitals, and gargoyles. But instead of drama, too often we see only incongruity. What is of the past cannot be of the present, except by the rosy light of nostalgia. Do we admire New York's older buildings because they are beautiful, or because they evoke a more gracious world? In an age when beauty is still equated with simplicity and efficiency, few people have the time or inclination to notice, let alone examine, the details that make the city of the past a symbol of values we are supposed to have outgrown.

I do not hold much of a brief for postmodernism, except as a bridge to something as yet unguessed. It is too self-conscious, and perhaps in compensation, too self-mocking. Self-mockery is not a strong or healthy foundation on which to build a new visual world. Humor is, but only as part of a spectrum of delight whose other extreme is wonder, and wonder demands a certain measure of innocence. Irony is too knowing, self-mockery is the enemy of delight. At best, postmodernism may play a similar role in architecture and design to the role Pop Art played in the revival of figural painting. It may provide a way, a kind of back door, for traditional forms to reenter our culture, without our having to confront them directly and unironically, and without our having to face the implications of our systematic loss of innocence over the last century or so.

In 1992, the huge Matisse exhibition at the Museum of Modern Art cast a vivid and challenging light on these issues.[1] Matisse is the most innocent of the great modernists, and the most sensuous. Instead of creating a fragmented, intellectualized world of his own, as so many of his contemporaries did, Matisse kept his work firmly grounded in the pleasure of seeing. Most important, he conceived that pleasure as the sum of equal parts. Flowers, wallpaper, and the patterns on a dress have the same visual strength as a human figure; or the image may be complete without any figure at all. It is no surprise that Matisse admired and was influenced by Persian miniature painting.[2] To judge by the results, it was not the Persian artists' uncanny mastery of detail that captured his imagination. Matisse could work that way, but he was just as comfortable with broad areas of color defined by a few strong brushstrokes. Rather, it was the inclusiveness of their vision, in contrast to the more selective, human-centered art of classical antiquity and the Renaissance.

The well-known decorative strain in Matisse's art is neither more nor less than a deep respect for the totality of visual experience, ornament included. The exhibition left no doubt that he came to this unified vision early, and never abandoned it. If this were all, we might applaud Matisse's independence at a time when ornament was almost universally derided, while recognizing that his career was no more than a footnote to the history of ornament. But his importance for the understanding of ornament goes much further. The crowds that poured into the exhibition affirmed an instinct which modernists and postmodernists alike may have trouble acknowledging: the longing for visual pleasure in its most direct forms, unmediated by intellection, rebellion, irony, or other self-consciousness. From the Renaissance through romanticism to modernism, genius has taken on increasingly dark and subversive connotations, becoming in our century virtually synonymous with a merciless attack on artistic and cultural convention. It is worth recalling that early in his career Matisse was one of the artists branded as *fauves* (wild beasts). If his work no longer shocks, it is not because his style changed, but because it remained so consistent. As the public became more accepting of bold colors and abbreviated forms, Matisse kept faith with the public as few "revolutionary" artists have done. Far from discarding his once-radical idiom as it became the stuff of convention, he worked for almost half a century to establish and refine the new convention. What had been most demanding in his art, he made the most accessible. Few great innovators have used their powers in this way, and perhaps only Mozart surpasses Matisse as a complex giver of simple pleasures.

Beyond the importance of ornament in his paintings, the pleasure of Matisse *is* the pleasure of ornament. It is the pleasure of familiar things, often simplified, often combined in new ways, but above all intensified, and presented as beautiful or amusing or delightful in themselves. We do not delight in a painting like *Woman in a Purple Robe* (fig. 1) because it tells us something about a woman's body, or about cloth or flowers or wallpaper, but because of the relationship of form and color Matisse distilled from these things.

Matisse's art is not just a helpful analogy to ornament. His flowing, irregular shapes and contrasting colors have long been familiar to textile, fashion, and interior designers, and through them to the public. We may not even realize how closely our tastes are bound up with his decorative contribution, for the supposedly difficult and sub-

Fig. 1. Henri Matisse. *Woman in a Purple Robe*. Oil on canvas. French, 1937. Houston, Museum of Fine Arts, 77–141. Gift of Audrey Jones Beck.

versive character of "great" art does not translate easily into "mere" ornament. More than that, ornament is a suspect category from the start. Ours is still the culture that enshrined the rejection of ornament as a momentous step, perhaps the crucial step, away from the tyranny of the past.

Two principles underlie Matisse's sympathy for ornament, and his intuitive understanding and adoption of its methods. One is inclusiveness, the other an impulse to reduce forms to their essence, to abstract and intensify them. The two seem contradictory, but only if we equate inclusiveness with meticulous detail, something Matisse never did. Like the artist's own career, the catalogue of the 1992 exhibition records the long coexistence and fruitful interaction of these principles. Near the end of Matisse's life, however, a change took place which the earlier work only hints at. Beginning in the late 1930s, Matisse made collages of cut-out paper (plate 1).[3] Over the years, he expanded his work in this medium, and used it almost exclusively in the last years before his death in 1954. Physically, it was an adjustment to his difficulty in holding a brush or maneuvering around an easel. Stylistically, the cut-outs emerge quite logically from his increasingly abstract painting of the late 1930s and 1940s. But if the cut-outs themselves are easily explained, their power is not. Even surrounded by the other works from which they grew, they look radically, qualitatively different from anything Matisse did before. The reason, I think, is that the new technique upset the balance of representation and decoration which Matisse had maintained for so many years. When he began to "paint with scissors" (his own phrase) using paper he had already colored, he abandoned the modulation of paint. At the same time, the process gave his forms a new strength and autonomy, since each became a distinct if subordinate "work."

With the shift to clearly defined two-dimensional forms, Matisse went from depicting ornament to creating it. Many of the cut-outs were maquettes for decorative projects: stained glass, religious vestments, book illustrations. Others, no different stylistically, were complete in themselves. Not all of the cut-outs qualify as ornament. Exactly which ones do is a subjective judgment, but I use the term for those in which the representational element is weakest, the play of two-dimensional forms most graceful and complex. Matisse's ornamental cut-outs have both the distinctiveness and the universal, contemporary appeal to restore the sense of direction that modern decorative art has lost. Unfortunately, they have yet to fulfill this potential. They are widely recognized as a breakthrough, but in abstract art, not ornament. Even in the 1992 retrospective, the relatively few cut-outs on display said more about Matisse's extraordinary powers of invention than about the consistency of his ornamental vision.

Yet Matisse's influence on ornament has already been incalculable. Shortly after seeing the exhibit, I happened to glance at the openwork decoration (if I may use so grand a term) on an inexpensive plastic laundry basket. The pattern of flowers and leaves, simplified to the very limit of recognizability, was derived if not actually copied from a Matisse cut-out. I doubt that many people have bothered to notice the pattern, let alone recognized its source. They were not really meant to. The goal was convenience for both maker and user: the decoration requires less plastic and allows the laundry to air. Visual stimulation is a very distant third, if it enters the picture at all. This is an extreme case, but it shows how thoroughly, yet how subliminally, Matisse has shaped our visual language. There has always been a movement of styles from "high" art to the culture at large, but is Matisse's ornament destined only for this? He created an ornamental style unique to the twentieth century. Can we afford to let it sink, unexamined, into the realm of the barely seen? Or should we give it the same attention *as ornament* that we are prepared to give it as an outgrowth of painting, and hope to adapt it, build on it, and perhaps someday surpass it?

Needless to say, Matisse is not the only source of ornament open to us now. But because he is so close to us in time and cultural assumptions, and so much in the public eye, his work illustrates not just the opportunities but the difficulties of readjusting to ornament. When we think of ornament, to praise or condemn, we usually think of patterns: integrated, composed of distinct motifs, orderly and predictable even at their most intricate. For Matisse, the essential unit of ornament was the individual form or motif, not the pattern. Arrangements are subjective, rarely repetitive, never intricate. The individual forms are unpredictable and only occasionally, ambiguously, representational. This approach is by no means unique in the history of ornament, but it is especially appropriate to the twentieth century, because it meets cosmophobia halfway. Drawing on the whole experience of modernism, it makes a telling contrast to the angular, repetitive, often machine-inspired forms of art deco, a far more literal-minded attempt to bring ornament into the new mainstream (fig. 2). There is good art deco ornament, but it is traditional ornament with the trappings of modernism. It can never have fooled or convinced a hard-line modernist, someone for whom modernism and ornament were incompatible by definition. Matisse's ornament has done precisely that.

Traditional pattern-based ornament is far more alien to the modern spirit. Two textiles illustrate the difference. The first is Turkish, from an Ottoman court workshop of the sixteenth century (plate 2). It is one of the world's masterpieces of textile art, a triumph of controlled contradiction. The pattern is simultaneously windswept and frozen. Every form that could delight by simple grace is skewed or interrupted. There are no clear pathways for the eye; every movement sends us off at a tangent, or racing back the way we came. Details give no chance for rest or quiet exploration, but spin us round and launch us back into the endless rhythm of stems and leaves and flowers,

Fig. 2. Sloan and Robertson. Façade of the Chanin Building, 1929. New York, 122 East 42nd Street. Author's photo.

never gentle, never awkward, never familiar, sparking with energy never to be released.

The second textile, a scarf woven in Scotland in 1980, has nothing in common with the first but the material, silk (fig. 3). We would expect enormous differences between the product of an imperial workshop and that of an independent weaver in a small town, but this contrast goes beyond function or cost, workshop or clientele. The two textiles represent opposing conceptions of handicraft. For the Turkish weaver, material and technique were means to a goal. That goal was the most accurate possible recreation of a specific pattern in colored silk. The process made no allowance for spontaneity; any deviation was an imperfection and nothing more. Weave structure and the texture of individual threads are suppressed for the same reason: they distract, and therefore detract, from the virtuoso display of precision. In the case of the scarf, materials and technique are an end in themselves. The straightforward, relatively loose weave, and the thick, nubbly threads, combine regularity and randomness. Structure does not conceal materials, and materials do not conceal structure. There is no deliberate subtlety, but there is subtlety nonetheless, in the irregular texture of the cloth which a predetermined pattern would have overwhelmed.

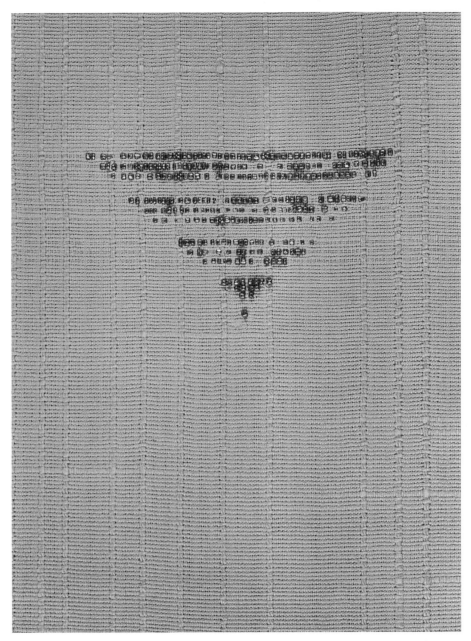

Fig. 3. Detail from a scarf. Silk with metal beads. Scottish, 1980. Private collection. Author's photo.

Only one element is intrusive or "artificial," in the sense that it does not follow directly from structure or materials. The rough triangle of beads is ornament, however rudimentary. Since the scarf was made decades after modernism had banished ornament, this must be a survival of the old decorative impulse, which the revolution was never quite able to eradicate. It is just what we might expect to see if that impulse were completely severed from the tradition which had nourished it for thousands of years.

Set directly against the Turkish silk, or any number of ornamental works from centuries past, the beaded decoration is a pathetic remnant. In its own terms it is more: an unpredictable yet harmonious flourish, a reminder of the human presence behind the "natural" interaction of structure and material. Yet the comparison is hard to shake off. Are we looking at a free choice, or at a culture that has "forgotten" how to make ornament? The idea of stylistic change as a process of learning or forgetting, rather than as a shift in priorities, has a strong grip on the popular imagination. I have heard adults explaining to children that medieval artists had forgotten, or not yet learned, the right way of depicting this or that subject. Doubtless there are people who still regard the entire history of abstract art as a sham, a cover for the lost ability to draw or paint "real" pictures. This is not a fruitful approach, but it is not ipso facto ridiculous. Social and cultural change *can* bring about a loss of traditional skills, and the offsetting gain is not always evident.

Twentieth-century cosmophobia is a complex phenomenon, with ideological roots more than two thousand years old. I have devoted the second half of this book to the origins and history of this prejudice, and the reasons why it crystallized decisively in the early 1900s. For the moment, it is enough to reflect on what it means to live with the results. Ornament is all around us; we have chosen not to notice it. This is a matter of taste, of pleasure, but the change has a much deeper social basis. Ornament was bound up with wealth and display, with power, luxury, and personal magnificence (fig. 4). Today, few of us have the opportunity to cultivate magnificence, so we rarely learn to appreciate it. More often we do just the opposite, making our lack of susceptibility a badge of both egalitarianism and sophistication. If personal magnificence is impractical, the ornament which evokes it is merely obsolete. If personal magnificence is *vulgar*, then ornament too is touched by vulgarity: a far more serious taint, clingy, contagious, and hard to eradicate.

For "consumers" of art there is a huge gulf between our time and the bygone age—only a couple of lifetimes past!—when *more* was more. For artists there is a different gulf, but equally wide. The issue is originality. Several years ago I taught a seminar on

Fig. 4. Giovanni Busi, called Cariani. *A Member of the Albani Family*. Oil on canvas. Italian, c. 1520.
London, National Gallery, NG 2494. Reproduced by courtesy of the Trustees of the National Gallery.

textile history at the Rhode Island School of Design. I had taught there before, and was alert to the differences between an artist's point of view and an art historian's, but a situation arose for which I was unprepared. The students in my class were all senior textile majors. They knew their craft but not its history, and were hungry for information. Still, it was the end of their senior year: the last thing they wanted was to have their perspective changed. I had just taken the class through the history of a pattern, a particularly rich history spanning almost two thousand years. By way of conclusion, I reminded them that all this history was theirs, that every motif, every variant could provide a model for them to use as they saw fit. Dead silence, thick with perplexity, quickly hardening into disapproval. What, I asked, was the matter? A forest of hands shot up, and the first voice spoke for all: "But we're supposed to be *original*. All our teachers say so!"

The story has no dramatic ending, but it led eventually to this book. In thinking about ornament I had taken the link between past and present for granted, never realizing how completely the twentieth century had severed that link. In this sense our culture really has forgotten how to make ornament, not because it has lost the ability but because it has forgotten how to learn. Refusal to imitate has cut us off from thousands of years of experience, insight, and technical refinement. There is nothing original about groping in the dark when you can reach out and turn on the light.

The strange thing is that for many people who practice a craft today, originality is not really a necessity and imitation is not really a disgrace. By and large we respect imitation, and give it an important place in our lives. The child with a coloring book, the knitter following a pattern or the cook following a recipe, the hobbyist who spends hundreds of dollars on a kit to build a model ship and hundreds of hours assembling it, all take pride in the work and the product. It is *theirs* even if they had no part in the original conception. In effect, they put themselves in the honorable position of a journeyman or subordinate artisan carrying out the instructions of a master. For every Barbara Walker, who not only analyzes and reconstructs old knitting patterns but creates new ones of her own, there are thousands who select a pattern and adapt it to the shape of a garment and the texture of a yarn, and many thousands more who rely on a single set of instructions for the style of the garment, the technique of making it, and the choice of yarn and decorative stitches.[4] Their pride is none the less, and their craftsmanship is just as real.

True apprenticeship with all its rigors is extinct in the modernized West, and in any case it could never be an option for the great majority of makers today, who as amateurs must spend most of their time doing something else. Following directions can provide a sense of vicarious apprenticeship. In the best cases there is an almost personal rapport with the expert, and a sense of community among the followers, a dim but discernable echo of the solidarity of guild membership. The innovative knitter Kaffe Fassett designs kits for sale which make it possible to recreate his designs, but he also leads workshops in which amateur knitters learn to adapt his design principles to their own styles. I sat in on one of these workshops, and was impressed not only by the sense of camaraderie among students of very different backgrounds, but by the absence of either "slavish" imitation or jealous resentment of the master.

Fassett, incidentally, is a model for the reintroduction of ornament into modern craft. Mining both the past and the world around him, he eclectically rather than systematically takes whatever looks promising and adapts it to his own vision and technique. His work is no less original when it takes off from a Turkish caftan than when it captures the play of sunlight on a stone wall. His enormously popular books teach largely by example, but I doubt that many people recognize them as lavishly produced modern counterparts to the model books which codified and transmitted ornament for centuries. Published patterns are rarely meant to be copied literally. They provide a "bass line" (as in music) on which artists have always been free to improvise.[5]

Lack of time and patience is another cliché that distances us from ornament. If our speeded-up society leaves no time for labor-intensive pursuits, it is only because it has trained us to demand quick results. Knitters, model builders, and do-it-yourselfers of all kinds have fought this trend by learning to work in short stretches of time, staying with a project for weeks, months, or even years. A remarkable illustration comes from the annals of telescope making. This is not a popular hobby like knitting or woodworking, but enough people do it to keep several companies in business providing materials. Some telescope makers buy their components ready-made. Others do it all themselves: grind their own lenses or mirrors, fabricate their own tubes, and so forth. As this book neared completion, I happened to read an amateur astronomer's account of how he built an off-axis Newtonian telescope from the ground up. The off-axis Newtonian is an esoteric design, a reflecting telescope whose optics are tilted to keep the secondary mirror from obstructing the light path. It requires a secondary mirror of unusual and exceptionally precise shape. Meanwhile, the asymmetrical tube must be built up from individually shaped staves of wood, then covered with fiberglass and epoxy. What makes this particular project so special is not that it took only a year to complete, or that the result was a unique and beautiful work of craft as well as a serviceable instrument, but that the maker had *no previous telescope-making experience*.[6]

A tour de force on the first attempt is exceptional. The capacity for sustained precision is not. Turning to a very different field of endeavor, before the age of computer animation, a full-length cartoon required millions of drawings, and took a team of draftsmen years to complete. In a less common style of animation, made famous recently by the "Wallace and Grommit" cartoons, three-dimensional figures must first be made, then posed and photographed again and again. A gesture worth a second of running time may need a dozen separate adjustments. With multiple characters, scenery, and special effects, twelve hours of work yield perhaps five seconds of completed film.[7] Clearly, if we neglect ornament as a creative outlet, it is not because we lack the patience for it, or because we think it demeaning to follow directions. We do not make ornament because we do not want ornament, because we have been schooled to mistrust or despise or simply ignore it.

To understand ornament we must understand our fear of it. To understand cosmophobia, we must understand ornament itself. By showing how ornament works, how it delights, the meanings it can carry, I hope to convey something of what we have lost. By showing how and why we lost it, I hope to break the spell, to open up a range of choices long avoided as taboo. This is a book for people who want to make, buy, or simply look at ornament, but do not know where to start; for those who know what they like, and want to look more closely at *why*. It is also a study of the mystique that has surrounded ornament, especially in the last two hundred years: the symbolic meanings attributed to it, sometimes correctly, more often not; the belief in its power to educate or mis-educate; and above all, the way it came to embody the human dignity of work against the onslaught of industry.

By itself, no amount of understanding will revitalize ornament. The reason is simple. Traditional ornament requires skill in drawing, and the modern West has largely forgotten how to draw. This is not a value judgment on modern art, but a statement of fact. It will remain true as long as we refuse to teach children the "right" way to draw—and teach it early!—for fear of inhibiting their creativity. It scarcely matters what the "right" way is, provided enough people agree on it to ensure consistency. The full rebirth of ornament is a matter of practical training. Language, science, and music all have rules. First you learn them, then you create. Why should art be any different?

Without draftsmanship we are limited to technologically assisted copying and image manipulation. Given the power of our technology this is not so bad, but it shrinks and distorts the picture of what ornament can be. We can adapt any style of ornament to our needs, but if we rely on programmed variations, however sophisticated, we cannot make it fully and finally ours. On paper or on a computer screen, that transformation comes only when the hand has learned to shape whatever the mind conceives. Drawing is the bridge between imagination and execution, between the pride of the designer and the pride of the maker. Without it, our enormous reservoir of skill and patience remains almost untapped.

PART I

What Is Ornament?

I

How Ornament Works

I HAVE SAID that ornament is the art we add to art. That is a beginning, but not a working definition. Figure 5, a wardrobe attributed to the French cabinetmaker André-Charles Boulle (1642–1732), illustrates ornament in its simplest sense, though the ornament itself is anything but simple. Two things stand out. First, ornament is separable from the functional shape of the object. If you want to know whether a particular feature of an object is ornament, try imagining it away. If the object remains structurally intact, and recognizable, and can still perform its function, the feature is decoration, and may well be ornament. If not, it is *design*.[1]

Design is as much a part of the creative process as ornament. Few objects have their shapes so completely dictated by function that any purely artistic change would make them useless. Figure 6 is a Chinese teapot from the factories at Yixing, famed for their inventive designs in unglazed stoneware. Although the pot itself dates from about 1980, the shape is one of the oldest in the Yixing repertory, credited to the eleventh-

Fig. 5. Attributed to André-Charles Boulle. Armoire. Ebony, with gilt bronze, brass, and tortoise-shell. French, late seventeenth or early eighteenth century. New York, The Metropolitan Museum of Art, Fletcher Fund, 1959 (59.108).

century statesman, poet, and connoisseur Su Dongbo. That shape is as much a display of artistic freedom and imagination as Boulle's ornament, yet it follows a completely different principle. Except perhaps for the stepped handle of the lid, there is not a single feature of which we can say *this is decorative, not functional; the teapot would work just as well without it.* Yet far from being a "generic" teapot, it is individual to the point of eccentricity.

Determining that a feature is not design does not automatically make it ornament. There is another criterion, based on what the feature looks like and how it is meant to be seen. All ornament is decoration, but not all decoration is ornament. Decoration is the most general term for the art we add to art. Used in this way it implies no judgment—"*mere* decoration"—on the quality or seriousness of a work. It simply means that one work of art has been added to another, and is therefore physi-

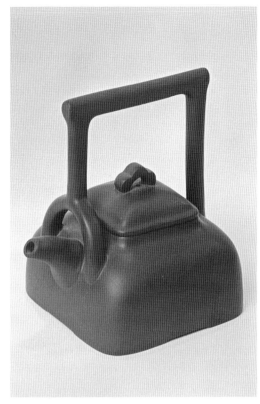

Fig. 6. Yuan Fen (signature). Teapot. Stoneware. Chinese (Yixing) c. 1980. Private collection. Author's photo.

cally and visually dependent on it. Michelangelo's *Last Judgment* is part of the decoration of the Sistine Chapel, but it is not ornament. *Ornament is decoration in which the visual pleasure of form significantly outweighs the communicative value of content.* Ornament can and often does have representational, narrative, and symbolic content, but visual pleasure must be paramount. If a piece of decoration seems to demand more information than the forms themselves convey—if, in effect, one cannot enjoy it without knowing the story—it is probably not ornament.

In the Western tradition, and to a remarkable extent in others, symmetry, repetition, flattening, the drastic simplification or complication of outlines, and the fragmentation, transformation, and recombination of organic forms in defiance of nature are hallmarks of ornament. Without denying content, they restrain it so that form predominates. In figure 5 the decoration includes human faces, animal feet, and a few architectural details, but most of the forms are based on plants. Not real plants—they are simpler, flatter, much more regular and symmetrical. They grow out of lines and shapes and each other, not out of pots or vases or the ground. The faces and feet are not part of complete figures: the faces are surrounded by leaves; the feet actually turn into leaves. Each door is symmetrical from left to right, and partly symmetrical from top to bottom. The two doors are identical, adding another level of symmetry. The test of separability tells us that the added forms are decoration, not design. The "story test" tells us that the decoration is likely—in this case overwhelmingly likely—to be ornament, and the suppression of content by symmetry, flattening, and so forth confirms this beyond doubt.

It is not always so easy. Adam van Vianen's silver cup of 1614 (fig. 7) could be design, decoration, or ornament, or a perfect mixture of the three. Most of the added features are so closely worked into the functional shape that they are scarcely separable, physically or visually. To all appearances there is no story—how can there be, with so little representation?—yet the recognizable elements are strange enough to raise all kinds of doubts. What do these forms mean? What is the cup really *about*? The support in the form of a monkey is an obvious parody of the giant Atlas holding up the sky, itself a standard theme for cups during the Renaissance and later. But why use such a theme here? The handle is recognizable as a seated female figure bending forward—in thought? in grief? or simply looking down? Is the continuation of the handle supposed to be her long hair, or something else? Can we even be sure the figure is female? The rest of the decoration is marine: the swirls on the body and lid are a conventional way of representing sea water, and the grotesque face below the handle would have been familiar as a sea monster. Is there a connection? These questions may recede into the background, but they never quite disappear.

The bowed figure may be Andromeda, a princess in Greek myth whom the gods condemned to be eaten by a sea monster as punishment for her mother's boastfulness. If so, van Vianen presents the story in a deliberately indirect and fragmented way, not least by omitting Andromeda's rescuer, Perseus. Perseus is the link between Atlas and Andromeda. According to legend, Atlas lived in North Africa, where the story of Perseus and Andromeda takes place. After killing the Gorgon Medusa, whose gaze turned living creatures into stone, Perseus stopped in Atlas's domain and asked for food and shelter. Atlas refused, and turned him out by force. Provoked, Perseus took Medusa's head from the bag in which he carried it and transformed Atlas into a mountain. Resuming his journey, he saw Andromeda chained to a rock in the sea, killed the monster (in a fair fight this time), and married the princess.[2]

Fig. 7. Adam van Vianen. Covered cup. Silver. Dutch, 1614. Amsterdam, Rijksmuseum, RBK 1976–4.

Not only do the mountains of western North Africa still bear the name of Atlas, they are inhabited by a distinctive kind of monkey, a macaque better known as the Barbary ape. Although van Vianen's monkey has a tail and Barbary apes do not, the representation is otherwise quite accurate. There are no monkeys in the story itself, but the depiction of Atlas as a Barbary ape is more than a generic parody or even a symbol of the place. The cup is a visual riddle. What, it first asks, is the connection between "Atlas" and "monkey"? The answer is "mountain," or more fully, the transformation of Atlas into a mountain, where this kind of monkey lives. The agent of that transformation is Perseus, who provides a further link to the sea monster, and the seemingly disconsolate figure surrounded by water. He is not shown because he is the real solution to the riddle.

If this is so, the cup and its decoration cannot be considered ornament. Yet the style says otherwise. The narrative elements, if we can even call them that, are too abbreviated to hold the visual and emotional center. They may allude to the story, but that is very different from illustrating it. The story is a pretext for the artist to conjure images of dissolution and fluidity from solid metal. Seen in this way, the delight in form and elaboration for their own sake may be enough to tip the balance in favor of ornament.

Van Vianen's cup is an extraordinary object, even by the standards of an age and a craft which reveled in the bizarre.[3] Few works in the "familiar" Western tradition raise such fundamental questions about the nature of ornament itself. Outside the Western orbit, we might find ourselves asking these questions routinely, not because the artists were more interested in them, but because their conventions of form and content are unavoidably strange to us. Despite its accessibility, ornament is not a universal language. Like spoken language, it has many different "families" and innumerable local "dialects" and "idioms," often mutually incomprehensible.

If the differences between ornamental styles seem far less glaring than between languages, it is because so much less depends on comprehension. Without a shared language the most basic human interactions are difficult; complex ones are impossible. We need not fear such dire consequences from our failure to understand or appreciate a particular style of ornament, but it can signal a subtler breakdown in communication. It is hard to like what we do not understand, and often easier to justify our dislikes than to overcome them. Hence such epithets as barbaric, decadent, primitive, and vulgar, applied not just to styles of ornament but to the people or peoples who flaunt them. Taste in ornament can be one of the many barriers between one civilization and another, between groups within a society, or between a society and its own past.

Ornament is as culture-bound as any other art. If it were not, if it had some magical property of transcending all cultural differences (a property even music and cooking, the arts that act most immediately through the senses, do not have!), could Western culture have become disillusioned with ornament to the point of wanting to give it up completely? I should not have to belabor this point, but ornament has a way of raising extravagant hopes. The reasons are not hard to see. In representational painting and sculpture, pleasure is inseparable from subject matter. Our responses may include a visceral one in which nothing matters but "pure" form and color, but recognition intrudes almost at once. We cannot help noticing human beings, animals, landscapes, and so on, even if we do not know exactly what is happening. The more we recognize, the more sharply our response is focused. Ornament does not work that way.

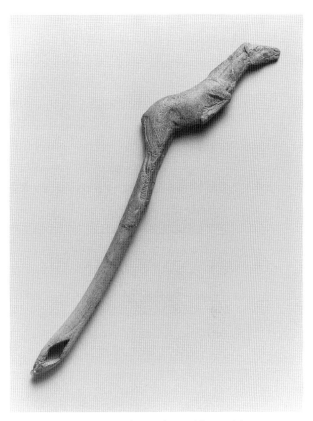

Fig. 8. Spear-thrower. Reindeer antler. Middle Magdalenian, c. 13,000–11,000 B.C. Saint-Germain-en-Laye, Musée des Antiquités Nationales.

Although it often has recognizable subjects, these matter less than the purely formal effects—otherwise it would not be ornament—and there is a great deal of ornament with no recognizable imagery. Since it is independent of representation, ornament seems to bring us close to the underlying, universal character of artistic form.

This line of thought is tempting, but it leads straight into a minefield. If art has formal properties that transcend representation, they must be the basic properties of art itself. Not only should they exist independent of representation, historically they should precede representation. It is unlikely that they do. Upper Paleolithic Europe (between about 35,000 and 10,000 B.C.) is the earliest culture from which a significant artistic legacy survives. Its representational art, including much that can be seen as ornament (fig. 8), is diverse and sophisticated; its nonrepresentational ornament is much less so.[4] From its very richness, we know that Upper Paleolithic art is not the "beginning" of art. Prehistorians may someday tell us conclusively whether art began with representation or with pure form, but in the meantime we should not rely on inference—least of all inference from later ornament. Although ornament is old, it is not primitive. Quite the opposite. Even the earliest surviving ornament must have been refined over thousands of years. This is a process involving not just changes in taste but the discovery of new materials and techniques, fluctuations in economic prosperity, and a great variety of cultural contacts and influences through migration, trade, conquest, and the spread of religions—not to mention historical revivals and rediscoveries. The chance of any form surviving unchanged from the dawn of art is vanishingly small. Even the simplest form may have a complex ancestry.[5]

There is another danger in the belief that ornament operates on a primitive, instinctual level: it is self-reinforcing. Bilateral symmetry is a good example. Since it is a feature of ornament worldwide, it must be attractive in a way that transcends cultural differences. If we ask why, the obvious answer is that it satisfies a universal human need for closure or completion. This explanation is so intuitively "right" that every case of bilateral symmetry seems to confirm it. But of all the ornament we know, relatively little is bilaterally symmetrical. To invoke a universal need, we must explain why it is manifest in some cases but not in others. Can we ever be sure that symmetry has always implied closure and completion, or that closure and completion have always mattered so much? In fact, strange as it seems, bilateral symmetry has been an important principle of ornament for no more than four or five thousand years.

My aim is to introduce ornament, not to explain it. I am writing about the ornament that people have chosen to make, and the ways they have chosen to use it, not about the fundamental impulse to decorate—about *how* ornament works, not *why*. Even this is no simple question. What effects does ornament achieve? By what devices does it achieve them? This is the visual side of the question, but there is also a historical side. The two are inseparable. How do the effects and devices differ from one culture to another? How do they evolve? And to complicate things still further, what happens to ornament when cultures interact? These questions can all be answered, but not with universal laws. Each case is different, and demands a different combination of visual and historical analysis. This is the basis of art history. We take it for granted when we look seriously at painting and sculpture, and at other arts like furniture that may include ornament, but rarely when we look at ornament itself.

For all its variety and fantasy, ornament is not the crystallization of a spontaneous, anarchic rush of feeling. Wherever practiced, it is a highly conservative art, bound by a network of conventions. Conventions are arbitrary yet fundamental rules governing every aspect of life, including art. Sitting on chairs instead of floor cushions is a convention. So is wearing neckties, putting pictures in frames, concentrating decoration around the doorways of buildings, or knowing that a character in a movie is pregnant because she faints for no apparent reason. The Valentine's Day heart is a convention within a convention: it looks nothing like a human heart, and the heart is not the organ of sentiment. The use of ornament is itself a convention, though its individual forms, styles, and applications vary with time and place. Every culture is a repository of ornamental forms, often very long-lived. Innovation is almost always a matter of reinterpreting or recombining them.

Conventions can sometimes be sidestepped, and familiar forms can be deployed in ways that designers a century earlier could not have imagined. But even ambiguous or fantastic ornament is rarely a break with convention. Far more often it *is* the convention. Convention is not hostile to change, but it acts as a brake on change, limiting it to what the culture can easily assimilate. Because ornament changes slowly, it can be hard to see how it is changing at any given point, or to identify a single artist's contribution. Did figure 9, for example, start out with fish, plants, a mask, or a set of abstract forms? How much credit goes to the person who made this particular object, how much to a succession of artists stretching back for generations, even centuries?

The building blocks of ornament are individual forms known as motifs. A motif is anything used as a motif; it is not defined by its origin or shape, or the presence or absence of representation. A nonrepresentational motif may be a simple geometric form, or something elaborate and capricious (fig. 10). Among representational themes, plants and parts of plants, animals, human beings, even entire scenes, have provided inspiration for ornament, and have been rendered in a huge variety of ways, some naturalistic, some barely recognizable. Ideas for motifs may even come from other artifacts. The Japanese excel at this kind of ornament (fig. 11).

When motifs are repeated, combined, or otherwise arranged in a more or less orderly way, the result is a pattern. Ornament does not always mean patterns. A motif may stand alone and still be ornament (fig. 10), or a combination of motifs may have no apparent order, in which case a more general term like arrangement or composition is preferable to pattern. For that matter, ornament can exist without discernable motifs, though this is a specialty of the twentieth century and rare in earlier periods. Nevertheless, the great majority of ornament throughout history has consisted of motifs arranged in patterns. They can be as simple as a checkerboard, or as carefully contrived as a Per-

Fig. 9. Stencil. Paper. Siberian (Nanai), early twentieth century. New York, American Museum of Natural History 2A19830. Photo: Denis Finnin.

Fig. 10. Bridle ornament. Wood. Siberian, from Pazyryk, fourth century B.C. St. Petersburg, Hermitage. Photo: after Sergei I. Rudenko, *Frozen Tombs of Siberia* (Berkeley: University of California Press, 1970).

sian rug (fig. 12 and plate 3). Simple motifs may be used to make a complex pattern, or complex motifs to make a simple one. There is no limit to the number of possible combinations and effects. The delicate floral patterns in figure 12 act as motifs within a much larger, bolder pattern.

The more delicate the pattern, the less likely it is to hold a viewer's attention over a large area. Without a strong internal framework it will convey lushness and intricacy rather than coherent organization. This explains why so much ornament is arranged in a kind of hierarchy: motifs, patterns, patterns of patterns. At one or more levels in the hierarchy we can expect to find forms that stand out by virtue of their size, color, theme, or technique, and provide a visual anchor, a base from which to explore the more subtle forms all

Fig. 11. Sword-guard (*tsuba*), with images of stirrups. Iron. Japanese, c. 1800. Photo: after Christie's, New York, *Japanese Swords and Sword Fittings from the Collection of Dr. Walter Ames Compton*, part 1, March 31, 1992.

around. In plate 3 the horizontal, vertical, and diagonal rows of medallions make a series of squares, rectangles, diamonds, X's, and asterisks, of various sizes. They often overlap and cannot be held in mind simultaneously, since focusing on one inevitably throws most of the others out of focus. Two visual anchors counteract this effect: the repeated motif of dragon and phoenix in a lobed medallion, and the diagonal lines of blue medallions connecting every second dragon medallion in each horizontal or vertical row.

Plate 3 embodies so many of the basic principles of ornament, it could almost have been designed as a teaching aid. It illustrates the most important types of motif (animal, floral, and nonrepresentational); the arrangement of motifs to make patterns; the use of complete patterns as motifs, resulting in a hierarchy of ever-larger patterns; the use of simple forms to achieve complex effects and complex forms to achieve simple effects; the eye's tendency, when confronted with an ambiguous pattern, to move continually among the possible interpretations; the increase in ambiguity as a pattern is extended and made more complex; and the need for a framework of strong, relatively simple forms to act as anchors.

Fig. 12. Detail of pile rug (cf. plate 3). Silk warp and weft, wool pile. Iranian, first half of the sixteenth century. New York, The Metropolitan Museum of Art, Hewitt Fund, 1910 (10.61.3).

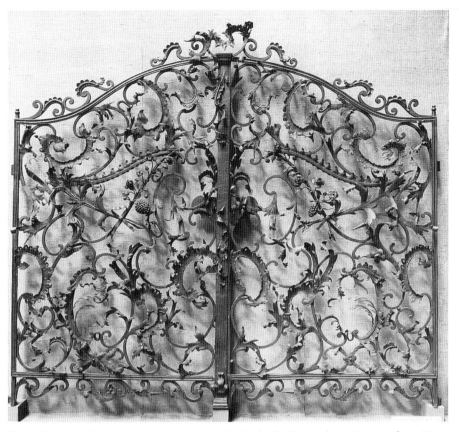

Fig. 13. Gate. Iron. German, eighteenth century. New York, The Metropolitan Museum of Art, 88.13 a-d. Gift of Henry G. Marquand, 1888.

The same principles, the same ways of looking, apply to much more elusive forms. They extend even to the rococo, the whimsical and demanding style of eighteenth-century Europe, which seems at first glance to defy analysis (fig. 13).[6] What makes the rococo almost unique is the combination of clarity and fluidity in the parts, and apparent chaos in the composition as a whole. (Chinese ornament of the Han dynasty does much the same thing, but without the wealth of fantastic imagery.) This effect depends on a characteristic arrangement of curved lines, most clearly seen in a simple iron trivet (fig. 14). Unlike most rococo ornament, the trivet is neither complex nor especially graceful, making it an effective first guide, a skeleton key to the rococo. Each of the trivet's seven identical supports is made up of short, simple curves which intersect, overlap, and counterbalance one another. From this formula comes the ingenious play of shapes in figure 13, and others of still greater complexity.

Fig. 14. Trivet. Steel. Spanish, eighteenth century. London, Victoria and Albert Museum, 1742–1892. Courtesy of the Trustees of the V&A.

Figure 13 is a typical piece of very good rococo ornament. It does not tell us everything about the style, but it shows us how to look. At least as important, it shows us how *not* to look. With figure 12 we could move in an orderly way from the parts to the whole. Here, we cannot. Except for the obvious symmetry between the left and right halves of the gate, there is no predictable pattern, nothing to "solve." There is no obvious visual anchor; no meaningful beginning, middle, or end in either a spatial or temporal sense. There is only movement.

At first it probably registers as incoherence. The individual lines are C curves like those on the trivet, only much more graceful. (The plant forms are an added flourish, ornament applied to ornament.) But because of their number and arrangement, these simple forms open up a vast range of possibilities. Starting at any point on any curve, follow it visually in either direction. It may flow directly into another curve, transforming the C shape into an S shape, or its reverse Ƨ. It may do the same thing at a more acute angle, producing an abbreviated double spiral Ƨ. It may divide, giving the viewer a choice of paths. It may run tangent to another curve, encouraging a "jump" and a dramatic change of direction. Or it may simply end, sending the viewer back to reenter the arrangement somewhere else. As one becomes used to this visual roller-coaster ride, other shapes and relations begin to emerge. The composition is full of echoes, but they are never exact. The "same" forms may appear several times, changed in size, rotated any number of degrees, or disguised by foliage.

These effects can tempt the eye away from strictly linear pathways, but not forever. They are too fragile, too easily reabsorbed into the "confusion" of the whole. As a result, all the effects I have described are present at once. At any given point the choices are limited, but the ultimate effect is a sense of movement without constraint or repetition. It is not meant to be brought under control by reference to a basic, comprehensible framework. The authority of the composition, what keeps it from dissolving into incoherence, is not in the whole but in the balance between grace and tension in the individual forms.

Such volatile ornament demands the most precise control of line, specifically of the ways in which curved lines create and channel visual momentum. Of all the possible lines, some are too short to create momentum. Others are too long, and dissipate theirs. Too sharp a curve or too abrupt a change of direction demands a slowdown just as surely as in driving, while gentle curves often lack energy. Too dense an arrangement obscures the flow of individual lines, while too much open space changes the tone from sumptuous to austere: not a bad thing in itself, but a challenge to which few designers have been equal. Balancing all these factors would be a remarkable achievement in pen and ink. In iron it is a triumph of vision and virtuosity, even if the metalsmith had a finished drawing to work from. But this accomplishment is far from unique. The eighteenth century was an age of virtuosity, and not just in metal.

There are textiles in which this command of line is scarcely more than a starting point (plate 4). Color adds another dimension, but the full richness of rococo textile art comes from the reflective properties of weaves and fibers. Depending on the weave structure, metallic thread or colored silk can appear either restrained or luminous. But the effect is not constant. Different weaves respond to different lighting conditions. Colors that look sober in direct light can shine like jewels when the light comes at an angle. Even when the changes are less dramatic, their ornamental implications go deep. If a single color is rendered by two different weave structures, in some lights it will register as one color, in others as two. Since colors define shapes, these textiles have the equivalent of two or more distinct patterns, which appear and disappear with every movement of the light, the viewer, or the cloth itself.

Words are a poor guide to such complexity, and even a trained eye can go astray. With enough patience, however, we can find our way into the most complex patterns. The method works for any style of ornament, but is especially gratifying when applied to the rococo. Perhaps more than any other style, rococo ornament has been maligned as irredeemably frivolous. There is a satisfaction akin to poetic justice in realizing that beneath the frips and flourishes—dissolving rocks, weird perspective effects, and idiotic cherubs—rococo ornament is brilliantly calculated and as tough as nails.

The textile in color plate 4 exemplifies two major properties of ornament—*intricacy* and *ambiguity*. Intricacy is formal complexity. An intricate pattern is intrinsically hard to read because the sheer density of elements keeps us from seeing how the pattern is organized. Ambiguity is the tendency of some patterns to send mixed signals: they can be read in two or more ways at once. Ambiguous patterns can be intricate, as we have just seen, but they do not have to be. In fact, ambiguity can often give a pattern the

Fig. 15. Floor mosaic. Roman, second century. Ostia, Ministero per i Beni Culturali e Ambientali. Photo: Archivo Fotografico della Soprintendenza Archeologica di Ostia.

fascination of depth and inexhaustibility while sparing the maker the enormous labor of intricacy. I do not mean that ambiguous patterns are easy to do. The best ones require a boldness and an intuitive sense of balance that are often missing from more formally complex works.

In figure 15, a second-century Roman mosaic, the individual motifs are simplicity itself, but the pattern is in constant flux, from squares to crosses to hexagons and back again to squares. Although the Roman artist needed only black and white, the addition of color to an ambiguous pattern enhances the effect significantly. In a flat-woven rug from Turkey (plate 5) the arrangement of forms is visually ambiguous but consistent. The distribution of colors, however, is arbitrary. Inevitably we try to reconcile the two sequences, but they never coincide. Instead, the unpredictable relation of form and color accentuates the ambiguity of the pattern by suggesting new combinations of motifs. The effect is almost kaleidoscopic.

Fig. 16. Inlaid felt rug. Kazakh, twentieth century. Almaty, National Museum of Kazakhstan.

Another way of creating ambiguity is to design the ornament so that the background itself forms a pattern. This works best with a simple color scheme: the eye moves continually between a dark pattern on a light ground, and a light pattern on dark (fig. 16). The result is simultaneously elusive and dynamic. In recent times this technique has been a specialty of north-central and northeast Asian ornament, but its roots are almost certainly Chinese.[7]

A variant, especially popular in medieval Islamic art, is beveling. The word means cutting on a slant, and unlike the other devices we have seen so far, it requires an actual third dimension, as in woodcarving or stucco relief (fig. 17). Ordinarily, in low relief the spaces left by the pattern are simply cut away to a uniform depth, so that the pattern stands out, physically as well as visually, from a lower, darker background. In beveled ornament, the cut-away parts slope down gradually, either at an oblique angle or on a curve, so that little if any of the field can be decisively identified as *not* pattern.

Fig. 17. Doors. Teakwood. Iraq, ninth century. New York, The Metropolitan Museum of Art, 31.119.1–2, Fletcher Fund, 1931.

Instead of being complementary, as in the previous example, pattern and ground are indistinguishable. Follow the pattern far enough and it will shade into its converse. The bottom of the groove may then leap into prominence as the only fixed element in the pattern, but this too is mutable. Like everything else in beveled ornament, the distinctness of the groove is relative, and it can change dramatically with the angle and intensity of the light.

As we have moved from the rug in plate 3—almost a textbook anthology of ornament—to more narrowly focused effects, ambiguity has emerged as an emblem of ornament's possibilities. In the examples we have seen so far, it has implied a degree of volition, whether conscious or intuitive. Specific forms of ambiguity serve specific decorative purposes. Since patterns are cultivated for their ability to please, we may assume that when ambiguity plays a major role in a pattern, it was on some level intended to play a major role in the pleasure which that pattern gives. But on another level, ambiguity is an essential property of *all* ornament. The business of ornament is to transform shapes and surfaces, by whatever means, into something other than what they really are. In the case of flat surfaces, the change is a matter of illusion, and representational drawing and painting provide the model. Not only can drawing and painting be vehicles of ornament in their own right, but as the quintessential arts of illusion they directly inspire those "decorative" arts that strive for similar effects, such as mosaic, pictorial weaving and embroidery, and engraved or

Fig. 18. Printed textile. Cotton. English, 1834. London, Victoria and Albert Museum, Circ. 305–1956. Courtesy of the Trustees of the V&A.

inlaid metalwork. In the most extreme cases there is an illusion not only of space but of real creatures to fill it (fig. 18).

The kind of out-and-out illusionism that invites us to look deep into what is actually a solid surface is rare in ornament. Ambiguity, however, is present whenever the surface is disrupted, even by patterns with only the faintest suggestion of three-dimensionality. The effect is much stronger when ornament physically disrupts the surface, or modifies the shape of an object. In figure 19, for example, the surface is worked with multiple patterns on multiple levels of relief. To ask which is the "real" surface is like asking which is the "real" pattern in plate 5. It is the wrong question to ask, because any attempt to answer it sets off the process of change. The number of possible answers is finite, but the succession is potentially endless. This also makes it

Fig. 19. Intersecting arches from the Aljafería, Saragossa. Stucco. Spanish-Islamic, eleventh century. Madrid: Museo Arqueológico Nacional. Museum photo.

the *right* question to ask. To receive an ambiguous answer, we must ask the kind of question designed to elicit a straightforward one! Inquiry is the key to enjoyment.

Not even the building blocks of ornament are secure. No artist is capable of perfect repetition. Small changes in the rendering of basic motifs can add up to large changes in the finished pattern. The differences are likely to be greater when two artists interpret the same motif, and greater still when they work in different media, or different techniques within a medium, or when they are separated by space or time. There is no way of predicting in advance which of these factors will cause the biggest change.

In 1571, the Mughal emperor Akbar ordered the building of a new capital, known as Fatehpur-Sikri, near Agra in northern India. For reasons still unclear, the city was abandoned less than a generation later; it survives as a huge and glorious ghost town, an outdoor museum of Mughal architecture and ornament.[8] Figure 20 shows a detail from one of the palaces there, in red sandstone, the Mughals' preferred medium for monumental building and carving. In the 1980s the Japanese weaver Ichiro Arai used the same patterns in a textile (fig. 21). It is not quite a direct copy. The various patterns have been rearranged to make a succession of vertical bands. More subtle changes include the substitution of grapes for pomegranates on the vine, a strangely literal-minded touch for such a sophisticated designer. (Real pomegranates grow on trees, not vines. In ornament they grow any way the artist wants them to!) Nevertheless, the cloth very nearly matches the original stone in color, a rich weatherworn red, and in texture, thanks to the use of fibers that shrank at different rates when the cloth was washed, giving it a genuine third dimension. Considering the differences between stone and cloth, India and Japan, the late sixteenth century and the late twentieth, it is a remarkably faithful adaptation.

Fig. 20. Detail of a doorframe and exterior wall. Red sandstone. Indian, sixteenth century. Fatehpur-Sikri, House of the Turkish Queen. Author's photo.

Fig. 21. Ichiro Arai. Detail of a woven textile. Japanese, c. 1985. Providence, Museum of Art, Rhode Island School of Design. Gift of Ichiro Arai. Photography by Erik Gould.

Far more striking are the differences between the front and back of Arai's textile (fig. 22). This is something we usually take for granted. If a textile with a pattern in the weave has a distinct front and back, the pattern is meant to be seen from one side only. That side is the front; in normal use the back does not show. Here, however, it is not easy to choose between the two sides. On one side both pattern and ground are relatively smooth, and the relief just sufficient to make a clear demarcation between them. On the other, the pattern is crinkly, the relief much higher, and the distinction between pattern and ground far less defined. By definition the materials are identical in both, the process the same, the manufacture simultaneous. Yet different aspects of the same process yield equally valid but thoroughly different interpretations of the same ornament. The more closely we look, the less it matters that the patterns are "the same." With effects so different, the idea of sameness becomes meaningless.

Figure 23, from a classic study of early Germanic ornament, shows how much the interpretations of a single pattern can differ.[9] The object is a small bronze plaque. It

Fig. 22. Reverse of fig. 21.

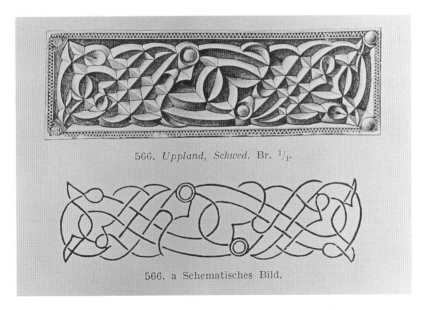

566. *Uppland, Schwed.* Br. $^1/_1$.

566. a Schematisches Bild.

Fig. 23. Two renderings of an ornamental bronze plaque. Germanic, sixth century.
Stockholm, Statens Historiska Museum. Photo: after Bernhard Salin, *Die altgermanische thierornamentik* (Berlin: A. Asher, 1904).

depicts two highly stylized dragonlike creatures coiled together; the pattern is the same when turned 180 degrees. But what is the pattern? The line drawing tells us almost everything, and almost nothing. Without it we might be hard put to identify animal forms at all, yet it bears little relation to the object. In the bronze, every outline is beveled on both sides. There are no level surfaces, only ridges and valleys. The schematic drawing equates the pattern with the tops of the ridges. Since the drawing is meant to help us identify the stylized animals, the equation is justified: only those lines give a recognizable image.

But how important is that image in the overall picture? The more complete (shaded) drawing makes it clear that the beveled surfaces are anything but a passive background to a linear composition. Wherever the animals' bodies cross, they interpenetrate—outlines, bevels, and all. Each crossing makes a tiny, irregular beveled polygon, which belongs structurally to both bodies, but is visually separate from them, and interrupts them. Since this happens many times, the pattern breaks up into a dazzling play of facets like the inside of a geode. The fluidity, even the integrity of the animal forms evaporates, and pattern and ground (what little ground there is in the line drawing) become indistinguishable.

This much abstraction at the expense of representation is extreme even by the standards of early medieval art, and fleetingly recalls the most self-consciously decorative expressions of cubism and futurism. But fascinating as the interplay of motif, pattern, and object may be, we should remember that we have never seen the object, only what appears to be a scrupulously accurate drawing of it. Is the drawing really so accurate? I am not talking about willful or even careless distortion; the problem is emphasis. Working with two variables, shading and contrast, the illustrator has opted for contrast. Highlights and shadows are defined as sharply as possible, subject to the need for some shading to remind us of the transition between the peaks and valleys.

No direct violation of reality is involved, as it would be if light and shade were applied arbitrarily: all the effects are consistent with a raking light from the top left. But how often could we expect to see the object in such a light, from the distance at which we read a book? The illustration, remember, gives the plaque in its actual size, an inch by three and a half inches. The depth of the beveling is to be measured in tiny fractions of an inch. If we move the plaque or raise the light source even a little, so that light strikes the surface more directly, the contrast is gone. This is not to say that exaggerated contrast is somehow intrinsic or unique to drawing. Photography could easily give the same effect, and the result would be just as contrived.

There are three lessons here for students of ornament. First, any representation of a pattern or motif is bound to distort by emphasis or omission. The only completely accurate illustration is the object itself. Second, distortion by emphasis or omission is not only inevitable, it is also very useful. The crystalline surface of figure 23a and the sinuous outlines of figure 23b are complementary aspects of the same ornament. In theory there could be others. Learning to "read" an unfamiliar style is a process of continual adaptation. The more we look, the more we learn to see. Anything that speeds this process is a welcome aid.

Third, and most important, we must not confuse ornament as interpreted by illustrators, or even the object itself under controlled conditions of isolation, distance, and light, with ornament in the real world for which it was made. *Sometimes* an accident

Fig. 24. Textile. Silk. Byzantine, sixth century. Aachen, Cathedral treasury. Photo: Ann Münchow.

of light would have brought out all the contrast in a beveled surface. *Sometimes* a contemporary would have glimpsed the whole stately pattern of a Byzantine silk fabric (fig. 24, p. 45). But for the most part the ornament that we analyze so closely was caught up in the great muddle of display: half-hidden, overlapped, in shadow, in motion. Our standards are not so different today. Choosing a pair of earrings or a necktie, we do not pause to analyze their decoration. We do ask, almost without thinking about it, whether they "go" with the day's outfit, or with our image of ourselves. This is a shorthand for analysis, possible because the items are completely familiar. If the conventional "fit" is not perfect, we will probably choose something else.

What I have called the muddle of display is the prerogative of those for whom aesthetic choice is second nature; in other words, those for whom the field of choice is their own culture. Today, most of us approach historic ornament as something *not* of the culture. The assumption that we can come to terms with ornament by separating it, physically or mentally, from its original setting is the clearest sign of our distance from it. Distance, in turn, creates uncertainty: if ornament was not made to be analyzed, and we cannot know it except through analysis, have we made the wrong start? The answer is that if no one cared how patterns looked, there would have been no incentive to create or vary them. Even if the only purpose of ornament were to highlight precious materials and conspicuous labor, it would not succeed unless people saw it, on some level, as a positive addition. Ornament with no aesthetic value of its own, however subliminal, is a contradiction in terms. It follows that studying a pattern in isolation, mentally exposing its subtleties layer by layer, is neither more nor less than a necessary step toward seeing the pattern as it was meant to be seen.

How Ornament Evolves

ORNAMENT IS ALWAYS changing. For art historians this change has been many things: a reflection of large-scale social and cultural change, a sign of foreign influence, a measure of the passage of time, and an artistic phenomenon worth studying for its own sake. For makers and consumers of art, change is a historical process in which everyone participates. Whether we know it or not, whether we try to prevent it or join in willingly and try to steer it, change goes on. For both artists and patrons, knowledge of the process is not an abstraction but a practical asset. What *has* happened is a guide to what *can* happen. It does not set a limit on creativity, as though nothing new were ever possible. Quite the opposite. The more we know about the history of ornament, the more choices we have, and the more likely we are to move beyond mere recombination, into invention.

But the history of ornament can be hard to know. Three small iron plaques from Iran (fig. 25) sum up both the process of change and the difficulty of interpreting it.

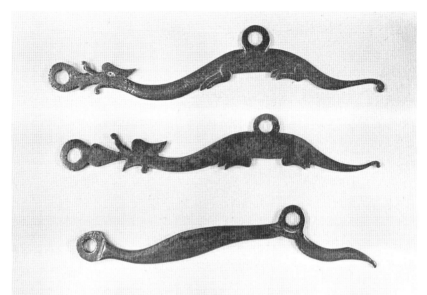

Fig. 25. Three plaques. Iron. Iranian, date unknown. Private collection. Author's photo.

The first plaque (top) is easily recognizable as a dragon. The outline is distinct, details such as eyes and scales are filled in, and the body is even modeled in low relief. The second plaque preserves the outline, but the surface is flat and featureless. The third plaque is once again worked in relief, but the outline has been radically simplified. Without the first two as a guide, we might not recognize it as a dragon.

The differences are obvious, but their implications are not. All we know about the three dragons is that they were bought from a dealer in Isfahan in 1973. Did the same artist make all three? Or were they made at different times and in different places? Did the artist, or artists, move from literal to simplified to abstract rendering, or the other way around? In either case, were there intermediate stages which, if we could fill them in, would make the progression less dramatic? If all three styles were available and equally accepted, the plaques could have been made in any order, within the briefest span of time. The whole idea of a sequence would then be a later construction, a modern image of stylistic evolution imposed by a collector or dealer.

The history of ornament is a succession of individual problems to be solved by a combination of knowledge and intuition. Ornament can and does evolve from simple to complex, and from complex to simple. Any small group of objects with a shared motif or pattern can suggest a sequence, but only a knowledge of the context can tell us whether that sequence is real. Local tastes and traditions, economic and social stratification, and the idiosyncrasies of artists and workshops, ensure that many different evolutions go on at the same time. They may influence one another or coexist without interacting at all. Often they appear to run in opposite directions. The more complex and cosmopolitan the society, the more strands its network of traditions is likely to have, and the more difficult it is to guess the whole picture from a few examples. This can be true even of one's own culture, where all the evidence is theoretically available. How much more so when the evidence has been ruthlessly, capriciously "edited" over many lifetimes by the destructive forces of war, reuse of precious materials, and dumb attrition.

Some patterns stay in fashion for centuries, even millennia. Like languages, religions, or systems of government, successful patterns not only survive cultural change but lend themselves to the kind of experiment that makes them a positive expression of change. Details of the process may be lost, but the broad outline is usually traceable. Few pattern types are more consistent over the centuries than the *ogival pattern* in textiles, yet few give more evidence of fruitful experiment, or have shown themselves more adaptable to changing tastes. Strictly speaking, it is a pattern type and a motif in combination. The former is known as the ogive, the latter as the pomegranate. Neither term is particularly helpful. An ogive is a pointed arch, as in Gothic architecture. The units that make up the ogival pattern can be described (I confess it would not have occurred to me) as two pointed arches set base to base, making an elongated medallion with pointed ends. When repeated in staggered rows, these medallions fit together exactly, but it was at least as common to have alternating rows of larger and smaller medallions enclosing different but closely related motifs. These motifs are usually plant-derived, but their occasional resemblance to pomegranates is incidental. They can also look like thistles, pinecones, pineapples, potted plants, bouquets of flowers, palmettes, or any combination of these things.[1]

We first see the combination of ogive and pomegranate around the year 1000, in a silk textile from Byzantium or Muslim West Asia (fig. 26). By the fourteenth century a lively but insubstantial and fragmented version of the ogival pattern had become established in Italy (fig. 27). Fifteenth- and sixteenth-century designers removed every trace of lightheartedness. Reinstating the original strong outlines, they gave their patterns the self-conscious magnificence of "official" art (fig. 28). In the sixteenth and seventeenth centuries, designers focused increasingly on the frame, often breaking it up into separate floral units. When the pomegranate is large and deeply notched, it can seem about to merge with its frame. Only the barest hint of ground separates them (fig. 29).

In this period the Ottoman Turks ruled not only modern Turkey and the lands of the eastern Mediterranean, but all of North Africa, and Europe as far west as the Balkans. Since the Italian city-states, notably Venice and Genoa, traded extensively with the

Fig. 26. Textile. Silk. Byzantine or Islamic, c. 1000. Munich, Bayerisches Nationalmuseum.

Fig. 27. Textile. Silk. Italian, fourteenth century. London, Victoria and Albert Museum, 7084–1860. Courtesy of the Trustees of the V&A.

Fig. 28. Textile. Silk. Italian, fifteenth or early sixteenth century. Providence, Museum of Art, Rhode Island School of Design, 35.553. Gift of Howard Sturges. Photography by Del Bogart.

Fig. 29. Textile. Silk. Italian, third quarter of the seventeenth century. Venice, Musei Civici Veneziani, 3216.

Fig. 30. Textile. Silk. Turkish, first half of the seventeenth century. Washington, D.C., The Textile Museum, OC1.57. Acquired by George Hewitt Myers in 1951.

Turks, it is no surprise that Turkish and Italian weavers used many of the same patterns. Unlike most other Islamic ornament, which emphasizes elaboration and delicacy, Ottoman ornament has a fierce and unpredictable strength. In all of Islamic art, only the Ottomans used bold, simple forms consistently and with confidence, sometimes alone but often combined unsettlingly with more intricate ones. The best Ottoman ogival patterns have an energy of unresolved conflict which the more staid Italian versions usually lack (fig. 30).

Back in Europe, the coalescence of ogive and pomegranate continued in the eighteenth century. The so-called lace-patterned silks (fig. 31), whose heaping up of detail

Fig. 31. Textile. Silk. English, c. 1728. London, Victoria and Albert Museum, 28A-1879. Courtesy of the Trustees of the V&A.

nearly obscures the pattern, have a long pedigree. A more original interpretation took shape in the 1730s under the influence of the French weaver Jean Revel (fig. 32, p. 54). Previously, although woven cloth might incorporate actual three-dimensional effects (e.g., pile weaves and thick metallic threads), illusionistic ones were confined to a few bent leaves and intertwined stems. For all their sumptuous elaboration, ogival patterns from before the eighteenth century are resolutely two-dimensional. Revel's pioneering work on color modulation changed this, allowing weavers to model any pattern in light and shade with a subtlety approaching that of painting. The idea of a pattern as a linear construction is suddenly obsolete: what matters is the texture and positioning

Fig. 32. Attributed to Jean Revel. Textile. Silk. French, c. 1735.
London, Victoria and Albert Museum, T. 187–1922. Courtesy of
the Trustees of the V&A.

of objects in three dimensions, not the play of forms across a flat surface. In some cases the ogival network is no more than a peg on which to hang a collection of precisely drawn, delicately shaded, and highly individual flowers, leaves, fruits, and related artifacts such as vases.

By all rights this should mean the end of the pattern type, but in the eclectic climate of the nineteenth century its historical associations proved irresistible, and it was revived. Medieval, Renaissance, baroque, rococo, and Islamic versions jostled one another as never before. The social climate, too, had changed. Sheer cost once made these textiles a badge of wealth and power. Now, not only was personal magnificence largely a thing of the past (in a more "democratic" age even fabulous wealth rarely adorned itself ostentatiously), but new production techniques, mechanized weaving and even printing, had placed "aristocratic" patterns within the reach of virtually anyone who aspired to some measure of elegance. The ogival pattern had become bourgeois.

This is the incarnation that we meet in upholstery and wallpaper today. It is also what drew the notice of nineteenth-century design reformers, of whom William Morris is only the best known. Seeing it as a link to the Middle Ages, their lost Eden of craftsmanship, designers of the Arts and Crafts movement began stripping away the accrued lushness of centuries. This process continued as the nostalgic historicism of the Arts and Crafts shaded into the self-conscious fluidity of Art Nouveau (plate 6). The results were still ornate but rarely ponderous, and represent a genuinely new stage in the pattern's history. If they are derivative, it is only in the sense that all ornament is inseparable from its tradition.

THE recognition of change has shaped the modern art-historical study of ornament. A new era of scholarship began in 1893 with Alois Riegl's book *Problems of Style*.[2] Riegl presented the history of ornament as a gradual evolution of forms in response to equally gradual changes in a culture's "artistic impulse" (*Kunstwollen*). This was a radical idea in its day, and *Problems of Style* is a polemical book. Riegl was setting out to refute the prevailing view that ornament flowed directly from materials and technique.[3] He could not have chosen a worse time for his methodological breakthrough. In the course of only a generation, the ever-accelerating shift from the ideal of individuality-within-convention to that of individuality-*against*-convention, the doctrine of truth to materials, and the revolt against ornament itself, turned *Problems of Style* into a document from another age.

Twentieth-century artistic practice, including craft practice, has been largely indifferent to the history of ornament, and often bitterly disdainful of it. Art historians have followed a different path to the same destination. Formalism, the belief that an art can meaningfully be studied in terms of its formal principles alone, is in deep disrepute, and Riegl is the archformalist. His idea of a *Kunstwollen*, a disembodied impulse shaping the history of art, was meant to counter a rigid technological determinism, but is now seen as mechanistic. Marxism dealt a crippling blow to a school of thought which downplays social, economic, and technological factors. More damaging still is the ease with which formalism can be made to subvert its original humanizing purpose. If styles have a life of their own, independent of outside forces, what room does that leave for the artist? Formalism is only a step away from a "selfish gene" theory of art, in which an artist is a style's way of reproducing itself.

Riegl's place in art history is secure, but his argument was denied a great part of its birthright of influence. *Problems of Style* was eclipsed, not refuted. Many of the assumptions he set out to disprove are still in force, and his insistence that style is independent of technique is as controversial today as it was a hundred years ago.[4] Since materials and techniques often have distinctive visual properties, they are bound to influence the artistic outcome. But only sometimes, and within limits. A useful example is figure 33, a Zulu basket made of insulated wire. The basic pattern consists of four interlocking zigzag spirals, but changes in the direction of the weave turn it into something much more complex. This is usually the limit of technical influence. A particular pattern may be easier to achieve in one technique than in another, but techniques rarely create whole

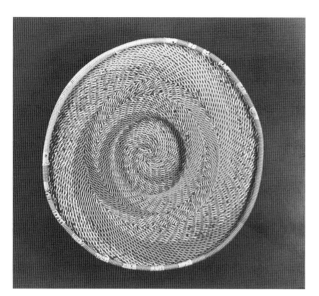

Fig. 33. Basket. Insulated wire. South African (Zulu), c. 1990. Private collection. Author's photo.

patterns, any more than they create images in painting and sculpture. Art is created by artists. Whether they regard the limitations of a particular craft as a supportive framework or as an obstacle to overcome has more to do with the interaction of individual talent and convention than with the "true" nature of the craft.

The textile technique known as ikat is a good example. Ikat is the art of tie-dyeing warp or weft threads, or both, off the loom, in such a way that when the threads are woven into cloth the dyed areas come together to produce a pattern.[5] It is a demanding technique, since it requires precise calculation at the dyeing stage and many small adjustments during weaving. No amount of work will make the colored threads come together exactly. The patterns always have blurred outlines in the direction of the warp, weft, or both. At first glance this is a clear case of technique influencing style. Central Asian and some Japanese ikats, in particular, conform to the popular image of an ikat style, an image they helped create as ikats were increasingly discovered by Western collectors and designers over the past generation (fig. 34). But not all ikats look the way the technique "says" they should. Weavers in the Indian state of Gujerat practice the enormously difficult technique of double ikat with such precision that blurring is for all practical purposes eliminated. The delicate repeat patterns in which these weavers specialize can be almost indistinguishable from patterns made with single-colored threads on a multiharness loom: only close inspection reveals the telltale irregularities (fig. 35).

Many viewers today will find this virtuosity misplaced. Why spend time and skill overcoming the limitations of a craft when it is precisely those limitations that make it special? It is a hard question to answer objectively. For more than a hundred years, the belief that technique should influence style has shaped the practice and appreciation of craft. Yet this belief is based on a misunderstanding of ornament. Ornament is artificial by definition. For a given technique, no one style is more "natural" than another. There is always a choice, to go with the limitations of the craft or against them.

Fig. 34. Ikat textile (detail). Silk. Central Asian, nineteenth century. Providence, Museum of Art, Rhode Island School of Design, 1992.127.4. Gift of Natasha B. Ford. Photography by Del Bogart.

Fig. 35. Ikat sari (detail). Silk. Indian, nineteenth century. Washington, D.C., The Textile Museum, OC6.53. Acquired by George Hewitt Myers.

Physically, these limitations are real: some things are harder to do than others. But as aesthetic imperatives they have only as much power as we choose to grant them. The decision to let style follow technique in order to produce the most "natural"-seeming effect is an aesthetic decision, whether we make it ourselves or let the culture make it for us. It is neither more nor less natural than the belief that a technique can do anything you want it to; the history of ornament abounds in both.

The Byzantine pattern type known as the *medallion style* is both a triumph of the silk weaver's art and a reminder of how unpredictable the interaction of style and technique can be.[6] Deceptively simple, the pattern consists of horizontal and vertical rows

Fig. 36. Floor mosaic. Roman, first half of the third century. Tunisia (Thuburbo Maius, "Maison aux Communs"). Photo: Dumbarton Oaks, Washington, D.C.

Fig. 37. Tapestry fragment. Wool and linen. Late Roman, c. fifth century. Washington, D.C., Dumbarton Oaks Collection, 73.2. Photo: Dumbarton Oaks, Washington, D.C.

of identical medallions enclosing human and animal figures (fig. 24). Repetition conceals a precise balance of movement and stasis, of ornamental and pictorial form. Even small-scale versions, with medallions no more than a few inches across, have a stateliness which is both rich and austere. The largest examples have medallions over three feet in diameter. Increasing the size of a motif may not increase its impact; often the result is merely incongruous. The large medallion silks are among the few successful attempts to raise ornament to a monumental scale.

The medallion style appears quite suddenly around the beginning of the sixth century. From then until at least the eleventh century, Byzantine medallion silks and their derivatives were synonymous with ultraluxurious textile production throughout most of Eurasia. Because they have no obvious antecedents in Roman textile art, and because their static magnificence conforms to an "oriental" rather than a "classical" stereotype, scholars have assumed that the Byzantines borrowed the pattern type from Persia. In fact, a closer look at Roman decorative art reveals a fascination with repeated motifs, especially with repeated *frames* of all kinds. It is strongest in the many floor mosaics that use rows of identical polygons as frames for portraits, genre scenes, and a variety of ornamental motifs (fig. 36).

In textiles, especially clothing, Roman taste favored isolated patches of decoration on a plain ground. Within these limits, the love of framing and repetition ran almost as strong as in mosaics (fig. 37). Today we associate repetition with mechanical processes, but these Roman textiles were tapestry-woven, a technique that allowed no mechanization. All patterns had to be built up laboriously by hand, thread by thread. In this respect tapestry closely resembles mosaic: repeating patterns are neither harder nor easier than nonrepeating patterns of similar overall complexity.

Although the Roman fascination with framing and repetition is independent of technique, the birth of the medallion style looks like a textbook case of technical influence. Around the fifth century a new invention, the drawloom, made it possible to raise and lower any combination of warp threads in a predetermined sequence. Once the weaver has completed the exacting task of figuring out the combinations and isolating the many groups of threads, even an elaborate motif can be repeated with no more artistic (as opposed to purely manual) effort than would be needed to weave it once.

The drawloom was the perfect tool for weaving silk. In part the reason was technical: the naturally long threads encourage repeating patterns, and their fineness rewards a dense and complex weave. In part it was economic: drawloom weaving is capital intensive, and therefore suited to a luxury material with a guaranteed market. Although the establishment of sericulture in sixth-century Byzantium eliminated the need for Chinese imports, the luxury value of silk was undiminished, and the finest grades of cloth remained an imperial prerogative for hundreds of years.

Since the preference for framing and repetition was well established in Roman art, the new technique did not so much create a new style as distill the old one into its definitive form. It would be easy to conclude that style and technique came together seamlessly to produce the medallion silks, but we must not oversimplify. In one major sense, the drawloom was an obstacle to the growth of the medallion style as we know it. Fluid, unbroken curves are hard to make on a drawloom. Every curved line is a succession of tiny (or not so tiny) right-angle steps. The smaller the individual steps, the smoother the curve appears from a reasonable distance, but the more operations the process requires. A big, bold circle is the most unforgiving of shapes. Like a sharp outline in double ikat, the almost perfect circles of the best medallion silks are a tour de force in defiance of technique.

The medallion style spread with amazing rapidity. The Chinese began weaving medallion silks in the late sixth century. By the eighth century their versions were as splendid as anything the Byzantines produced (fig. 38). Throughout the history of ornament some of the most important stylistic changes occurred when a pattern was passed from one culture to another. At one end of the spectrum, a person travels to a faraway place, finds something interesting and brings it back, or copies it and brings back the copy. The cultural exchange goes no further, and the artifact survives, if it survives at all, as the record of a single adventure. At the other end of the spectrum, an artifact is made in large numbers and traded on a large scale (or on a smaller scale among an influential elite, as were the medallion silks), becomes popular, inspires copies and adaptations, and ultimately becomes part of another culture's mainstream. Given the power of historical accident, it can be far easier to recognize a cultural borrowing than to know how it came about.

This is true of any kind of artifact, not just ornament. A Caucasian cookbook published in 1976 describes a classic dish from Georgia, east of the Black Sea. It is pheasant cooked with walnuts, wine, grapes, orange juice, and tea. Although the combination is distinctive, the ingredients are not unusual—except for the tea. Tea is sometimes used as a flavoring in East Asia, but in West Asia and Europe it is almost unheard of. I was therefore astonished to find the same ingredients in a recipe from Catalonia, a region of northeastern Spain.[7] Although the methods of preparation differ somewhat, the dishes are essentially the same, and each is presented as typical of its region. There must be a historical link, and a fairly recent one, since tea was unknown in Europe before the seventeenth century. Was it once a common dish, perhaps of Ottoman origin, now surviving only in a few small areas? Or was it carried from Georgia to Catalonia, or Catalonia to Georgia, in a period of intensive trade or other contact between the two areas? Or was it a lone traveler's cherished recipe?—in which case it may have spread no further in its new home than a family or small community. In theory, a little research should settle the issue. The danger is in leaping to conclusions from the coincidence itself.

A second example comes from anthropology. It has the character of an "urban legend," something many people know but are unable to pin down with names and dates. The kind of pitfall it illustrates, however, is not just real but omnipresent. Some time ago, perhaps in the 1930s, an anthropologist visited some Blackfoot Indians and asked

Fig. 38. Woven silk textile. Chinese, eighth century. Nara, Horyuji. Photo: after Ryoichi Hayashi, *The Silk Road and the Shosoin* (New York: Weatherhill/Heibonsha, 1975).

Fig. 39. Fragment of a doorway. Marble. Roman, second century. Istanbul, Archaeological Museum. Author's photo.

to hear their tales and legends. One of the stories they told him was remarkably close to the episode in the Old English poem *Beowulf* in which the hero battles the monster Grendel. Delighted, the anthropologist published an article called "The Beowulf Legend among the Plains Indians." Several years later another anthropologist visited the same group, and once again asked to hear their legends. They told him several, but not the "Grendel" story. When he asked about it, none of his informants remembered any such story. Finally, the oldest member of the group explained: "A long time ago one of your people came and asked to hear our stories. We told him some, then asked to hear some of his. He told us the Grendel story. Later, another of your people came and asked to hear our stories. But we didn't like him, so we told him the same story back again."

Being played for a fool by informants with their own agenda is every fieldworker's nightmare, but the anecdote makes a more important if less amusing point. There are no true and false borrowings, only successful and unsuccessful ones. In slightly different circumstances, the story of Beowulf and Grendel could have become a living part of the Blackfoot repertory of tales, just as pheasant with walnuts and tea became known as a traditional recipe two thousand miles from its original home.[8]

Small-scale borrowings can be fascinating, but it is the success stories that shape the history of ornament. The medallion style is one of them. Another is the vine scroll. In plain language this is an imaginary vine whose tendrils form a predictable series of loops or spirals. In and around them, the artist is free to add a variety of other plants

Fig. 40. Decorated arch. Stucco. Italian, eighth century. Cividale, Tempietto. Author's photo.

Fig. 41. Relief carving with floral scroll. Indian, sixth century. Sarnath, Dhamekh Stupa. Author's photo.

and animals, often naturalistic in themselves but with no regard to scale or ecological compatibility (fig. 39). Starting in the Greco-Roman Mediterranean, in less than a thousand years it found its way into every major Eurasian art tradition, with a distinctive form and emphasis in each (figs. 40, 41). Interlace, another pattern type of Roman origin, proved almost as adaptable, and played a central role in both Christian and Islamic

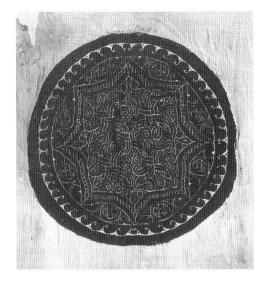

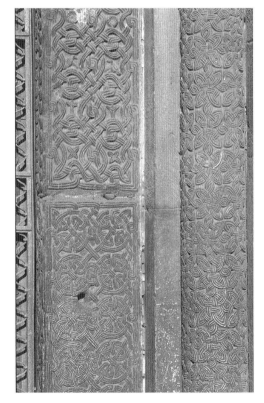

Fig. 42. Tapestry roundel. Wool and linen. Late Roman, late fourth or early fifth century. New York, The Metropolitan Museum of Art, 89.18.151, Funds from Various Donors, 1889.

Fig. 43. Church portal (detail). Stone. Italian, eleventh-twelfth century. Milan, S. Ambrogio. Author's photo.

Fig. 44. Ewer. Brass. Islamic (Mesopotamia), mid-thirteenth century. Baltimore, The Walters Art Museum, no. 54.456.

ornament throughout the Middle Ages (figs. 42–44).[9] A decorative form of Arabic script known as square kufic, developed in the twelfth and thirteenth centuries and used mainly on buildings (fig. 45), found its way quickly to German-speaking Central Europe—as the basis of an embroidery style (fig. 46).

The most recent of the great borrowings is the so-called paisley pattern. Few people who put on a paisley blouse, scarf, or tie are aware of its origin, but the pattern's history is well known.[10] The common feature of all paisley patterns is a motif like a curved teardrop, which may be large or small, rounded or immensely elongated. Often referred to simply as a "paisley," or sometimes as a "pine," the motif is more correctly called a *boteh* or *buta*. This is the Persian word for a flower, but the motif itself is Indian.

Fig. 45. Tombstone. Limestone. Iranian, 1352. New York, The Metropolitan Museum of Art, 35.120, Rogers Fund, 1935.

Fig. 46. Embroidery with scenes from the life of St. Margaret (detail). Nettle cloth with silk and metallic thread. German, c. 1290. Helmstedt, Kloster St. Marienberg. Photo: after Marie Schuette and Sigrid Müller-Christensen, *The Art of Embroidery*, trans. Donald King. (London: Thames and Hudson, 1964).

Fig. 47. Relief of flowering plants (detail). Marble. Indian, 1631–47. Agra, Taj Mahal. Author's photo.

Fig. 48. Border from a shawl. Mountain goat wool. Indian (Kashmir), mid-eighteenth century. London, Victoria and Albert Museum, I.M. 165–1913. Courtesy of the Trustees of the V&A.

The paisley pattern began in the seventeenth century as a fairly naturalistic rendering of a flowering plant, an altogether typical motif in Mughal decorative art (fig. 47). Among many other uses, we find it repeated along the borders of shawls, a specialty of Kashmir, which were increasingly favored as *men's* garments in India around this time. During the eighteenth century the *boteh* lost much of its original resemblance to a plant. The foliage became more elaborate and "busy," while the increasingly well-defined outline took on the familiar teardrop shape (fig. 48). In the second half of the eighteenth century, European women adopted the Kashmir shawl as a high-fashion

Fig. 49. Shawl (detail). Silk and wool. European, 1840–50. Washington, D.C.,
The Textile Museum, 1964.59.1. Gift of Mrs. Robert G. Trumbell.

accessory, for reasons having at least as much to do with its material as with its decoration. The traditional Kashmir shawl was made from the wool of Himalayan goats—
the original cashmere—and its softness was legendary. Since the goats were wild or
half-wild, and the best quality wool was gathered from bushes and rocks in the spring-
time after the goats had shed their winter undercoats, it is no surprise that demand far
outstripped supply.

The weaving process was a match for the material. It is called twill tapestry, because
the entire textile, both the pattern and the plain twill ground, was handwoven as tapes-

Fig. 50. Shawl. Wool. French, mid-nineteenth century. New York, The Metropolitan Museum of Art, 26.179. Gift of Mrs. Edwin E. Butler, in memory of her father, Dudley B. Fuller, 1926.

try. An elaborate shawl could take more than a year to weave. Under pressure from the European market, Kashmiri weavers turned increasingly to such labor-saving devices as dividing the work of a single shawl among several people, or substituting hand embroidery for the even more time-consuming twill tapestry. They also responded to European taste by increasing the size of the *boteh*. During the crucial second quarter of the nineteenth century it became much more than a border motif. Patterns consisting of multiple *botehs* of different sizes, overlapping or elaborately intertwined, grew inward from the edges of the shawl until the plain ground was reduced to a tiny area at the center, or disappeared completely (fig. 49).

It is difficult to separate Indian and European currents in this rapid evolution. Not content with commissioning shawls from Indian manufacturers, the Europeans did their best to produce "Kashmir" shawls of their own. Part of the effort focused on the texture of the cloth. Since no European wool was soft enough, there were repeated attempts to establish breeding populations of Himalayan goats. However, the animals either died en route or responded to the gentler European climate by producing inferior wool. Efforts to imitate the Kashmiri patterns were more successful, especially after the widespread adoption of the jacquard loom—essentially an automated drawloom—in the 1820s. Paris and Lyon became shawl-weaving centers, as did Norwich in England and Paisley in Scotland—hence the use of the word "paisley" for the shawl or its pattern.

Fig. 51. Vase. Cameo glass. American (Honesdale), c. 1901. New York, The Metropolitan Museum of Art, 69.91.1, Anonymous Gift Fund, 1969.

The middle decades of the nineteenth century mark the height of European achievement in shawl manufacture. At this point the interaction of the two styles becomes too complex to chart, with Indian weavers imitating European shawls based on Indian shawls commissioned for the European market. In the most elaborate European examples, the density of the pattern overwhelms the individual *botehs*, which dissolve into floral and architectural fantasies of rococo inspiration. More often the *boteh* retains some vestige of its earlier form, but is enormously elongated in sweeping curves bearing no resemblance to traditional Indian ornament (fig. 50).

It is important not to think of European shawls as mass-produced imitations of Indian originals. Even when the patterns are almost identical, the combination of technique and national style produces very different effects. Seen close up, the surface of a twill tapestry shawl is full of energy, which seems to evaporate as soon as we move from details to large-scale motifs and patterns. In contrast, jacquard shawls look flat and stilted on the level of detail, but come to life when we can see the whole pattern.

Although both versions had their strengths and weaknesses, the Indian shawls were consistently in greater demand as luxury items. Presumably they were valued for their exotic origin, not for any intrinsic quality, especially since few of the later shawls made for export had the delicacy of pattern or the remarkable softness of the best early pieces. The European fashion for shawls ended abruptly in the 1870s, but the *boteh*, detached from its original contexts and historical associations, has persisted into our own time as one of the most fertile and vigorous creations in the recent history of ornament. The shawls themselves have an importance beyond illustrating how the interaction of two cultures can transform a motif. The more adventurous of their designs bridge not just a cultural gap but an art historical one: between Victorian ornament and Art Nouveau (fig. 51).

Occasionally an individual artist has changed the history of ornament. The unknown Roman or Byzantine weaver who first used a drawloom to weave a pattern of circles was one such innovator. Adam van Vianen, whose challenge to the integrity of visual form prepared the way for the rococo, was another (fig. 7). So was Jean Revel of Lyon, who expanded the horizons of textile design in ways that go beyond the creation of individual patterns (fig. 32). But these are exceptions. The ogival pattern may go back to an inspired breakthrough by a single artist, but the paisley pattern does not. Ultimately even the biggest changes lead back to the conventions of ornament, not away from them. Artists assimilate a new idea or pattern or technique, combine it with what they already know, and the process goes on. Change is no less significant for being gradual. Only a succession of artists, emulating and improvising on each other's work, can bring out the full richness of a pattern.

From Function to Meaning

IN SEARCH OF UNIVERSALS

IN 1983 THE Polish American Congress issued a medal commemorating the 300th anniversary of the defeat of the Turks at Vienna. This battle, in which King John III Sobieski of Poland played a major role, marked the westernmost advance of Turkish power, and was thus a turning point in the military struggle between Christendom and Islam. The obverse of the medal bears a portrait of the king, with the inscription: John III Sobieski Savior of Christianity. The reverse shows the king on horseback, in full armor, holding the Polish flag; an inscription reads: Poland Still Vigilant. In view of the political situation in Poland in the 1980s, the symbolic message is obvious. The medal is an expression of solidarity with the Polish people, and of confidence in their ultimate victory, through national pride and Christian faith, over an ungodly occupying power.

None of this is explicit: it depends on the viewer's ability to see the present in the past and the past in the present. Yet despite its cleverness, sincerity, and topicality, the

Fig. 52. Winnowing tray. Wood. Suriname, 1980. New York, American Museum of Natural History, neg. no. 2A12491. Courtesy of the Department of Library Services, American Museum of Natural History. Photo: A. Singer.

medal probably struck many viewers as no more than a curiosity. It is as though communication by symbol or allusion were ipso facto irrelevant because it requires a sense of history to mediate between seeing and understanding. How easily we forget that in many cultures previous to our own, such mediation was taken for granted. A culture's reliance on allusion and symbolism can be a measure of its alienness, even when, like Renaissance Europe, it is part of our direct ancestry.

If symbolic communication using portraits of real people is alien to modern thinking, how much more so is symbolism in ornament. Naturalistic imagery is specific, so it is at least reasonable to assume that its symbolic associations will be specific. By this standard, ornament is doubly inaccessible. We are unaccustomed to approach it with the seriousness, or the openness to new systems, that we bring to the representational arts; and the ubiquity of ornament in premodernist art is itself a bar to specificity. It is one thing for visual forms to be familiar—we can imagine this leading to greater ease of symbolic association—but too great a familiarity becomes banality, the forms are taken for granted, and their very meaning becomes meaningless. In these terms, ornament and meaningful symbolic communication seem incompatible. The use of ornament for specific communication depends on a paradox: the attachment of meaning to forms that are stripped of meaning.

Nevertheless, there is a surprisingly widespread assumption in today's world that ornament can and does, or at one time could and did, convey important symbolic messages. Western viewers of ornament apparently crave meanings, and what they crave, they find—or create. An apt illustration comes from Sally Price's book *Primitive Art in Civilized Places*. The Maroons of Suriname, descendants of escaped slaves, have a distinctive style of ornamental wood carving (fig. 52). According to Price, foreign scholars and collectors continue to find meanings in the patterns even when the artists insist there are none. One investigator went so far as to say that a pattern must have meaning *because* the Maroons deny that it has! Another case involves a Maroon man who

sold wood carvings to tourists in the 1960s. He soon realized that his customers wanted to know what the carved motifs "meant." Since they had no traditional meaning, but were purely decorative, he bought a book of Maroon motifs, with foreign interpretations, and copied the illustrations in his carvings. Himself illiterate, he "simply showed the book to his customers so they could look up the meanings of their purchases." His business prospered.[1]

The story illustrates the importance of commerce in artistic creation, and the difficulty of ever establishing an "authentic" meaning. These seem very different issues, but they can be closely related. We rely on native informants, speaking directly or through documents, to confirm meaning in the art of cultures foreign to our own, including those of our own past. Implicit in this reliance is the assumption that their testimony is "true." Yet here the testimony is false on two different levels. The artist-informant did not believe the information he gave his clients (strictly speaking, he did not give it to them, but allowed them to take it for themselves), and this information was itself derived from foreign interpretations whose accuracy was compromised by cultural prejudice. I have said that there are no true or false cultural borrowings, only successful and unsuccessful ones. In this case the issue is not the borrowing itself, but the demonstrably false conclusions to which it leads.

Everyday meanings, as distinct from esoteric ones, should be exempt from chicanery. If a foreigner points to a tree and asks what it is, we have no reason to say it is a cat. But the situation might be very different if we knew he believed that we use the same word for tree and cat (however incomprehensible or silly his reasons might seem to us), and wanted to go on believing it, and would pay generously to have his belief confirmed. How many times might this sort of thing have happened in the past? How many documents that we regard as testimonies to meaning in ornament are really testimonies to the age-old principle of giving the customer what he or she wants?[2]

More is at stake here than the trustworthiness of a given document. The search for meaning even when native informants deny it, and the creation of a market for meanings, cast doubt on the validity of interpretation itself. Yet interpreters of human behavior on all levels, including artistic creation, have asserted a right and a duty to find meanings beyond what their subjects openly state. Can we afford to renounce this? Quite apart from the cynical quip that a lot of scholars and critics would lose their jobs if we agreed to believe only what artists said about their own works, we would have to resign ourselves to a certain literalism in our aesthetic responses. Just as composers are not always the best performers of their own music, someone whose primary talents are visual may put far more into a work than he or she is capable of explaining in words. The various interpretative disciplines were created in recognition of this fact.

In his book *The Sense of Order*, E. H. Gombrich explains the enthusiasm for meaning in terms of the "spell . . . cast by mysterious symbols of which the meaning has been forgotten. Who can tell what ancient wisdom may be embodied in these enigmatic shapes and forms?" He also compares the search for meaning in ornament to "the hope that in tracing back the roots of any word we would arrive at the true and original meaning—its God-given meaning as it were."[3] Gombrich finds these connected impulses at least as far back as the eighteenth century, and there is no denying their power. In an essay entitled simply "Ornament," published in 1939, Ananda Coomaraswamy approaches the problem of meaning in ornament from just this point of view. Tracing the history of words for ornament, especially in Sanskrit and Greek, he concludes that the original meaning of the concept (we cannot speak of the original meaning of the word, since Coomaraswamy deals with several different words) was something like *completion:* "whatever was originally necessary to the completion of anything, and thus proper to it, naturally giving pleasure to the user; until still later what had once been essential to the nature of the object came to be regarded as an 'ornament' that could be added to it or omitted at will." For Coomaraswamy, necessity implies meaning; indeed, we cannot fully appreciate the implications of his approach for visual ornament unless we remember that he applies exactly the same terms to language and verbal expression: "Sound and meaning are indissolubly wedded; just as in all the other arts of whatever kind there was originally a radical and natural connection between form and significance, without divorce of function and meaning."[4]

At first, Coomaraswamy's insistence that all ornament had an "original" communicative function, now lost, seems no more than a particularly apt illustration of Gombrich's point. But there are other elements in it that help explain why the problem of symbolism looms so large in any modern attempt to understand ornament. Coomaraswamy ends with an appeal, not for interpretation, or the recovery of lost secrets, but for communication, and in the terms of his argument communication is linked with necessity. In other words, by arguing that ornament once was, and should again be, a means of communication, he rejects the separability of functional and ornamental form, and by extension the modernist insistence that functional form is defined by the absence of ornament.

If ornament once had meaning (the argument would run), then it once had an identifiable and necessary function. We have lost the meanings, and even the general

Pl. 1. Henri Matisse. *Composition, Black and Red*. Paper collage. French, 1947. Wellesley, Massachusetts, Davis Museum and Cultural Center, Wellesley College. Gift of Professor and Mrs. John McAndrew, 1958.11. © 2001 Succession H. Matisse, Paris/Artists Rights Society (ARS), New York.

Pl. 2. Textile. Silk. Turkish, second half of the sixteenth century. Washington, D.C., The Textile Museum, oC1.68. Acquired by George Hewitt Myers in 1952.

Pl. 3. Pile rug. Silk warp and weft, wool pile. Iranian, first half of the sixteenth century. New York, The Metropolitan Museum of Art, Frederick C. Hewitt Fund, 1910 (10.61.3). Photo: © 1989 The Metropolitan Museum of Art.

Pl. 4. Textile. Silk. Italian, early eighteenth century. London, Victoria and Albert Museum, T32–1910. Courtesy of the Trustees of the V&A. Photographer: David McGrath.

Pl. 5. Flat-woven rug (*cicim*). Turkish, late nineteenth century. Washington, D.C., The Textile Museum, 1989.10.97. Bequest of Arthur D. Jenkins.

Pl. 6. G. C. Haité. Printed textile. Linen and cotton, c. 1890. London, Victoria and Albert Museum, T56–1953. Courtesy of the Trustees of the V&A.

Pl. 7. "Carpet page" from the Lindisfarne Gospels. British Isles, c. 700. London, British Library, Cott. Nero D IV, f. 26V.

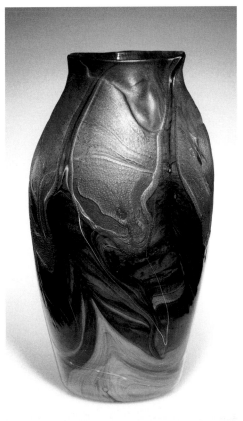

Pl. 9. Louis Comfort Tiffany. Vase. Glass. American, 1893–96. New York, The Metropolitan Museum of Art, 96.17.17. Gift of H. O. Havemeyer, 1896. Photograph © 1989 The Metropolitan Museum of Art.

Pl. 8. Kelly Miller. Tattoo. American, 1991.
Photo: © 2001 William DeMichele.

Pl. 10. Barbara Todd. *Adam's Boat*. Quilt. Canadian, 1994–95. Possession of the artist. Photo: Robert Keziere.

awareness of meaning in ornament, and as a result ornament has lost its function and even become the antithesis of function. But so long as we are able to recover meanings, we retain the ideal of ornament as something necessary and functional, and the hope of restoring it to this former state.

Until very recently, ornament *has* been functional, and it *has* been a means of communication. Where Coomaraswamy and others have gone wrong is in assuming that if ornament communicates it must communicate symbolically. To believe that the "lost" function of ornament was to

Fig. 53. Capital. Marble. Late Roman/Byzantine, fifth-sixth century. Istanbul, Archaeological Museum. Author's photo.

convey a host of specific meanings is a particularly modern kind of romanticism. We are simultaneously uncomfortable with symbolism and fascinated by it. Because we believe ourselves incapable of using symbols, we are eager to find them in other cultures. We define ourselves by what we have lost, and we yearn for it.

Communication need not be symbolic, any more than function need be mechanical. Before one even selects a pattern or motif, the *decision to use ornament* conveys a wealth of meaning, no less real or powerful for being inchoate. Elaborating an object beyond a certain point means disguising its original character. This is one of ornament's basic functions. Decorated capitals have been in continuous use in Western building for thousands of years, transforming a simple structural unit into a wealth of floral, animal, and even human forms (fig. 53). Late Gothic fan vaulting is often so complex that pattern effectively conceals structure (fig. 54). Nor is it uncommon to find ornament used to deny the very solidity of the surface it adorns, through the direct challenge of illusionism (fig. 18), or else by imparting such a complex texture that a viewer sees little else (fig. 55).

These transformations affirm a pervasive, age-old dissatisfaction with structural necessity as the sole determinant of artistic form. The primary function of ornament—and it is a function, make no mistake—is to remedy this dissatisfaction by introducing free choice and variation into even those parts of a work that appear most strictly shaped by structural or functional needs.

Fig. 54. Interior of King's College Chapel. Cambridge, England, 1446–1515. Photo: A. F. Kersting.

GRANADA...557 bis Vista interior de la Sala de Embajadores.(Alhambra). J. Laurent y Cⁱᵃ Madrid.
Es propiedad   Déposé

Fig. 55. Interior of the Sala de Embajadores. Spanish-Islamic, second half of the fourteenth century. Granada, Alhambra. Courtesy of the Fine Arts Library, Harvard College Library. Photo: J. Laurent.

Displays of virtuosity often evoke a complex or even contradictory response by calling attention to the conditions they surmount. The fan vaulting in King's College Chapel reminds us of the weight and solidity of stone, precisely because the architect has gone to such lengths to make it seem light and insubstantial. In figure 56, the elegance of the scrolls and figures suggests a soft, easily worked material. For a moment one accepts the illusion, but a new and heightened appreciation of the achievement follows with the realization that the ornament was chiseled out of steel. In each case, ornament emphasizes both a problem and the artist's ability to solve it.

Considerations of status frequently affect the character and applications of ornament, as when ornament is used to transform ordinary goods into luxurious ones. Such transformation has often been a response to sumptuary laws. These laws, of a type

Fig. 56. Filippo Negroli. Burgonet. Steel. Italian, 1543. New York, The Metropolitan Museum of Art, 17.190.1720. Gift of J. Pierpont Morgan, 1917.

once common to a variety of cultures, are intended to promote the economic and moral health of a society by limiting the consumption or display of luxury goods by its citizens. Implicitly and often explicitly, sumptuary laws have reinforced established social structures by restricting luxury on the basis of class or rank. In England in the reign of Elizabeth I, for instance, only those of the rank of baron and above, Knights of the Garter, and Privy Councillors were allowed to wear cloth of gold or silver, tinseled satin, silk, cloth mixed or embroidered with gold or silver, or foreign woolen cloth.[5]

Given the pervasive desire for social and economic advancement, and for display as a confirmation of that advancement, it is hard to imagine an enterprise more doomed than the enforcement of sumptuary laws. The techniques used to circumvent the laws were often straightforward, as in the later Roman Empire, where the finest grades of

Fig. 57. Dagger hilt. Gold. Chinese, fourth century B.C. London, © The British Museum, 1937.4–16.218. Reproduced by courtesy of the Trustees of the British Museum.

purple dye from the *Murex* shellfish, the so-called Tyrian purple, were an imperial pre-rogative. (We are accustomed to thinking of purple as the color of royalty, but it is important to remember that the luxury value of murex purple came first: rulers arro-gated it to themselves because it was beautiful and expensive.) Here, the solution was simply to imitate the prohibited color as closely as possible by other means; apparently this was permitted so long as one did not wear anything that looked like a *completely* purple garment.[6] Of the many thousands of decorated textile fragments preserved from the Late Roman period by the dry sands of Egypt, the great majority are decorated wholly or primarily in purple, usually through combinations of madder and indigo (many of these appear dark purplish-brown today), some presumably with lesser qual-ity murex dye.

No matter how pleasing the color purple in its non-murex forms may have been, there is no way to explain its popularity except by its resemblance to the pigment which sumptuary law and economic reality had placed beyond reach. In other words, thou-sands upon thousands of citizens clothed themselves in a semblance of wealth, aware that they were deceiving no one, just as they were not deceived by their neighbors' use of the same expedient. Yet for centuries the *idea* of purple as a symbol of luxury was so compelling that on some level the difference between semblance and reality did not matter.

Whereas ornament may confer glamour on everyday materials, precious materials lend some of their own glamour to ornament.[7] This is especially true of gold, but there is a complex reciprocity here. The prestige of gold is not just due to its rarity but to the kinds of things that can be made from it. Gold has a low melting point, is malleable and ductile to a very high degree, and does not tarnish. The challenge it conveys is to exploit opportunities, not to triumph over difficulties. In view of the importance of gold as a symbol of wealth and status, it is worth noting that its physical properties allow the creation of extremely lavish effects using relatively small amounts of the metal (fig. 57). In such cases the most labor-intensive forms of ornament may have been economical as well as ostentatious.[8] Modern Western society places an enormous premium on fine handwork, but in many parts of the world, even today, gold jewelry is priced accord-ing to weight, not workmanship.

Another function of ornament is to express reverence for the sacred. Texts from var-ious historical periods touch on decorative art and its relation to religious devotion, but almost always they focus on the object rather than on the way it is decorated. A passage from the thirteenth-century author Durandus, for example, describes how on festivals curtains are hung up in churches, for the sake of the ornament they give; and that by visible, we may be led to invisible beauty. These curtains are sometimes tinctured with various hues . . . so that by the diversity of the colours themselves we may be taught that man, who is the temple of God, should be ordained by the variety and diversity of virtues. A white curtain signifieth pureness of living: a red, charity: a green, contemplation: a black, mortification of the flesh: a livid-coloured, tribulation. Besides these, over white curtains are sometimes suspended hangings of various colours: to signify that our hearts ought to be purged from vices: and that in them should be the curtains of virtues, and the hangings of good works.[9]

Although the word "ornament" is not used in our technical sense, but in the most general sense of decoration, there is little doubt that some of the textiles were ornamental. Frustratingly, the text gives no clue to what they looked like, beyond their predominant colors, or to what, if anything, their motifs or patterns meant in religious terms.

If luxury were not an almost universally understood metaphor for the sacred, we would not find it in sacred contexts. It would have its place in the secular realm, giving pleasure and conferring status, but the incentive to assimilate religious and luxury art simply would not exist. The fact that it does exist opens the door to the complex interaction of religious and secular art. Luxury in religious art is veneration made visible and tangible. It is an offering up of that which is most demanding of effort, skill, and expense. The underlying assumption is that anything less would be unworthy of the deity *or* the worshipper.

In the Judeo-Christian tradition, this attitude has found its most overt expression in the Old Testament, in accounts of the construction and decoration of the Tabernacle and Temple, and in a verse from Psalm 26 (Psalm 25 in the Vulgate, from which it was known to medieval Christians): "Lord, I have loved the beauty of thy house." Clear as they are, these precedents were the cause of much controversy throughout the Middle Ages. Against the examples of Tabernacle and Temple, it was argued that such elaborations may have been necessary to the Jews, but that since Christianity had superseded Judaism, Jewish ceremonial and display were no longer needed. Similarly, the words of the Psalm, which became a touchstone of the dispute, were taken to refer to a mystical rather than a physical dwelling.[10]

Regardless of its desirability, the power of luxury in religious art was taken for granted. In 735, St. Boniface wrote to the abbess Eadburgha: "And I beg you further to add to what you have done already by making a copy written in gold of the Epistles of my master, St. Peter the Apostle, to impress honor and reverence for the Sacred Scriptures visibly upon the carnally minded to whom I preach."[11] Even St. Bernard of Clairvaux (1090–1153), founder of the Cistercian order and one of the most eloquent critics of religious luxury, could recognize its usefulness in winning over the "carnally minded": "Bishops have a duty towards both wise and foolish. They have to rouse the devotion of the carnal people with material ornament, since they are incapable of spiritual things."[12] He also recognized that wealth attracted wealth: a well-ornamented shrine received more donations. Four hundred years later, a more comprehensive statement of the connection between aesthetic and religious experience appeared in the proceedings of the Council of Trent (1545–63), among the formulations that defined the doctrines and practices of Catholicism in the face of the growing Protestant threat:

> And since the nature of man is such that he cannot without external means be raised easily to meditation on divine things, holy mother church has instituted certain rites, namely, that some things in the mass be pronounced in a low tone and others in a louder tone. She has likewise, in accordance with apostolic discipline and tradition, made use of ceremonies, such as mystical blessings, lights, incense, vestments, and many other things of this kind, whereby both the majesty of so great a sacrifice might be emphasized and the minds of the faithful excited by those visible signs of religion and piety to the contemplation of those most sublime things which are hidden in this sacrifice.[13]

In these examples, luxury in religious art is meant to have a religious effect, even on worshippers whose outlook was fundamentally "carnal." However, the more lavish a work of traditional religious art, the more likely it is to include, implicitly or explicitly, some element of self-glorification by the patron. Patronage on a grand scale is often a continuation of politics by other means. For the West, the consecration of Solomon's Temple in the tenth century B.C. set the precedent. It was a magnificent royal ceremony, intended to bind the kingdom together under Solomon's power as well as God's. The Temple and its furnishings were part of a huge architectural complex that included Solomon's own palace.[14] Fifteen hundred years later, descriptions of the church of Hagia Sophia (Holy Wisdom) in Constantinople (fig. 58), built by the Byzantine emperor Justinian between 532 and 537, echoed the lavish detailing of materials and workmanship in the biblical account. The echo is certainly deliberate. Hagia Sophia

Fig. 58. Interior of the Church of Hagia Sophia. Byzantine, 532–37. Istanbul. Author's photo.

was built not just as a place of worship but as a focus for imperial ceremony, and a symbol of the wealth and splendor of the Christian empire. On first entering the church, Justinian is said to have exclaimed, "O Solomon, I have surpassed thee!"[15]

Ornament appears in both accounts. For example, 1 Kings 7.15–22 tells how Hiram of Tyre cast two bronze pillars for the temple:

He also made two capitals of molten bronze, to set upon the tops of the pillars; the height of the one capital was five cubits, and the height of the other capital was five cubits. Then he made two nets of checker work with wreaths of chain work for the capitals. . . . Likewise he made pomegranates; in two rows round about the one network, to cover the capital that was on top of the pillar; and he did the same with the other capital. Now the capitals that were upon the tops of the pillars in the vestibule were of lily-work, four cubits. The capitals were upon the two pillars and also above the rounded projection which was beside the network; there were two hundred pomegranates, in two rows round about; and so with the other capital.

Justinian's court poet Paul the Silentiary tells how

the mason, weaving together with his hands the slabs of marble, has figured upon the walls connected arcs laden with fruit, baskets and leaves, and has represented birds perched on boughs. The twining vine with shoots like golden ringlets winds its curving path and weaves a spiral chain of clusters. . . . And above the high-crested columns . . . is deployed a tapestry of wavy acanthus, a wandering contexture of spiky points, all golden, full of grace. It encompasses marble shields—disks of porphyry glittering with a beauty that charms the heart.[16]

Holiness, self-aggrandizement, and in a different vein the refusal of structural necessity are ideas that ornament can convey by its very presence, regardless of the choice of motifs. This kind of communication is less precise and less versatile than communication by symbols, but has one overwhelming advantage: it is almost completely independent of cultural conditioning. Standards of luxury vary with time and place, but the equation of luxurious display with both temporal and spiritual power appears to be constant. This should be the full extent of universal or near-universal meaning in ornament. More precise correspondences of form and meaning depend on cultural convention. They cannot, by definition, be universal. Nevertheless, the quest for universal meanings, like the quest for perpetual motion, is irresistibly tempting. Several attempts, while never quite successful, have broadened our awareness of how form and meaning can relate.

Among the most intriguing pioneers in this endeavor were the art critic John Ruskin (1819–1900) and the psychologist Carl Jung (1875–1961). Both fell into the fatal and probably inevitable trap of circularity. The problem is not in the way they applied their insights, but in the assumptions on which those insights rest. Both Ruskin and Jung offered a connection between form and meaning that is not culture-bound, but only if one first accepts a set of axioms that *are* culture-bound.

If this book has a hero it is Ruskin, though the reasons may not be clear until later. Blessed with an imagination as immediate and vivid as a child's, a passion for intellectual rigor (by his own eccentric standards), and a magical ability to evoke the visual in words, he taught the modern West how to look at art. Above all, he was an uncompromising moralist, for whom every work of art, great or small, had implications for the working of society and the health of the human spirit. His goal was to show his contemporaries how to see these implications—and act on them. For Ruskin, "all noble ornamentation is the expression of man's delight in God's work." This is not sentimental religiosity. When Ruskin speaks of God's work, he means it literally. God's work is the natural world, and "beautiful ornament, wherever found, or however invented, is always either an intentional or unintentional copy of some constant natural form."[17]

From the role of certain forms in nature, Ruskin inferred a series of correspondences of form, meaning, and function, such as "the peculiar fitness of the circular curve as a sign of rest, and security of support, in arches." Thus "the other curves, belonging especially to action, are to be used in the more active architectural features." He would have disdained these one-to-one correspondences as an end in themselves. A rigid symbolic system, in which every circle had to mean "security," would have appalled him. His concern was not with the meanings of individual forms, but with the ways in which certain very broad categories of form shape our view of the world. Good ornament, for Ruskin, began with God's work, because natural forms can be intrinsically beautiful, and because contemplation of God's work leads to contemplation of God. In contrast, "all ornament is base which takes for its subject human work [i.e., artifacts as the basis of motifs and patterns]. . . . For to carve our own work [i.e., carve images of it], and set it up for admiration, is a miserable self-complacency, a contentment in our own wretched doings, when we might have been looking at God's doings."[18] The argument is both moral and aesthetic: if we become so involved in our own work that we recycle it endlessly without looking for inspiration outside ourselves, we not only lose touch with God (and become even more self-centered), but we will also lose touch with God's work (and produce uninspired and derivative ornament).

This is very much the way Ruskin's mind worked. The connection between art and morality is fundamental and unambiguous. The kind of art we make and enjoy, down to the smallest detail, determines our stature as human beings, measured by our aspiration to something beyond ourselves. In the final analysis, Ruskin could not have cared less for the literal imitation of nature. It is the underlying forms of natural things, reduced to their essence, that lead back to the divine. Ruskin recognized the importance of subject matter, to the extent of making a basic moral distinction between ornament based on natural forms and ornament based on artifacts. But his brilliance as a moralist of ornament lay in his willingness to bypass subject matter for the implications of irreducible form.

Jung, in contrast, believed in the universality and immutability of certain symbols, which he called *archetypes*. The difficulty is obvious. Symbolic thinking is a human universal, but individual symbols are culture-bound. Universal symbolism should therefore be a contradiction in terms. Jung's achievement was to find a way around the contradiction. It was and remains a highly controversial achievement, but this does not detract from its originality. Jung defined his archetypes as

> forms or images of a collective nature which occur practically all over the earth as constituents of myths and at the same time as autochthonous, individual products of unconscious origin. The archetypal motifs presumably derive from patterns of the human mind that are transmitted not only by tradition and migration but also by heredity. The latter hypothesis is indispensable, since even complicated archetypal images can be reproduced spontaneously without there being any possibility of direct tradition.[19]

In other words, Jung believed that symbols themselves, not just the capacity for symbolism, were innate: that they were transmitted biologically. If this is true, universal symbols not only can exist, they *must* exist. Wherever people go, certain specific ideas and images go with them. No other modern theory of culture makes this claim.

We do not know enough about the biological basis of thought to prove Jung either right or wrong. But even the possibility that he was right gave the study of symbolism an excitement that was altogether new. Although Jung never made a study of ornament per se, probably no one had a greater influence on the appreciation of ornament in the twentieth century. Jung shares Ruskin's assumption that subject matter is ultimately irrelevant. Only irreducible form can transmit irreducible meaning. For Ruskin, irreducible form could be manifest in a bold outline or a minute detail. For Jung, it was in the absence of detail. With all individualizing details stripped away, archetypes are not just universals but constants. Requiring neither conscious choice nor reference to a known tradition, they are reminders of what is innately and essentially human.

Not all symbols are archetypes, and not all archetypes are ornament. Archetypes need not even be visual, though many have a visual aspect. An example is the number four in its various incarnations, of which the most important is a circle divided into four parts. Jung found that this figure, which he called the quaternity, played a major role not only in the dreams of his patients but in Western religion and esoteric thought:

> Although the quaternity is an age-old and presumably prehistoric symbol, always associated with the idea of a world-creating deity, it is—curiously enough—rarely understood as such by those moderns in whom it occurs. . . . as a rule I discovered that they took it to symbolize *themselves* or rather *something in themselves*. They felt it belonged intimately to themselves as a sort of creative background, a life-producing sun in the depths of the unconscious. . . . The use of the comparative method shows without a doubt that the use of the quaternity is a more or less direct representation of the God who is manifest in his creation. We might, therefore, conclude that the symbol spontaneously produced in the dreams of modern people means something similar—*the God within.*[20]

The visual image that most concisely expresses the idea of the quaternity is the figure Jung called the *mandala*. The word is Sanskrit for circle, and as a technical term in Hindu and Buddhist art, it refers to a specific type of devotional image in tantric practice, with multiple pictures and religious symbols arranged concentrically. For Jung, it included a very wide range of images with a relatively small number of underlying characteristics, such as "circular, spherical or egg-shaped formation," "a center expressed by a sun, star, or cross, usually with four, eight, or twelve rays," or "squaring of the circle, taking the form of a circle in a square or vice versa."[21]

The examples Jung illustrated—the work of his patients, or in a few cases his own work—suggest an even more basic similarity: they are self-contained, concentric, and possess some form of symmetry. Many possess the qualities of ornament, often very good ornament, but the implications of his method for the study of ornament go far beyond specific examples. Since individualizing detail is irrelevant, images or patterns that appear very different may be, in essence, not just similar but *the same*, on the level of meaning as well as form. In other words, the creations of different artists, workshops, provinces, or entire cultures or historic periods can be shown, through similarities on the level of irreducible form, to express the same definable and consistent truths of human nature.

This principle is frustratingly immune to proof or disproof. Ornament often consists of a simple organizing framework filled in with multiple levels of detail. As a result, it is easy to find works that differ widely in appearance, but when stripped of detail conform to the same irreducible structure. The more we are prepared to disregard individualizing detail, the more likely we are to see the patterns in terms of underlying universals. The greater the possibility of establishing such universals, the greater the incentive to ignore detail. Jung's theory of archetypes is seductive because it promises so much, but the price is our acceptance of an untested and possibly untestable theory of the mind.

The theory of archetypes is an especially daring expression of an impulse that shaped many branches of scholarship in the late nineteenth and early twentieth centuries but is now unfashionable. I mean the impulse to look at such human phenomena as social behavior, religion, language, or art, not in the context of a single culture but worldwide, in the hope of discovering the underlying principles of those phenomena and ultimately of civilization itself. The most powerful expression of that approach was Sir James Frazer's *The Golden Bough* (1890; revised version 1913). Drawing on a huge body of evidence, including classical texts, modern European folklore, and ethnographic reports from all over the world, he revealed an archaic substratum of socioreligious beliefs and practices, centering on the seasonal death and rebirth of vegetation, and on magical practices intended to reinforce this cycle and ensure continuing fertility.

Frazer's approach was historical insofar as he sought to recapture an early stage of human thought and institutions. But it was only implicitly historical. Much of his evidence cames from contemporary rather than ancient sources, and in any case he was concerned with defining his phenomena and showing what they meant and how widespread they were, not with where and when they started or how they spread. But whenever a distinctive cultural trait occurs in widely separated areas, or among people with different styles of thought, the question of origins is bound to arise. Anthropology offers three explanations, or categories of explanation: independent invention, convergence, and diffusion. Of these, only diffusion bears directly on the relation of form and meaning in ornament, and the possibility of universal or near-universal symbolism.

We have encountered diffusion before. The Georgian-Catalan recipe for pheasant with walnuts and tea is an example. Ornament based on square kufic script (figs. 45–46) illustrates diffusion on a larger scale, including its vulnerability to historical accident. If the diffusion of ornamental forms is unpredictable, how much more so the diffusion of meanings. Can we be sure that meanings are diffused at all? At best, we must prove it on a case-by-case basis. Sometimes this is impossible, sometimes merely very hard. Ornament has always been associated with luxury objects, whose compactness and high value-to-weight ratio make them easily or at least profitably portable in both trade and plunder. Forms transmitted in this way are unlikely to carry their specific meanings with them, unless the cultures are already closely linked. The diffusion of ornament is then only part of a much deeper pattern of influence. Historically, such patterns of influence are most often associated with the spread of religions; conquest and trade do not enforce the necessary degree of consistency.

An important challenge to this view appeared in an article by Rudolf Wittkower, entitled "Eagle and Serpent."[22] Using the evidence of art, literature, and mythology, he traced the theme of combat between an eagle and a snake from West Asia in the third millennium B.C. to the Greco-Roman world and Christian Europe; to India, Southeast Asia, and the Pacific; and through Northeast Asia to aboriginal North and South America. (An eagle in combat with a snake was the central omen and symbol of the Aztecs, and survived the Spanish conquest to become the symbol of modern Mexico. This is the best-known version of the theme in the New World, but as Wittkower showed, it is far from the only one.) In all these migrations, Wittkower found the visual form inseparable from a symbolic meaning based on the solar associations of the eagle and the chthonian associations of the snake: "the struggle of the eagle and the serpent always represents the fundamental opposition of light and darkness, good and evil."

If Wittkower is right, the association of specific forms with specific meanings can defy distance, time, and cultural change. Diffusion is capable, by itself, of creating a ubiquitous if not universal symbol (Wittkower's account omits Africa). The argument is convincing for Western art, where the theme of eagle and snake is well documented, with written texts to confirm its meaning. It is the eastward spread of the motif that strains credibility, especially the suggestion that it traveled as far as Mexico with its symbolism unchanged. (Among other problems, the symbol would have had to pass through a region where, owing to the cold climate, snakes were unknown.) As though in recognition of the difficulty, Wittkower hedged his diffusionist bets with an almost Jungian appeal to racial memory:

Fights between eagles and snakes have actually been observed, and it is easy to understand that the sight of such a struggle must have made an indelible impression upon human imagination in its infancy. The most powerful of birds was fighting the most dangerous of reptiles. The greatness of the combat gave the event an almost cosmic significance. Ever since, when man has tried to express a struggle or victory of cosmic grandeur, the early memory of this event has been evoked.

This suggests another possibility. Why resort to "early memory" or "imagination in its infancy"? Eagles eat snakes. I have seen this myself, if only in a wildlife documentary; even on the screen it is a powerful, almost uncanny vision. Wittkower treated the combat as though it had no existence outside art and mythology. If that were so, we could safely accept his conclusions, but the combat is a recurring natural event. As a result, although we know that it has a consistent symbolic meaning across an enormous cultural, geographic, and chronological range, we do not know why. We still lack proof that the union of a particular form and meaning can survive diffusion on a global scale. Wittkower's evidence admits other explanations, and a chain is no stronger than its weakest link.

We are back where we started. No universal laws govern the relation of form and meaning. Intuition tells us that consistency of form implies consistency of meaning, but the most unshakable symbolic associations may be culturally determined. Americans associate the color white with weddings, but in East Asia white is the color of mourning. In Western cultures the owl is a symbol of wisdom, but in South Asia it is a symbol of stupidity. A culture could exist in which the snake stands for heaven and the eagle for earth, or in which they stand for different things altogether. It would be no stranger than the transformation of the cross, originally an instrument of torture pure and simple, into a symbol of salvation.

The more specific the interpretation, the greater the need to confirm it empirically. But absolute confirmation is rarely possible. Meanings go unrecorded if they are too esoteric *or* too commonplace. Even clearly documented meanings are transitory; they can change as decisively within a culture as between cultures. We all know that baby girls wear pink and baby boys wear blue. The colors have an identifying function which our society considers both important and immutable. Yet as recently as 1918, boys wore pink and girls wore blue.[23]

Ornament, Meaning, Symbol

IN SEARCH OF SPECIFICS

BEYOND ITS IMPLICATIONS for social status, aesthetic choice, and religious veneration, and the tempting but uncertain profundities of irreducible form, ornament has conveyed many specific meanings, each requiring a different interpretative approach. From the start, we should avoid confusing interpretation with recognition. Ornament frequently occupies a shadowy area between representation and abstract form. In an eighteenth-century Caucasian rug (fig. 59) it requires some effort to see the indistinct shapes in the main field as animals, alone or in combat. The style seems gradually to have slipped away from naturalism, whether by inclination or neglect, and one feels that much more of this trend would have left the forms unrecognizable.

The drift from image to abstract motif suggests that many such motifs originated in representation, and that the original content remains latent in the transformed motif, an anchor of specificity for those who can recognize it. The impulse to interpret a motif in terms of representational content is very strong, and undeniably satisfying: it gives

Fig. 59. Pile rug. Caucasian, probably eighteenth century. Present whereabouts unknown. Photo: after Lefevre & Partners auction announcement, 1982.

the sense of having broken through appearances to the motif's "real" nature. The problem is that every abstract motif need not be derived from a representational one, and that even when a motif did come into being in this way, we cannot be sure how long or how accurately its original context was remembered.

Sometimes we must learn a new visual language to know what, if anything, the pattern represents. As with verbal languages, the syntax can be so complex, or the idioms so localized, that even a "native speaker" cannot always be sure of reading correctly. Chilkat blankets or robes of the Pacific Northwest (fig. 60), for example, depict animals in a highly conventional way, with disconnected elements corresponding to eyes, ears, wings, fins, and so forth. Far from being random, the arrangements supposedly conform to well-established rules. Yet two accounts of these robes, based on the testimony of tribe members, have identified the same pattern in fundamentally different ways.[1] Such ambiguity in compositions that were assumed to be recognizable increases both the challenge and the satisfaction of mastering an unfamiliar idiom. But essential as this skill may be to understanding a given ornamental style, it is only in the most limited sense an end in itself. Knowing what a motif *represents* is not the same as knowing what it *means*. It is the

Fig. 60. Chilkat robe. Mountain goat wool and other fibers. American Northwest Coast (Tlingit), late nineteenth century. New York, American Museum of Natural History, neg. no. 327464. Courtesy of the Department of Library Services, American Museum of Natural History. Photo: Rota.

difference between learning the vocabulary and syntax of a new language, and understanding the subtleties of its literature.

Some conventions, like those of the Chilkat robe, are so unfamiliar and complex that by mastering them (insofar as their inherent ambiguity allows) one acquires not just a basic skill but a new way of seeing, and with it an important insight into another culture. At other times, an understanding of what the form literally represents is a matter of knowledge, not analysis. If we do not know the facts, we cannot possibly deduce the subject. Figure 61 shows a printed textile from contemporary Japan, decorated with a random-seeming arrangement of stylized figures. There is nothing immediately human

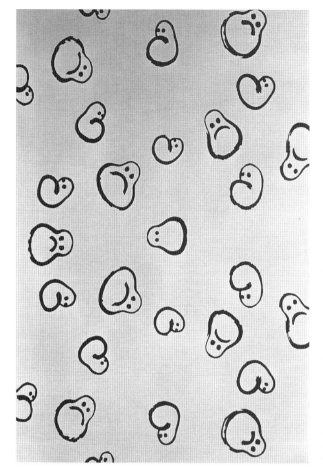

Fig. 61. Printed textile. Cotton. Japanese, c. 1985. Private collection. Author's photo.

about the outlines, and the eyes and mouth which distinguish one of them are rudimentary even by cartoon standards. A Japanese, however, would instantly recognize that the three different figures not only represent human beings, but the same human being, namely Bodhidharma (Daruma in Japanese), the founder of Zen Buddhism.

Bodhidharma probably lived during the sixth century, but he is far more a figure of legend than of history. He has long been the subject of both serious, naturalistic images and playfully simplified ones, of which our textile is an extreme case. The simplified images are widely incorporated into Japanese popular culture and the decorative arts, where they have a specific and thoroughly recognized meaning as symbols of good fortune. In fact, they bear the same relation to the Bodhidharma of religious history as Santa Claus bears to his original, St. Nicholas of Myra.

The Daruma cloth is a paradigm for ornamental symbolism in its simplest form: stylized figures in which we learn to recognize an individual, who in turn evokes a specific abstract idea. But symbolism rarely works so neatly. In the previous chapter we looked at the ways in which ornament can express very general ideas, like luxury or holiness. There is no sharp break between this largely implicit communication and more precise connections of form and meaning. An example is the dragon robe, an essential piece of formal wear in China during the Ming (1368–1644) and Qing (1644–1911) dynasties. As the name implies, these robes were decorated with woven or embroidered dragons (fig. 62). Dragons have a better defined and more enduring place in Chinese than in Western mythology. Unlike their Western counterparts, Chinese dragons are not malevolent, and they are associated

Fig. 62. Portrait of a Manchu nobleman. Hanging scroll, ink and color on silk. Chinese, probably second half of the eighteenth century. Present whereabouts unknown. Photo: after Gary Dickinson and Linda Wrigglewsorth, *Imperial Wardrobe* (Berkeley, Calif.: Ten Speed Press, 2000).

Fig. 63. Hans Memling. *The Virgin and Child with St. Anthony Abbot and a Donor.* Oil on wood. Flemish, 1472. Ottawa, National Gallery of Canada, 6191.

with water, not fire, but they are certainly powerful and mysterious, and are considered the highest celestial symbol.

As a garment motif, the dragon implied superiority in the wearer's position or aspirations. But one small detail conveyed, at least in theory, a far more specific message about the wearer's social standing. Chinese art depicts dragons with three, four, or five claws on each foot, but sumptuary laws dictated that only members of the imperial family were entitled to wear the five-clawed variety. As with purple in the Roman empire, jealous safeguarding of an imperial prerogative led to costly and even dangerous emulation of a status to which most wearers could not realistically aspire. Five-clawed dragons often appear on garments (and other objects) that are obviously not imperial. The desire to wear an imperial emblem gave rise to an amusing piece of casuistry. The Chinese word for a five-clawed dragon is *long* (*lung*); a dragon with four or fewer claws is a *mang*. Those accused of wearing the forbidden *long* dragon sometimes argued that the creature in question was not a *long* but a *mang* that happened to have five claws![2] There are also dragon robes in which the threads forming the creatures' fifth claws have been carefully unpicked to avoid the imputation of lèse-majesté.

These "sumptuary" meanings can be unexpectedly complex. A particular textile pattern, first cousin to the ogival patterns we saw in Chapter 2, appears repeatedly in European paintings and tapestries of the fifteenth century.[3] From the people who are shown wearing it, we can see it was a mark of lofty position. It is also consistently associated with images of the Virgin and Child, not as a garment but as a backdrop or curtain behind the figures (fig. 63). Social significance has become religious significance, as often happens with emblems of status, but the process does not end here. The pattern survived for centuries, and its religious associations seem not only to have survived with it, but to have intensified. In the sixteenth century it appears on the pope's chasuble in a context that evokes the ritual authority of the papacy.[4] A painting by the seventeenth-century Dutch artist Pieter Saenredam shows an uncut strip of patterned cloth in an otherwise bare church interior. The textile can only be meant as a symbol of sacredness, a nonfigural "icon" in an age of rampant iconoclasm.[5]

Ironically, the social meaning of the pattern seems to have outlived the religious meaning. John Singer Sargent's portrait of the collector Isabella Stewart Gardner uses an enlarged version of the same pattern for a backdrop (fig. 64). In a gesture altogether appropriate for the woman who built an Italian Renaissance palace in Boston to house her collection, artist and patron reached back to one of the preeminent symbols of status in the Renaissance. But they got it only half right, and the mistake reminds us of how precise such symbolism could be. The painting raised a number of eyebrows, primarily because people thought it sexually daring, but also because of the textile pattern's resemblance to a halo.[6] Those who objected on religious grounds were more correct than they knew. Did neither Sargent nor Mrs. Gardner realize that in her role as aristocratic patron she should have *worn* the pattern? To have herself portrayed standing in front of it verges on blasphemy.

Fig. 64. John Singer Sargent. *Portrait of Isabella Stewart Gardner*. Oil on canvas. American, 1888. Boston, Isabella Stewart Gardner Museum.

SOME kinds of meaning are inherent in the forms themselves, eliminating the need for conscious interpretation so long as certain principles are understood. Interlace—ornament composed of crisscrossing bands—is a good example. Although East Christian, West Christian, and Muslim civilizations evolved their own styles of interlace, they have a common origin in Roman art of the second to fourth centuries A.D. (figs. 42–44). This helps explain both their underlying formal similarities and the remarkably consistent ways they were used.[7] The most elaborate interlace patterns are among the very few kinds of ornament that are simply too hard for even a trained viewer to "read" without substantial effort. Such virtuosity fascinates by its intrinsic brilliance. It is also a strong indicator of luxury, since it implies the highest level of craftsmanship.[8] Thus complex interlace is part and parcel of visual display, whether the context is secular or religious. Yet its baffling intricacy suggests an additional purpose, which was apotropaic.

The word is from the Greek *apotropaios*, and means "turning away evil," in the sense of bad luck, supernatural malice, and above all, the evil eye. The belief that certain people can inflict harm by a glance is widespread.[9] Interlace is connected to the evil eye through the folklore of knots.[10] The Latin word *ligatura* is only one of many words, in different languages, meaning both a knot and a spell. Often the knot is part of the spell, for a specific, usually inhibitory purpose; you undo the spell by untying the knot. This is the opposite of an apotropaic use, but knots could also protect against physical or magical harm. During the Western Middle Ages, people did use knots apotropaically, for example on trees as protection against wild animals, or on the person as amulets against the devil. Insofar as interlace is the representation of a real or fanciful knot, there is every reason to assume that it could have the same function.[11]

But how does a knot, real or fanciful, actually protect? The knot must be difficult to untie: physically, if it is real, or visually, by tracing and "solving" it, if it is fanciful. (Remember the talismanic Gordian knot, which could not be untied because its ends were concealed.[12]) This is part of a much larger complex of beliefs linking protection with difficulty or concealment.[13] People in traditional societies often avoid counting valued things, such as agricultural produce, for fear of laying them open to the evil eye. Unknown numbers have the power to baffle both human and supernatural evildoers. In the same spirit, some amulets incorporate either quantities of uncountably tiny objects such as grains of sand, or visual units whose fineness makes counting imprac-

Fig. 65. Title page of the Homilies of St. Augustine. Italian, c. 800. Heidelberg, Universitätsbibliothek, Cod. Salem. 10.12.

tical. This category of amulet also includes faceted stones and braided threads. In other words, visual elusiveness has the same protective power as uncountability.

Complex interlace is a labyrinth for the eye, but unlike true labyrinths, whether built or drawn, it has no entrance or exit as such—no "goal."[14] To solve it, you must follow not only its windings but also its crossings, and hold them all in mind together. This may once have been easier, or easier for more people, than it is today, when even among specialists there are few accustomed to analyzing complex ornament. Yet I doubt that the most elaborate forms were ever transparent. Complex interlace was meant to baffle. Precious objects decorated with interlace were more than just amulets, but their creators took for granted the need to incorporate magical protection. The essence of the evil eye is envy, and there is no stronger magnet for envy than a treasure, or its possessor!

The protective power of complex interlace explains its frequent association with the cross in virtually every branch of medieval Christian art. As the central symbol of Christianity, the cross was apotropaic in itself, but it was not the only protective sign. A page of an Italian manuscript from about 800 (fig. 65) illustrates the talismanic alliance of cross and interlace. The centrally placed cross divides the page into four rectangles. The arms of the cross are filled with complex interlace, the only "decorative" element. The text within the rectangles is as follows:

HEC ARMA	FIDES
INLESOS	SERVAT
FIDE	LES
REX	LEX
LVX	PAX
IN NOMINE	SC̄E CRVCIS
INCIPIVNT	OMELIE
SC̄I AVGVSTINI	DE NATALE DN̄I

The inscription is in three parts. The first, "hec arma fides inlesos servat fideles," is confusing because the Latin is corrupt. It means: "With this (defensive) weapon faith preserves the faithful from harm."[15] *This weapon* can only mean the cross, since (1) it must refer to something at hand; (2) there is nothing else at hand but the cross; (3) we know that the cross acted as a defensive weapon; and (4) there is an additional small cross immediately preceding the *hec,* as though to make the reference doubly clear. Indeed, this small cross is the key to the inscription. It is a kind of rebus. If we pronounce the word *crux,* not only does the sense become explicit, but the line itself is transformed into a complete hexameter verse.[16]

The second part of the text consists of the words "rex lex lux pax" ("king law light peace"). In contemporary poetry these are epithets of Christ, and often appear together. Here, grammatically isolated, they constitute a fourfold invocation of Christ, deriving additional force from the repetition of the letter X, itself an alternative form of the cross. The formula has much in common with traditional spells or charms: the repetition of like-sounding words, and the invocation of a deity by multiple names.[17] The third and final part of the title page is straightforward. It invokes the "name of the holy cross" for the beginning of the text itself.

In summary, the page features a single large cross. It explicitly describes the cross as a (defensive) weapon. It evokes Christ four times, in a manner strongly reminiscent of charms, adding four more crosses in the process. The text (homilies of St. Augustine) is said to begin in the name of the cross. It is hard to imagine the cross harnessed to a more single-mindedly apotropaic purpose, or a work of "high" culture more imbued with the superstitious anxiety of popular belief. Interlace is the only part of the composition whose magico-religious role is not explicit, but the cross and interlace are coextensive. It would not be going too far to say that the shield of the faithful in this manuscript is not just the cross, but the cross with interlace.[18]

The so-called carpet pages of early Hiberno-Saxon manuscripts offer a more lavish but equally clear illustration of the same principle. These pages consist entirely of ornament. In the Lindisfarne Gospels there are five of them, each a variation on the theme of cross and interlace (plate 7). They face the opening words of the introductory material—that is the beginning of the book itself—and of each gospel. In suggesting they stood guard at the vulnerable "doorways" of the book, I do not mean to deny them other functions: in particular, that of glorifying the sacred text by adorning it. But any pattern can adorn. A cross with interlace is more than just a cross with ornament. Interlace entangles the malevolent or envious gaze and keeps it from going any farther, while the cross literally puts the fear of God into the evildoer.

So far I have mentioned symbolism as little as possible. In general use, symbolism means that one thing "stands for" another, intentionally evoking a particular person, event, or idea. This definition sounds almost simplistic, but has the advantage of being very precise. In particular, it allows us to distinguish between different kinds of meaning. Interlace can be intensely meaningful, but it is not symbolic, it is *efficacious*. Even symbolism in the rigid sense includes many levels of understanding. Symbolism is bound up with myth and religion, history and politics. They nourish it, and it nourishes them. Less well known is the fact that even before these forces come into play, language itself can determine the content of symbols and how they are received.

In Mandarin, the standard dialect of Chinese, the word for a bat (the mammal) is *fu*. The word for "good luck" is also *fu*. They are writtten differently but are *homophones:* they sound the same. Since anyone (speaking Mandarin) who says "bat" is also saying "good luck," an image of a bat is automatically an auspicious symbol. Bats are common in Chinese ornament, and everyone knows what they stand for. Unlike mandarin ducks, which are symbols of happy marriage because they mate for life, the symbolism of the bat has nothing to do with the behavior of bats, real or imagined. It is purely a linguistic matter, and so basic that it requires no conscious act of interpretation, no intermediate "I get it" between the two meanings of the sound. The symbol is self-evident and self-sustaining in a way that no conventional symbol, however well internalized, can ever be. The Valentine's Day heart is a conventional symbol, and we have no trouble recognizing that it means love, but think of how much closer the connection would be if the word for "heart" happened to be pronounced "love."

Symbols of this kind are deeply embedded in the culture and are resistant to change, but they do not convey more meaning, or more valid meaning, than other kinds. The fact that they are self-evident does not make them *true*. And while the Chinese language is rich in homophones, not every homophone generates a symbol. The word for owl is *fu*, again a completely different word, again a homophone for good luck, but the owl remains a bird of ill omen. The symbol-making power of language operates only in the absence of stronger forces; it is powerless against superstition.[19]

Given the right circumstances, visual or any other symbolism can be manipulated, as literary creation manipulates language. Gerhart B. Ladner's essay, "Medieval and Modern Understanding of Symbolism: A Comparison,"[20] provides a concise guide to this process, though it makes no claim to universality, dealing only with the Christian and post-Christian West. Symbolism may be a universal faculty, but symbolic systems are as different as the cultures that use them. Ladner charts a way of thinking that appears radically different from our own:

> [T]he Western Middle Ages conceptualized a universe of symbols in which, with the sole exception of God, everything could signify something else. . . . Above all, material things signified spiritual things or even God himself.
>
> It was one of the fundamental character traits of early Christian and medieval mentalities that the signifying, symbolizing and allegorizing function was anything but arbitrary or subjective; symbols were believed to represent objectively and to express faithfully various aspects of a universe that was perceived as widely and deeply meaningful.

Strange as this system may appear, the popular Western idea of symbolism as a one-

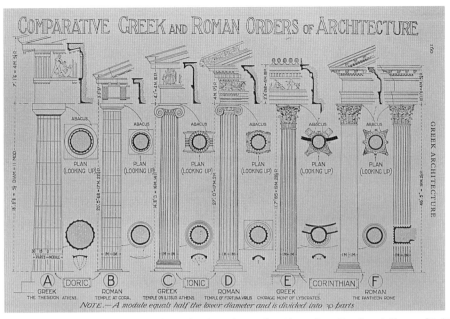

Fig. 66. Schematic drawing of the classical orders. Photo: after Sir Banister Fletcher, *A History of Architecture: Being a Comparative View of the Historical Styles from the Earliest Period* (New York: Batsford/Scribner's, 1896).

to-one relationship of thing and idea is its impoverished descendant. What is new is the idea that symbols are arbitrary, that individuals have the power to command or even create them. This change has allowed symbolism to survive as a mode of thought and expression, but it probably explains why encounters with the more "absolute" symbolic systems of traditional cultures may trigger feelings of spiritual inferiority.

Once a symbol is embedded in a culture it usually takes on a life of its own and remains meaningful until cultural changes make it obsolete. Yet symbols can change their meaning, or take on new meanings without losing their old ones. Wheel-shaped amulets were enormously popular in pre-Christian Gaul, because the wheel was an attribute of a Celtic solar deity assimilated to (and invoked as) the Roman Jupiter.[21] The same motif reappeared in medieval church art, as a symbol of the cosmic nature of Christ. This is not a survival of pagan *beliefs*. Christianity took over the motif and its cosmic associations, but shifted the reference (as it so often did) from Jupiter to Christ.

A visual symbol does not usually depend on knowledge of its origin, any more than the power of a word depends on our awareness that it is derived from French, Greek, or Arabic. We may need to know about the Celtic symbolism of the wheel to understand its use in medieval art, but a medieval worshipper did not. Sometimes, however, the origin *is* the meaning. An ornamental style often evokes the place or time in which it is supposed (correctly or not) to have originated, and this can be a mode of communication. Usually the message is a general one of exoticism, inviting the viewer to participate, if only as a consumer, in the adventure of trade with strange and inaccessible places. Sometimes the message can be more specific. Ancient Greek architecture relies extensively on columns for both structural and artistic effects. During the fifth and fourth centuries B.C., three distinct ways of combining columns with other structural and decorative forms came to predominate (fig. 66, p. 103). These combinations are known as the classical orders, and have become canonical, though not immutable, for all styles that emulate the principles of Greek architecture, notably in Rome and in Western Europe and its dependencies since the Renaissance.

Although modernism dealt an all but mortal blow to the classical orders as a serious vehicle of expression, we have no difficulty in recognizing classicism when we see it. More to the point, we have no trouble recognizing that in certain contexts it has a point to make. The prevalence of classical forms in government buildings, courthouses, libraries, and schools is an attempt to forge a link with the classical past as the presumed origin of all that is admirable in our civic and intellectual lives. The origin is the message, and the message is classicism itself.

The names of the three orders, Doric, Ionic, and Corinthian, connect them with places or ethnic groups, as evocative to the Greeks themselves as classicism is to us—and far more specific. Since both Ionia and Corinth had reputations for refinement and luxury (Corinth, famous for its prostitutes, was a byword for sexual pleasure), while the Dorians were fighters, the juxtaposition of "masculine" Doric style with "feminine" Ionic and Corinthian is almost as old as the orders themselves. These associations helped determine how the styles were used: Ionic or Corinthian for the interiors of buildings, Doric for the exteriors. But more important, the ability of each order to evoke a place made it possible for architecture to carry a political message. After the Persian War, the shift from Doric to Ionic in certain Athenian buildings reflected an attempt by Athens to mend fences with the eastern (Ionian) Greeks in the face of increasing political and military pressure from Dorian Sparta.[22]

IT is not always easy to keep creation and interpretation separate, and in a symbol-revering world there is no reason to do so. One creates by interpreting, and interpretation is more than a disinterested process of discovering what people once thought. An intuitive sense of rightness justifies grafting a new meaning onto a form that already has one, or has survived perfectly well with no meaning at all. If a new symbolic interpretation "works," it must in some sense have been there already, waiting to be discovered, like scientific laws today.

A book by George Hersey, with the delightfully old-fashioned title *The Lost Meaning of Classical Architecture*, illustrates the difficulty of using this process to revitalize symbolism for a culture that has lost its faith in symbols. In the first century A.D. the Roman author Vitruvius wrote a treatise on architecture, the only technical work on the subject to survive from Greek or Roman antiquity. Analyzing Vitruvius's terminology, Hersey found a consistent symbolic connection between details of Greek temple architecture and aspects of animal sacrifice. For example:

> Homer habitually refers to sacrifices as the offering of *meroi*, thighs; and so let us note that the three uprights in a triglyph were called by this name. The same is true in Latin: *femores* [*sic*]. (In Greek, furthermore, the word is close to the word for share or offering, which would trope the body part received in communion.) Since "glyph" means something carved or chopped off, a tri-glyph is or can be a thigh-bone chopped in three (*triglyphos* means thrice-cloven).[23]

The idea that parts of a temple symbolically depict the ritual performed within is intellectually exciting and intuitively satisfying, but there are problems. The triglyph is a simple, completely nonrepresentational form, a rectangle divided into three parts by two parallel vertical grooves. There is no evidence that it was originally intended as a symbol, or that it evolved from an earlier form in which the sacrificial reference was more explicit. Nor is it likely that the ancient Greeks, master anthropomorphizers of the divine, would have chosen to depict their most important religious ritual in this dryly abstract way. Yet we cannot simply ignore Vitruvius. Hersey concluded, reasonably enough, that at some time between the beginnings of Greek architecture and the time Vitruvius wrote about it, the symbolism of sacrifice was grafted onto the structure and ornament of the temple via the terms used to describe them.

If this were all, it would be no more than a footnote to the history of interpretation. The buildings themselves reveal no special flair for symbolism. A Greek temple is not a symbolic essay—let alone a poem—on the theology of sacrifice. But Hersey goes much further. It is he, not Vitruvius, who insists on a coherent system behind the strange coincidence of terms. To understand why, we need only recall that the alienation of modern taste from its classical roots began before modernism. In 1851, Ruskin wrote: "Do you seriously imagine, reader, that any living soul in London likes triglyphs?— or gets any hearty enjoyment out of pediments? You are much mistaken. Greeks did: English people never did,—never will." According to Ruskin, a nineteenth-century architect built in a classical style "because he has been told that such and such things are fine, and that he *should* like them."[24]

Ruskin's question about triglyphs is purely rhetorical; his not so hidden agenda included the systematic denigration of classical styles in favor of medieval ones. Hersey, however, rephrased it as a real question: "Why do architects erect columns and temple fronts derived ultimately from ancient Greek temples, when ancient Greek religion has been dead for centuries, when the temples themselves were not even buildings in the sense that they housed human activities, and when the way of life they expressed is extinct?"[25] The "civic heritage" explanation did not satisfy Hersey, who believes that only the vividness of its symbolic language could propel classical architecture through the millennia: the glamour of immanent meaning lived on when the meanings themselves were forgotten. He does not distinguish between ancient and modern classicism—the excellent photographs by which he illustrates the classical style are mostly of nineteenth- and twentieth-century buildings—and it is easy to see why. In his zeal to confirm the vitality and viability of classicism, he has performed the same kind of creative grafting that he uncovers in the ancient world.

This shows how imaginative the personal or arbitrary use of symbolism can be— and how artificial. The medieval approach to symbolism is every bit as vital, but less obtrusive because it tends to reflect cultural norms instead of trying to shift them. In a miniature from the Lambeth Bible, an English manuscript of the twelfth century (fig. 67), two separate ornamental traditions reinforce the message of theology, law, and figural art. Its subject is the so-called Tree of Jesse, the genealogy of Christ in the form of a stylized plant or tree. I say "so-called" because the text on which the image is based, Isaiah 11.1–2, does not actually mention a tree. It says, "A shoot will come out of the root of Jesse, and a flower will come up from the root" (my translation, based on the Septuagint and the Vulgate). The terms for root, shoot, and flower are generic, though the Latin *virga* and Greek *rabdos*, here translated as "shoot," seem to imply something stiffer than a herbaceous plant. The previous verses describe God's anger, and the leveling of great forests. This is probably the origin of the tree (as against plant) image, but the crucial iconographic step, which did not come until the eleventh

Fig. 67. *Tree of Jesse*. Miniature from the Lambeth Bible. English, twelfth century. London, Lambeth Palace Library, MS 3, f. 198.

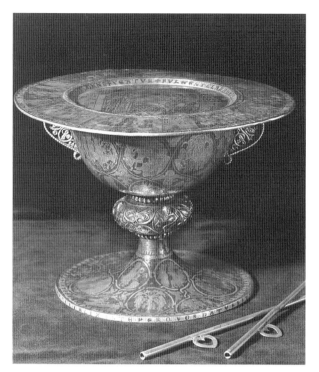

Fig. 68. Chalice. Silver with niello decoration. German, c. 1160–70. Vienna, Kunsthistorisches Museum, 8924.

or twelfth century, was the assimilation of the biblical "shoot" to a genealogical tree.[26]

Genealogy is an integral part of the biblical image. Jewish messianic hopes were closely associated with the lineage of King David. Jesse was the father of David, so the "shoot" means one of David's kin. The genealogies of Christ in the gospels of Matthew and Luke emphasize his descent from David through Joseph, his father according to Jewish law. Kinship diagrams, known as trees of consanguinity, were used extensively in Roman law and medieval canon law, to determine inheritance and to prevent marriages between close relatives.[27] These diagrams do have the form of stylized trees, although they show the ancestors at the top, forgoing the sense of growth that today seems essential to the tree as a metaphor for kinship.

Technically, Christ's descent from Jesse is through Joseph, but here the Virgin Mary forms the "trunk" of the tree, reflecting the pun of *virga* ("shoot") and *virgo* ("virgin"), and making her unequivocally the conduit between human and divine, prophecy and fulfillment.[28] There is also a connection with a device used in the same period for consanguinity trees, the "presentation figure." This is a human figure who stands behind the tree and is to some extent formally merged with it. Often shown as an emperor or pope, the figure apparently embodies secular or religious authority.[29] Depicted in this way, the Virgin is more than just a conduit: she validates the entire composition.

The miniature not only connects the pre-Christian and Christian worlds, but appropriates Old Testament history, making it culminate in Christ. It thus combines temporal progression and theological inevitability. This is where the ornamental traditions come in. The first is *medallion interlace* (fig. 68). Like the complex interlace of plate 7, it is of Roman origin (cf. fig. 36). There is a middle ground, but the two strains are usually quite distinct. For such a simple pattern type, medallion interlace has a remarkably precise and consistent function: to divide a surface into uniform, easily encompassed parts over which the eye moves in a predictable rhythm. Used as a framing system for significant images, it simultaneously connects and separates them, emphasizing their independence *and* their interdependence.

Images linked in this way do not become equivalent; they become *equipollent*. I did not coin the word, though it is rare in general use. "Equivalent" in its root sense ("of equal value") would have served, but usage has made it virtually synonymous with "identical." "Equipollent" means *of equal force,* and this is precisely the effect of medallion interlace. Formally or thematically, no one element dominates, except the interlace itself. At the same time, the devaluing effect of repetition allows recognizable figures and even whole scenes to function as ornament, with no loss of explicitness. The arrangement also tends to negate historic time. It is static and nondirectional, with no sense of progression and culmination. Each figure or scene exists in its own moment, but we know they are all connected: the pattern tells us so. Physical connection does not always imply symbolic connection, and medallion interlace cannot create meanings where none exist. What it can do is give physical form to connections that are allegorical or mystical instead of causal, sequential, or "logical" in any modern sense. And it is a constant reminder to be on the lookout for these connections.

The second ornamental tradition is the vine scroll (figs. 39, 40). In the Greco-Roman world, the grapevine symbolized Dionysus, or Bacchus, the god of wine. The intoxication of wine was a widely understood metaphor for religious ecstasy or transcendence. Dionysus was also associated with the idea of an afterlife, and his image, in human form or as a vine, plays an important role in Roman funerary art and beliefs concerning the dead. Myths in which Dionysus is killed but restored to life reinforce this connection.[30] Thus the vine in pagan art connotes bliss, resurrection, immortality, but how specifically it does so depends on the context. A vine motif on a sarcophagus, used in conjunction with scenes from the myth or cult of Dionysus, will have a symbolic directness that the same motif would lack if used by itself on the floor of a house or the doorway of a civic building.

For an emergent Christianity trying to create a visual idiom of its own within the Roman milieu, the vine scroll was a ready-made symbol. There is a general continuity between certain pagan cults (notably that of Dionysus) and Christianity in their emphasis on transcendence and blissful life after death. Christianity gave the connection of wine and transcendence a new meaning via the wine of the Eucharist, which mystically becomes Christ's blood and the means of salvation for the faithful. Christ also says to his disciples, "I am the vine, you are the branches. He who abides in me, and I in him, he it is that bears much fruit, for apart from me you can do nothing" (John 15.5). This gives the vine a clear symbolic reference which is exclusively Christian.

In the Tree of Jesse miniature, the allegorical shorthand of medallion interlace suggests a new level of complexity. In the bottom pair of medallions appear four Old Testament prophets, who foretold the coming of Christ. In the middle pair are female figures personifying the virtues of mercy and truth (on the left), and justice and peace (on the right), a reference to Psalm 85 (84 in the Septuagint and Vulgate). The two top medallions represent the Church and Synagogue, crowned and veiled respectively. A hand from above strips away the veil, signifying the Christian revelation which enlightens the Jews even as it makes their faith obsolete.[31]

St. Jerome's commentary on the Psalm explains the imagery.[32] The best-known translation of the verse, in the Authorized or King James Version, reads, "Mercy and truth are met together, righteousness and peace have kissed each other." Jerome's Latin version, however, has justice, not righteousness. His commentary explicitly equates mercy with peace, truth with justice. The two medallions in the miniature thus have the same meaning, and Jerome tells us what that meaning is. There are, he says, two believing peoples, the Jews and the Gentiles. The Savior was promised to the Jews but not to the Gentiles, who were outside God's law. Yet the Gentiles are able to share in salvation through Christ. Therefore truth corresponds to the Jews, to whom God gave what he had promised, and mercy corresponds to the Gentiles, to whom God gave what he had *not* promised. The meeting and amity of the virtues signifies the uniting of Jew and Gentile "under one shepherd, Christ," and the medallions depict that event as prefigured in the Psalm.

As an integrating framework for all these images, the vine-like "Tree" imparts a sense of movement upward, not only visually but in levels of actuality, from prophecy to prefiguration to fulfillment. Each image grows, physically and metaphorically, from the one below it. Together they represent an unmistakable hierarchy, but one in which no element is overtly subordinated or diminished. The structure and connotations of the tree establish the hierarchy, while medallion interlace negates it through equipollence. Each image has its place in an unshakably fixed pattern, just as each stage in the growth toward Christianity has a vital and eternal role in the divine plan of prophecy and fulfillment. The composition embodies Jerome's reminder that salvation belonged to the Jews by right. Thus the supplanting of Judaism by Christianity is depicted as growth. This message finds its clearest expression in the central figure of the Virgin, who holds the medallions of Church and Synagogue in balance, even as she gives birth to Christ, who will unite them. And since the vine had its own connotations of transcendence, culminating in Christ as the true vine, the sequence of prophecy and fulfillment takes place "in Christ."

This is symbolic thinking at its most elegant, with theology blending seamlessly into visual art. It is, however, a very specific kind of symbolic thinking: Christian, medieval, Western. To equate it with elaborate symbolic systems everywhere would be a great mistake. In one sense, however, it is typical. Its correspondences work on many levels, by no means all of them visual. Although the cues are visual, the responses they trigger are shaped by every kind of cultural expression, the more the better. Symbols that can be adequately expressed through ornament alone—demanding no reference beyond what the form invokes automatically—are almost by definition the most schematic, though the ideas they embody need not be. Ornament has its part to play, but we will not appreciate it until we realize it is only a part. Symbolism at its best is not a system of correspondences but a way of looking at correspondences. Both the correspondences and the ways of looking vary with the culture, because they are the culture.

PART II

Modernism and the Rejection of Ornament

Preface to Part II

IN THE FIRST half of this book I have tried to demystify ornament. The second half has a complementary purpose: to demystify the "ornament question." The phrase refers to the long and passionate debate that occupied theorists and practitioners of the decorative arts in the second half of the nineteenth century and the early years of the twentieth. The subject was ornament in all its ramifications: aesthetic, social, economic—anything that could affect its future as an art form. Even today, that debate shapes many of our assumptions about the relation between art and life. We are carrying out the mandate of another age.

How did ornament become the focus of such earnest speculation? How, above all, did a debate on the future of ornament end as it did, with a verdict that ornament had no future? The answer lies in the unique circumstances of nineteenth-century Europe and America. It was a time of unprecedented growth, not just in science and technology but in the study of human societies, past and present. Overwhelmed by new materials, processes, and historical examples, the design community struggled desperately to keep pace. Technical difficulties aside, each new development raised its own questions, sometimes fundamental ones, about what was beautiful, appropriate, practical.

Visible innovations were only the tip of the iceberg. The real challenge was the transformation of Western society by the process we now call modernization. Social scientists define modernization as the shift from animate to inanimate sources of power for the operations that hold societies together: production of goods, transportation, communication.[1] Although some inanimate sources of power had been in use for millennia—think of water-driven mills, or wind-driven ships—they were the exception. Muscle power, human or animal, was the rule. Only after the Industrial Revolution of the eighteenth century do we see the beginnings of a *modernized society*, a society so dependent on inanimate sources of power that even a partial failure of those sources could not be made up by a return to animate ones.

The transition to a modernized society was, and remains, the most profound large-scale socioeconomic upheaval in recorded history. As expanding technologies demanded new skills and devalued old ones, whole populations of skilled workers, such as hand weavers, lost their means of support. Mechanization pervaded even the most complex manufactures, and workers saw themselves as slaves, not masters, of the machines they operated. Where handicraft survived at all, it survived as a relic of an older, slower world.

The implications for ornament were clear from the start. How could a craft-based art continue to exist when craft was sliding toward extinction? The question acquired a special urgency from the belief that if society could find a way to preserve ornament in the face of modernization, ornament would return the favor and help preserve society. To put it another way, ornament symbolized certain aspects of preindustrial society that were considered essential to the quality of life: personal involvement in work, pride in a job well done, love of beauty in the built environment and in objects of daily use, and social continuity, the sine qua non for the teaching of traditional skills. By assuring a future for ornament, the design community would be safeguarding the virtues ornament embodied. In effect, they would be designating an area of life and art that was off limits to modernization. For some of the most influential participants in the debate, ornament was never just a set of decorative forms; it was a way of work, and ultimately of life, without which humankind might survive, but humanity could not.[2]

Then everything changed. In the first quarter of the twentieth century—almost overnight, historically speaking—belief in salvation through ornament gave way to an even more passionate belief that ornament itself was the problem. Two factors contributed to this about-face. First was the recognition that the debate on ornament, however well intentioned, was leading nowhere. A practical accommodation between ornament and industrial society, one that took full account of the social, economic, and psychological implications of both, was no closer to realization in 1900 than in 1850. Ornament was no longer just a symbol of preindustrial bliss; it had become the emblem of a society unable to move either forward or back. The revolt against ornament, when it came, was like the cutting of the Gordian knot, a drastic but brilliantly simple answer to a problem that had come to seem insoluble.

The other factor was cosmophobia, deep-seated fear and mistrust of ornament. Cosmophobia predates modernization by hundreds, even thousands of years, but modernization brought it closer to the surface than it had ever been. Cosmophobia raised the stakes, imbuing the debate on ornament with a sense of ultimateness that even the crisis of modernization cannot quite explain. Cosmophobia was the dark side of the ornament question. Harder to believe, it was the deciding factor in the debate. The visual culture of modernism is its legacy.

The modernist movement in architecture and design presented itself as a great victory for reason. Cosmophobia, in contrast, was irrational—when it was not overrational. Before its fateful alliance with modernism, it was protean and covert, attaching itself to all kinds of seemingly unrelated cultural anxieties. I doubt that even the most dogmatic modernist would condemn ornament as a threat to sexual morality, yet a recent study leaves no doubt that in the nineteenth century many influential thinkers saw ornament as the embodiment of morbid sexuality and the dangerously seductive powers of fantasy.[3] Exciting as it is to be carried back to a time when ornament *mattered*, the ways in which it mattered are a reminder that some of our most familiar received ideas are rooted in a very distant world.

The modernist revolt against ornament was not predestined, as many of its apologists would have us believe, but it was certainly overdetermined: it had many causes, any one of which could have been a sufficient cause. Of these causes, these hidden seams of cosmophobia, only the one involving sexual morality has been explored in detail. In the remaining chapters of this book I shall investigate some of the rest, and try to show how they came together. I doubt that I have found them all, but enough can be seen converging in the nineteenth century to explain the uneasiness that overshadowed the ornament question, and the dogmatism that still surrounds its resolution.

Chapter 5 reviews the basic modernist assumptions about ornament, and the state of ornament and the ornament question in the nineteenth century, with emphasis on the pivotal role of Adolf Loos in the development of modernist decorative aesthetics. Chapter 6 deals with the moral and religious dimensions of cosmophobia, including the association of self-restraint with cultural advancement, mistrust of the deceptive power of artifice, and fear that the unbridled imagination inherent in some kinds of ornament might undermine social and religious institutions. Chapter 7 explores the impact of machinery on nineteenth-century art and life, as seen in changing attitudes toward work, the huge increase in multiple production (including machine-made ornament) and the intellectual gymnastics by which not ornament but the abolition of ornament came to be equated with human dignity and social justice. Finally, chapter 8 expands on themes introduced earlier, to show that, far from rejecting ornament out of hand, modernism responded to the demands of its time by creating a new and versatile ornamental style.

The survival of ornament in a radically new guise is one of the great ironies of the modernist revolution in design. The other is that the ornament question was never resolved; it was only buried.

5

The Revolution That Never Happened

MODERNISM IS THE defining cultural movement of the twentieth century. It has touched every creative or interpretative discipline, and transformed many. So pervasive a movement resists definition, except in reductively simple terms. Insofar as modernism had a unifying goal, it was a new directness and authenticity of expression, free from both the familiarity and the artificially imposed restraints of old convention. To this end it sought, more aggressively than any previous movement, to overturn the outward forms that Western civilization inherited from antiquity and the Renaissance. It even sought an end to the *need* for such forms, to the idea of artistic validation through direct appeal to the past.

For some people, modernism remains a challenge, a threat, or merely impenetrable. Picasso's *Les Demoiselles d'Avignon* of 1907, Stravinsky's *Le Sacre du Printemps* of 1913, and T. S. Eliot's *The Waste Land* of 1921–22 have been cultural icons for almost a century, but this has not made them easy or relaxing works. Yet modernism, especially in architecture, still offers some people a vision of utopia. Others have recognized the vision but judged it misguided. And there are many for whom the important thing is not what modernism means, or meant, but the conviction that it is no longer modern, that it has lost its immediacy and begun to recede into history.[1]

Visually, and above all architecturally, we live in a world shaped by modernism. The city of steel and glass is a creation of the mid-twentieth century, with roots going back much further, yet it still embodies the dynamic, impersonal glamour of the New. On a street of Victorian houses, an aggressively modern house may still demand an effort of adjustment, whether it was built in 1920 or 1950 or 1990. Architectural styles do not cease to exist when they are no longer revolutionary. Books go out of print, paintings may vanish into museum basements, textiles simply wear out. Buildings are more conspicuous, and more durable. Unless there is compelling reason to pull them down, they remain part of our environment.

Ideas, like buildings, endure beyond their "proper" time. Even as the next wave gathers speed and sweeps past, all eyes upon it, their influence remains. My favorite example is from *Art and Industry,* by the noted English critic of art and design Sir Herbert Read. The book appeared in 1934 and remained in print for half a century. Read's subject is the relation between functional and decorative elements in mass-produced objects. His goal was to make that relationship harmonious, in part by specifying what was *not* harmonious. Near the beginning he illustrated a decorated craftsman's tool of the eighteenth century (fig. 69) with this caption:

> "Applied" Art. This rose-engine—a lathe for turning rose-pattern engraving on metal—precedes the industrial age (it was made in Germany about 1750); but it shows that already a division existed between form and decoration, and that machinery was thought of as something to be as far as possible concealed. It differs from a similar object a hundred years later in that the ornament which smothers the machinery is original contemporary ornament; but that does not justify its application.[2]

How many assumptions this brief passage embodies! The fundamental one is that ornament can be dismissed without reference to the goodness or badness of its execution. Ideology has conquered taste. The second assumption makes clear the ideological grounds for dismissal: ornament is incompatible with machinery. The third is implicit in the statement that "already a division existed between form and decoration." To Read,

Fig. 69. Lathe ("rose engine"). German, mid-eighteenth century. London, Science Museum, 24699.

such a division did not always exist. We have met with this nostalgia before, in the work of Coomaraswamy and others: the vision of a time when ornament mattered, and was thus inseparable from basic form.

A fourth assumption follows directly from this. For Read, the division between form and ornament apparently came about in the mid-eighteenth century, but the key word is "already." If the division *already* existed in 1750, then it is on the whole a more recent phenomenon, but by looking back to 1750 we can see its origins. From the context it is clear that Read had in mind the growing ascendancy of the machine during the late eighteenth century and especially during the nineteenth. In other words, the ascendancy of the machine caused, or at the very least exacerbated, a split between functional form and decoration. As a result, combining ornament with machinery is *wrong*. But why? The answer lies in assumption number five: that machinery is beautiful in itself. The efficiency of the machine confers an austere, dynamic, and forward-looking beauty of its own. Ornament is elaborate, fixed, and looks backward to the past. Thus polarized, machines and ornament have no common ground. Any attempt to combine them implies a wish to conceal or disguise the machinery. At best this shows insensitivity to the beauty of function; at worst it is cowardly or dishonest.

Read's dogmatic rejection of ornament frees him from having to ask whether the lavish decoration of the rose engine actually interfered with its function. For millennia people have made their living using decorated tools, played music on decorated instruments, and fought for their lives with decorated weapons. There is a principle of self-regulation at work here: if the decoration prevents efficient use, either physically or through unwillingness to risk damage, the object will not be used. At the same time, objects have always been made for delight and display. They may have the outward form of useful objects, but design, materials, or simple irreplaceability make them impractical for everyday use. Many swords were never intended for the battlefield, or even for the conventions of a formal duel. Their counterpart today is the thousand-dollar handmade pocket knife, or the restored antique car that is never driven, but lovingly carried from show to show on a trailer.

Many gradations are possible between pure utility and pure display.[3] A wealthy amateur might buy and use a decorated tool, untroubled by a loss of balance or durability which would lead a professional to reject it at once. Martin Matthews in his book on engine turning characterized Read's rose engine as "destined more for the Palace than the workshop," without implying that it was unworkable. Ornamental turning was a craft much favored by wealthy amateurs. Indeed, one type of specialized lathe in use during the nineteenth century was so valuable a work of craft in its own right that professional artisans could not afford to own it.[4]

Systematically eliminating ornament has not eliminated compromise. Simple design is not always practical design, as anyone who has shopped for stainless steel flatware already knows. The question of practicality is at once objective and subjective: "Does the device work well?" but also "Does it satisfy my particular needs, social and aesthetic as well as utilitarian?" This freedom of choice is incompatible with any single dogma, which perhaps explains why Read so unhesitatingly labels the rose engine a machine, not a tool.

Without exploring the full implications of the difference, it is safe to say that a machine is a device that operates more or less automatically when coupled with a suitable power source. A tool operates only under the worker's direct control. It is not just the efficiency of the machine, but its impersonality, which makes ornament incongruous. If the rose engine is a machine, then by the rules of modernism it must not have ornament. The more ornament it has, the more incongruous it appears, and the more completely it justifies the elimination of ornament from a machine-dominated world. But if it is a tool, we should not judge its suitability for ornament without taking into account the intentions of its maker and purchaser. As it happens, specialized lathes are known as "engines" or "machines," but they require precise human control, and are human-powered, via handwheel or treadle, in the manner of early sewing machines. Read's case is by no means as strong as he would like us to think.

Read's sixth and final assumption is that nineteenth-century ornament is without merit. He says of the rose engine: "It differs from a similar object a hundred years later in that the ornament which smothers the machinery is original contemporary ornament." In other words, the ornament we may expect to find in the mid-nineteenth century is *not* "original contemporary ornament." Read cannot mean that the actual decorations are of an earlier period, since this is demonstrably untrue. Rather, we must understand that the *kinds* of ornament used in the mid-nineteenth century are not *truly of their time* ("contemporary") because they are not the *unique creation* of their time ("original").

This goes beyond a judgment of good versus bad work. Read means that nineteenth-century ornament is fundamentally inauthentic. In effect, it consists entirely of reproductions. Originality is a difficult criterion for ornament, which tends to develop by gradual change in received forms, rather than by the sudden adoption of new ideas. We do not habitually dismiss Italian Renaissance ornament as inauthentic because of its debt to Rome, or Roman ornament because of its debt to Greece. What sets the nineteenth century beyond the pale? The difference must be qualitative. Read does not simply dislike nineteenth-century ornament, he considers it a nonstyle.

This view is inseparable from the twentieth-century prejudice against everything "Victorian." Although the term refers literally to the reign of Queen Victoria (1837–1901), in common use it evokes not just a period in English history, but a set of negative stereotypes by no means historically or culturally bound. They include smugness, hypocrisy, bigotry, sexual repression, class distinction, imperialism, sentimentality, and clutter. If the visual arts have suffered badly from this retrospective taint, it is perhaps because the charges of sentimentality and clutter—of all Victorian sins the least titillating—are so often justified.

Anti-Victorian prejudice provides the background for Read's sweeping, confident dismissal, but two other influences are at work that relate specifically to ornament. First is the issue of stylistic identity. If Read denies that the mid-nineteenth century produced "original, contemporary ornament," he is only echoing what designers and critics of that era said themselves. The search for a "true" or "authentic" style of architecture, and a style of ornament to go with it, was an obsession in the nineteenth century. Proponents of the neo-Gothic and neoclassic styles in particular gave them moral, religious, and political as well as aesthetic overtones in an effort to convince the public that one or the other style was the only right one for the time.[5] Implicit in this was the awareness that the time had no true style of its own. *Neo*classic, *neo*-Gothic: the forms were adopted from earlier periods—changed, recombined, but not "original." Designers of the mid-nineteenth century had an enormous range of choice. Foreign and historic styles were open to them as never before, but there was no style in which they worked instinctively because it was *theirs*. They knew this perfectly well, and it made them miserable.

The second factor is the new ascendancy of the machine. Beginning in the late eighteenth century, industrial technology made ornament widely available for the first time. As the process accelerated with expanding markets and increasingly sophisticated technology, manufacture crossed an invisible but crucial line. Instead of being produced by people, with the help of machines, ornament was produced by machines. Reacting against this development, critics as influential as Ruskin and Morris proclaimed that mass-produced ornament could not be authentic because it lacked the human imperfection, the almost imperceptible yet ever-present, self-renewing originality that only handwork could guarantee. Although the tension between technology and ornament was much more complex, ornament made *by* machines was thought at least as bad as ornament *on* machines. This view is still largely unquestioned.

On the one hand, then, we have the trap of eclecticism, the lack of a "genuine" ornamental style; on the other, the trap of mechanization, the dehumanizing of ornament in the process of manufacture. If we accept, as many Victorians did, that Victorian ornament fell into both traps, Read's dismissal of a whole epoch becomes not just understandable but inevitable.

It is important to remember that the passage from *Art and Industry* that I have analyzed in such detail is only a picture caption. I chose it because it compresses so many ideas into so few words, and because, as a caption, it was not intended to make a new point. Its purpose is to remind us of what we already know, or should know. Behind Read's brief summing-up lie two crucial questions. How did nineteenth-century ornament fall into the traps of eclecticism and mechanization, and how did modern design escape from those traps by turning its back on ornament? The answers are to be found in the second half of the nineteenth century; more precisely, between 1851, the year of the Great Exhibition in London, and 1908, when Adolf Loos first called for the abolition of ornament.

The Exhibition—its full title was the Great Exhibition of the Works of Industry of All Nations—defined the Victorian style in art, commerce, and technology. Arguably, it defined the Victorian style *as* art, commerce, and technology, in a new synthesis which only the Industrial Revolution made possible. Certain critics found this synthesis repugnant, and launched a debate on the nature of ornament and its place in the industrialized world. What began as a movement to reform ornament nurtured a more radical impulse. This impulse found a voice in 1908, when the Austrian architect Adolf Loos wrote an essay with the sensational title "Ornament and Crime." After more than fifty years of debate, it had become possible to repudiate ornament altogether. From this moment on, modern design was no longer a foreshadowing, but a reality.

If we identify the Great Exhibition as a turning point, we are following in the footsteps of Sir Nikolaus Pevsner. This enormously prolific art historian has probably done more than anyone else to establish a clear evolutionary path through the maze of styles and ideas in the second half of the nineteenth century. His best known work on the subject, *Pioneers of Modern Design*, was first published in 1936: almost exactly contemporary with Read's *Art and Industry*. It has been in print ever since.

As the title implies, Pevsner treated the nineteenth century as a prelude to the twentieth, or to what he regarded as the dominant themes in twentieth-century design. He sought to show how we came to be where we are. But if the end is a given, the beginning is not. Almost throughout history it is possible to find objects or buildings whose austerely "functional" form seems an anticipation of modernism. They strike a sympathetic chord because we see them with modernist eyes, but historically they do not lead to modernism.[6] The history of premodernist art (including, of course, architecture) is the history of art with ornament. The rejection of ornament is not an evolution over centuries, with undecorated forms gaining ever wider acceptance. Some modernist designers have found inspiration in selected historical forms, but in the larger sense the rejection of ornament is a rejection of history itself. In Pevsner's hands, the Great Exhibition becomes the emblem of forces that set Western visual culture on the path to revolution.

From a modernist standpoint, the Exhibition's direct impact was largely negative; it gave the reformers something to rebel against. But its real significance went much further. To understand this, we must understand what the Exhibition was like. We would recognize it as a World's Fair, though the term is much devalued today. Visitors to the New York World's Fair of 1939 remembered it for decades as an opening of new vistas. The London Exhibition had this effect on a far grander scale, in part because it represented a more diverse world, a world just beginning to "shrink" under the influence of modern advances in transportation and communication. But even more, the Exhibition owed its success to an almost magical harmony of content and presentation which made it one of the defining events of the nineteenth century. Coming at a time of enormous social change, it embodied many aspects of that change, but without ambivalence or anxiety. Its six million visitors reveled in a unifying, optimistic glow of progress that both reflected and focused the spirit of the time.

The scope of the Great Exhibition was universal, its aim political. The exhibits were divided into four categories: raw materials, machinery, manufactured goods, and fine arts. Examples came from all over the world, but inevitably the greatest emphasis fell on the industrialized West, and on England above all. One huge hall was filled with working machinery, and the dominant impression was of the world yielding up its resources (the "raw materials") to lay at the feet of British enterprise. This was precisely the effect the Exhibition's planners meant it to have.

To Pevsner the Great Exhibition stood for all that is worst in the Victorian age. Its mindset is a "stodgy and complacent optimism."[7] He saw its delight in the power of industry to transform the world as a mask for the hideous oppression of the poor,[8] and the exhibits themselves elicited his uncompromising scorn. I do not mean the machines, except those that happened to be ornamented, or the category of "Fine Arts," which was restricted to painting and sculpture, and in any case played a rather small role. At issue, rather, are the vast number of European and American "manufactured goods" whose design included some ornament. They may be functional or purely decorative. Many are hybrids, nominally functional objects with impractically lavish ornament, made as display pieces for the occasion. Together they form a category that has gone by various names: decorative art, applied art, industrial art; the first is in most general use today. Manufacturing processes ranged from traditional craftsmanship to the newest techniques of mass production. The published catalogue of the Exhibition, while by no means complete, nonetheless conveys the astounding range of objects and styles on display.[9]

These works, in Pevsner's view, defined a philistine culture spawned by unchecked industrial growth:

> It is sufficient to say that manufacturers were, by means of new machinery, enabled to turn out thousands of cheap articles in the same time and at the same cost as were formerly required for the production of one well-made object. Sham materials and sham techniques were dominant all through industry. Skilled craftsmanship . . . was replaced by mechanical routine. Demand was increasing from year to year, but demand from an uneducated public, a public with either too much money and no time or with no money and no time."[10]

The dismal quality of the exhibits was not limited to mass-produced goods. Handwork suffered in equal measure, since industrial society had discarded its one guarantor of good taste, the continuity of craft. Of a machine-made carpet, Pevsner wrote: "Eighteenth-century ornament may have influenced the designer, the coarseness and over-crowding are his original addition. Moreover, he neglected all the fundamental requirements of decoration in general and of carpet decoration especially; we are forced to step over bulging scrolls and into large, unpleasantly realistic flowers." A group of handmade silver vessels provokes essentially the same reaction: "The insensibility of the artist towards the beauty of pure shape, pure material, pure decorative pattern, is monstrous."

Only the exhibition hall itself, known as the Crystal Palace, earned Pevsner's admiration. The building was the work of Joseph (later Sir Joseph) Paxton, who up to that time had not been so much an architect as a designer of large-scale gardens and greenhouses. Adapting the principles of greenhouse construction, he conceived a structure of prefabricated iron and glass capable of enclosing the entire Exhibition, working machines and all (fig. 70). The Crystal Palace was an expression of Victorian confidence in new materials and new techniques, possible only with heavy industry, but the strength of that confidence carries it beyond its time. The Crystal Palace is widely seen as the first "modern" building: not only the first to rely on mass-produced components, but the first in which function was allowed completely to dictate form.

Fig. 70. Joseph Nash. Interior of the Crystal Palace. Lithograph. English, 1851. London, Victoria and Albert Museum, E.607–1949. Courtesy of the Trustees of the V&A.

It needed no ornament, and so received none. Although Pevsner recognized that the Crystal Palace had close technical antecedents (though none nearly so large or so much in the public eye), he called it "a triumph of logical construction, wholly independent of any architectural traditions," and placed its contemporary admirers "among the pioneers of *twentieth-century* design."[11]

Pevsner is the most cogent interpreter of the Exhibition and its influence. He made it a historical landmark and an ideological touchstone, the beginning of the modern movement and the epitome of all that modernism repudiated. To this end he relied on precise argument, eloquent description, and the freewheeling use of value judgments— a reminder that passions have always run high in the debate on ornament. His account of the Great Exhibition fans the flames of anti-Victorianism, as though in fear that the birth of modern design would lose its drama unless set against the backdrop of a culture gone apocalyptically wrong.

The optimistic tone of the Exhibition did mask a grim social reality, but this is only half the story. The human species has made two fundamental changes in its way of life. The first, eight to ten thousand years ago, was the Neolithic or Agricultural Revolution, the change from a nomadic existence sustained by hunting and gathering to a sedentary existence sustained by the domestication of plants and animals. The second was the Industrial Revolution of the eighteenth and nineteenth centuries, characterized by a shift from animate to inanimate sources of power.[12]

The human dimension of the Neolithic Revolution can only be inferred from archaeological remains. The Industrial Revolution is abundantly documented, and its conflicts and dislocations echo in our own world. *England in 1851 had just come through the most wrenching social change the world has ever known.* The Great Exhibition celebrated more than just survival. The building, the manufactures, the raw materials brought—some, already, by steam-powered ships—from faraway lands, were tangible symbols of victory. The technological revolution of the previous decades had been assimilated and harnessed, and the prize was economic strength. It was no small achievement, however terrible its human cost.

In "High Victorian Design," his detailed yet dismissive account of the Crystal Palace exhibits, Pevsner resorted to what I can only call a cheap shot. There are 130 illustrations, depicting an even greater number of objects from the Exhibition. Only fourteen of the illustrations are photographs of the actual objects, and six of the fourteen are of freestanding sculptures. (I stretch the definition to include a group of stuffed ermine arranged as a tea party.) In other words, only eight photographs represent the decorative arts, and two of these are details of the same work. All the other illustrations are taken from contemporary publications, especially the *Art-Journal Illustrated Catalogue*. They are wood engravings, produced quickly for general distribution. Their scale is small, their number great. The catalogue has 328 pages of illustrations, and most pages contain at least three or four images. Many have more. These illustrations are an acceptable guide to the general form of the objects, for identification, but when it comes to style and quality they are no guide at all, and were never meant as one.

If we accept the engravings as an accurate reflection of Victorian manufacture, of course we will see "sham materials and sham techniques." This is especially true of textiles, where color and texture are so important, but hardly an object escapes distortion. Whether he deliberately misleads us, or is himself blinded by his contempt for the culture as a whole, Pevsner fails to distinguish between the wood engravings and the works they reproduce. Contemporaries did not make this mistake. Matthew Digby Wyatt's *The Industrial Arts of the Nineteenth Century* (London, 1851) is a selection of objects from the Exhibition, handsomely reproduced: the equivalent of a coffee table book. The illustrations are much larger than those in the *Catalogue*, more carefully drawn, and in color. Unfortunately for comparison, only one of the objects chosen by Pevsner appears in both the *Catalogue* and Wyatt's publication: a statue of Andromeda by John Bell.[13] In the simplified engraving, the figure hovers between banality and outright incompetence. Wyatt's draftsman, using a different angle of view, conveys not just subtle modeling but an interesting eroticism. As for the elaborate pedestal, which is of more direct ornamental interest, the Wyatt illustration shows details that simply do not appear in the more cursory version.

Twelve years later, J. B. Waring's *Masterpieces of Industrial Art and Sculpture at the International Exhibition, 1862* presented a similar collection of objects in even more sumptuous and meticulous form.[14] We can hope for no clearer image of how the Victorians saw their own decorative art. Whatever these objects are, they are not "sham" anything. They are eclectic, lavish, and they freely mix representational and nonrepresentational forms. There is a softness in the facial expressions which may irritate us, and a surprising combination of stiffness and tentativeness in the ornamental lines. Color schemes often manage to be somber and discordant at the same time. These are the marks of a style, not of that strange bugbear, a nonstyle. By today's standards it is a difficult style to like, but that is beside the point.[15]

Pevsner also overplays the forward-looking aspect of the Crystal Palace itself. Extolling it as a precociously stark anticipation of the "machine aesthetic" is like visualizing the temples and statues of ancient Greece in the neoclassic purity of white marble. They were originally painted. I do not mean to suggest that the Crystal Palace was ornamented, but it *was* painted, and the painting was intended to negate the very effects Pevsner extols! Mary P. W. Merrifield, a contemporary specialist in colors and pigments, had this to say of its appearance:

> For practical purposes the effect of the interior of the building resembles that of
> the open air. It is perhaps the only building in the world in which *atmosphere* is
> perceptible; and the very appropriate style of decoration adopted by Mr. Owen
> Jones has added greatly to the general effect of the edifice. To a spectator seated
> in the gallery at the eastern or western extremity, and looking straight forward,
> the more distant part of the building appears to be enveloped in a blue haze, as
> if it were open to the air, the warm tint of the canvas and roof contrasts with the
> light blue color of the girders into which it is insensibly lost, and harmonizing
> with the blue sky above the transept, produces an appearance so pleasing, and at

the same time so natural, that it is difficult to distinguish where art begins and nature finishes.[16]

In other words, the structure may have been austerely functional, but this was not an end in itself. Owen Jones, who devised the color scheme, was one of the leading designers of his day, and subsequently author of the influential *Grammar of Ornament* (1856). In the Crystal Palace he used his skills, with evident success, not just to soften the effects of the structure, but to make parts of it disappear altogether. In absolute terms this is no different from the application of ornament: the structure is considered incomplete, or unattractive, without something superadded. I am not trying to belittle the Crystal Palace as an artistic or technological achievement, or to deny that it served as a beacon on the road to modernism. But if painting was integral to its effect in the way Merrifield describes, the Crystal Palace was more a product of its time than Pevsner would have us believe.

No one nation invented modern design. Nevertheless, the English have staked a claim, not to modern design itself, but to the debates and reforms that made it possible. English writers on the origin of modern design tend to approach the subject with particular fervor, almost as if they took it personally. In part this is Ruskin's influence: there is no more powerful writer on the moral implications of decorative art. But it is also the legacy of an active conscience. If the road to modernism began at the Crystal Palace, England has much to answer for. From a modernist standpoint the Great Exhibition was crucial because it was crucially bad, the low point in the history of design. There is an expiatory streak in English design criticism. To claim their fair share of credit for setting things right, the English must also accept the blame for setting things wrong.

It is hard to separate the event itself, the debates it inspired, and the efforts of twentieth-century writers like Read and Pevsner to weave the entire sequence into a canonical history of design. As a result, any account of the birth of modernism that starts with the Exhibition risks the charge of Anglocentrism. This is no reason to abandon the Exhibition as a starting point. Its symbolic position is secure, so long as we remember that the English view is not the only view.[17]

Let us move forward to 1908 and Adolf Loos (1870–1933), whose apparent equation of ornament with crime became a modernist shibboleth.[18] Surprisingly, Pevsner did no more than mention Loos's famous essay in a footnote, perhaps because Pevsner's subject was not the rejection of ornament per se, but the origins of the movement and style in whose name the rejection took place. Another historian of modern design, Reyner Banham, has no doubt of Loos's centrality:

He [Loos] had settled the problem of ornament as Alexander settled the Gordian knot, shockingly but effectively, and his ideas gained an empire wider than the Macedonian's wildest dream. It is impossible now to imagine how the Modern Movement might have looked as a decorated style, but it might have been just that, had not its creators had ringing in their ears Loos' challenging equation: "Ornament Equals Crime."[19]

Banham oversimplifies. Loos was one of the first architects to abandon traditional ornament in practice. He was also a brash and aggressive critic, and with "Ornament and Crime" he became the first to disown ornament in print. There is no doubt that his essay influenced the way people built and looked at buildings, but its influence was not immediate. For a decade the essay had limited circulation, and translations into other languages were either incomplete (the French version of 1913) or nonexistent (no English translation appeared until 1966). Its real influence dates from the 1920s, and owes much to Le Corbusier's enthusiasm for its ideas, and the Dadaists' enthusiasm for its quirky, sardonic bluster. Thus, instead of launching a new style as Banham insists it did, the essay reinforced a style already in existence. By 1931, when "Ornament and Crime" was reprinted in Loos's second collection of essays, its central idea was common coin. The rejection of ornament was no longer credited to Loos, and in his last years he felt cheated of the recognition he deserved.[20]

This puts the achievement of "Ornament and Crime" in a different light. It was not a cry in the wilderness, whatever Loos's friend and protégé, the painter Oskar Kokoschka, may have said.[21] Loos spoke for his time: better than he knew, and too well for his own good. He did not turn the tide of history, as he would have liked to think, but he defined the turning point. In 1908 he presented certain ideas in a challenging, even overbearing manner. Earlier, these ideas (even without the manner, but certainly with it) would have earned him dismissal as a visionary if not a crank. Now they fed a growing cultural mainstream.

Other misconceptions attend the essay. Despite the inspired sensationalism of the title, Loos never says that ornament equals crime. What looks like an equation is really an analogy. Loos means that ornament is anachronistic in the same way as crime, which some social theorists considered a holdover from an earlier stage of social evolution.[22] His main quarrel with ornament is economic.[23] Only in this area does he equate "criminality," in the metaphorical sense of outmoded habits of mind, with true criminality, which is palpably destructive:

The stragglers retard the cultural development of peoples and of mankind, since ornament is not just produced by criminals [here, people with outdated assumptions], but commits a crime by seriously harming men in their health, their national capacity, and hence their cultural development. If two men living side by side have similar needs, make the same demands on life, and have the same income, but belong to two different cultures [i.e., stages of cultural development], from an economic standpoint the following can be seen to occur: the man of the twentieth century becomes ever richer, the man of the eighteenth century ever poorer. I assume that both live according to their inclinations. The man of the twentieth century can cover his needs with a much more modest capital and therefore makes savings. The vegetable that he likes is cooked simply in water and topped with a pat of butter. To the other man it does not taste so good without honey and nuts and someone cooking away at it for hours. Ornamental plates are very expensive, whereas the white crockery which modern men like is cheap. The one accumulates savings, the other accumulates debt. So it is with whole nations. Alas, if a people lag behind in their cultural development! The English become richer and we become poorer.

In this scheme of things, eighteenth-century culture, with its love of ornament, is less "evolved" than twentieth-century culture, which has learned (in theory at least) to take pleasure in the absence of ornament. Since ornament costs more than no-ornament, a modern mindset promotes thrift, while an atavistic mindset leads to extravagance. Thus an evolved society—one that rejects ornament—is a prosperous society, whereas love of ornament is both a cause and an outward sign of cultural retardation. For Loos, "*evolution of culture is synonymous with the removal of ornament from the objects of daily use*" (the italics are Loos's own).

This is only one facet of Loos's argument. He also attacks ornament on aesthetic grounds, but glancingly, as though his heart were not in it: "To me, and to all cultivated people, ornament does not increase the pleasures of life. If I want to eat a piece of gingerbread I will choose one that is completely plain and not . . . a piece which is covered over and over with ornament." The practical implications of ornament mean more to him, especially the areas where cultural and economic realities collide: "Since ornament is no longer a natural product of our culture, and consequently represents either backwardness or degeneration, the work of the ornament-maker is no longer paid for at a proper rate."

The dictum that "ornament is no longer a natural product of our culture" echoes the fear that haunted the nineteenth century: it was no longer possible to create "authentic" ornament. For the Victorians, the alienation of ornament from industrial society was a paralyzing disability. They fought it on every ideological front—artistic, educational, social, religious. Loos stands the old fear on its head by recognizing and accepting cultural change. Ornament is equated with an earlier developmental stage, which "all cultivated people" have outgrown or should outgrow. And if the big abstractions of cultural change are not enough, there is always everyday reality. Time is money. Ornament is financially impractical for the consumer, and as society recognizes this and turns away from it, ornament becomes increasingly impractical for the producer as well. The conclusion is obvious—in Loos's terms, self-evident. To stand against the rejection of ornament is the sign of an obsolete set of values.

The suggestion that makers of ornament deserve any reward at all should alert us once again to Loos's pragmatism. Indeed, the essay is full of concessions to what Loos regards as pockets of backwardness still surviving in Europe (but not in America!). This pluralism does not sit easily with modernist teleology, and receives less attention than it might. But the success which Loos the critic achieved with his diatribe conceals a far greater inconsistency, and a wonderful irony. Loos the architect never renounced ornament. He did something much more original. He reinvented it, with a completely new character and direction for the twentieth century.

Loos loved to juxtapose the simplest forms with the most luxurious materials, especially rare woods and colored marble (fig. 71). Remember that in his scheme of things, giving up traditional ornament does not mean giving up pleasure, it means moving on to more sophisticated forms of pleasure. The beauty of materials asks for no superfluous work, and makes no overt reference to other styles (though the Japanese have a special appreciation for wood, and the Romans and Byzantines were connoisseurs of marble). It should therefore be completely free from the taint of ornament. But one critic at least has observed that Loos made nature his ornament.[24] This is more than a high-flown way of saying that Loos used natural substances for decoration. He carefully chose his stone and wood for their surface effects, which go far beyond "mere" color and texture but are not ornament in the traditional sense. Lacking both the order and content of art, these natural forms are not just unpredictable, they defy all attempts to reduce them to patterns. Traditional ornament, no matter how complex, can always be approached via the relation of parts to one another or to the whole. With Loos, the very idea of parts and whole is inapplicable.

Fig. 71. Adolf Loos. Façade of the Goldman and Salatsch Building ("Looshaus"). Austrian, 1909–11. Vienna, Michaelerplatz. Author's photo.

This new approach to ornament does more than exploit the properties of specific materials. Designers have learned to create their own forms in the same spirit, without relying on the materials. The resulting style has dominated Western decorative art in the twentieth century. I do not hesitate to call it *modernist ornament*, despite the apparent contradiction in terms. Loos gave modernism the only ornament it could accept, an ornament without images, patterns, motifs, or history. Even this was not enough. Cloaking his achievement in a diatribe against ornament itself, he gave us the only ornament we could pretend was no ornament at all. We went after the decoy and swallowed it whole, a feat of self-deception that shapes our visual culture to this day. With this recognition the historical picture changes. It is no longer meaningful to ask why Western artists, their interpreters, and their public suddenly turned their backs on ornament. The real question is why they found it necessary to believe they had done so.

6

The Flight From Enchantment

MORAL AND RELIGIOUS OBJECTIONS TO ORNAMENT

WESTERN COSMOPHOBIA IS inseparable from the belief that moderation is better than excess. The ideal of moderation extends to every aspect of life, and there is nothing specifically European about it. Yet it would be hard to exaggerate its role in shaping a distinctive European identity. The Greeks were the first Western people to articulate it, and since that time it has been linked to Greece and to the idea of European culture as the heir of Greece.[1] The words "Nothing in excess," inscribed on the temple of Apollo at Delphi, are a motto for all that is best in the Greek heritage.

But this is not all. In the fifth century B.C., moderation was a powerful weapon in the Greek campaign against the invading Persians. In retrospect, we can see that it was one of the most powerful propaganda weapons ever deployed. The Greeks did not stoop to depicting the enemy as a race of lechers, gluttons, or sadists. Their propaganda operated on a far subtler level. In the Greek view, the Persian people surrendered part of their human dignity by serving absolute rulers, while the Persian kings, by exercising absolute power, placed themselves above humanity. Both servility and self-aggrandizement were forms of excess, and each fed the other, allowing the Greeks to portray themselves as defenders not just of political but of human freedom, against an enemy whose values were fundamentally compromised.

The Greek word for foreigner, and especially for a Persian (their foreigner par excellence), is *barbaros*. Unlike our "barbarian," it does not imply an unsophisticated or brutal culture: the basic meaning is someone whose native language is not Greek. But there is one sense in which the Greeks did see the Persians as culturally deficient. To the Greeks, neither absolute power nor absolute submission was compatible with self-discipline, which required both autonomy and awareness of limits. This explains why, even though the outnumbered Greeks won a series of stunning military victories, the decisive psychological event of the war was not a battle. It was the Persian king Xerxes' effort in 480 B.C. to bridge the Hellespont, one of the two straits separating Europe and Asia.

The Persian army was to cross on two bridges of boats, but a storm destroyed them. Before rebuilding the bridges, Xerxes ordered his men to punish the Hellespont with whips, and to throw fetters into the water, in token of its subjugation. Just as the troops began to cross the new bridges, an eclipse of the sun took place. Assured that this portended the eclipse of his enemies, Xerxes pressed on. He was, of course, routed. His action had been a direct insult to the gods, especially the sea-god Poseidon, and retribution was inevitable.[2]

Not only did the war between Greece and Persia embody the conflict between moderation and excess, it still does. Where the Greeks saw Xerxes' "subjugation" of the Hellespont as an affront to the gods, we are more likely to see it as a failure to distinguish between a sentient being and a force of nature. In Greek terms, Xerxes' actions are foolishly arrogant; in our terms, they are infantile. In both, they define the non-European culture as the culture of self-will beyond all realistic limits. It is this utter lack of restraint on the part of the rulers, and the corresponding lack of autonomy on the part of the ruled, that gives the phrase "oriental despotism" its power.

These thoughts have led us away from ornament, but not so far away as it might seem. Phrases like "oriental magnificence" and "barbaric splendor" convey a love of display untempered by restraint. The first implies that such display is alien to Western civilization, the second that it is alien to civilization itself. Accustomed as we are to the axiom "less is more," we would do well to ask why unrestrained display is wrong by definition. There are many possible answers, but the underlying one is moral, not aesthetic. Restraint is assumed to imply a higher degree of individual or cultural maturity. A second, built-in assumption is that this maturity is the birthright of Europe, and defines it in opposition to the more extravagant cultures east of the Mediterranean. The Greek poet Simonides, in his epitaph for the Athenian soldiers who died fighting the Persians at Marathon, said that they "laid low the power of the gold-laden Medes [i.e., Persians]." Inappropriate love of display sums up the enemy's foreignness, and more besides. The Persian rank and file are unlikely to have gone into combat weighed down with gold, but it is hard to blink away the image of soldiers so splendidly adorned that they could not fight. More than six thousand Persians are said to have died in the battle, but only one hundred ninety-two Athenians.

Morally and geographically, the battle lines have changed little since that time. Despite centuries of "barbarian" rule in Europe, and the rise and fall of dazzlingly powerful and sophisticated empires in Asia, our cultural values are still shaped by the politics of twenty-five hundred years ago. The line between Europe and Asia was the western boundary of the old Persian empire, and is still the line separating West and East, moderation and excess. No matter that the Roman and Byzantine empires straddled that line for a thousand years, the link with Asia still pushes Byzantium to the margins of Western history. No matter that some European rulers have had more power over their subjects than Xerxes ever dreamed of; that few Asian palaces have matched the splendor of Versailles; that ancient Greek art was sometimes garish, and ancient Persian art was always elegant; or that the luxury arts of Japan include a cult of simplicity which the West is still learning to appreciate: oriental magnificence and oriental despotism still go hand in hand.

The idea of moderation as a sign of cultural maturity is quite recent, because the idea of cultural maturity is itself recent. I do not mean that the Greeks had no sense of their own or anyone else's historical development. Thucydides imagined the movement from a nomadic and piratical society to a sedentary one, in which individuals no longer needed to go constantly armed. "The Athenians," he said, "were the first to lay aside their weapons, and to adopt an easier and more luxurious mode of life; indeed, it is only lately that their rich old men left off the luxury of . . . fastening a knot of their hair with a tie of golden grasshoppers. . . . And there are many other points in which a likeness might be shown between the life of the Hellenic world of old and the barbarian of today."[3] Luxury comes with security, and is therefore an advance over the earlier, more precarious condition of life, but the ability to put luxury aside is a sign of even further progress. Two important things are happening here. One is that simplicity begins, insidiously, to displace moderation as an ideal to set against excess. The other is that by equating the barbarian (i.e., Asian) culture of his own day with the Greek culture of an earlier age, Thucydides gave the myth of Greek superiority a temporal dimension. Not only were the Greeks superior in their moderation, but they had taken a step their neighbors to the east had yet to take; they were *ahead*.

The idea that cultures advanced at different speeds along a single line of development did not gain currency in the Greek world. The myth of the Golden Age—a bygone age of simplicity and ease—had too strong a hold on people's imaginations, and the prevailing view was of a world in decline, with luxury a poor compensation for what humanity had lost.[4] Nor did the Christian idea of sacred history, with its absolute distinction between those within the faith and those outside it, allow for a view in which cultures differed only in their speed of development. Not until the more skeptical climate of the eighteenth and nineteenth centuries did the idea of development come into its own as a way of relating all the world's cultures, regardless of time or place. In the 1750s, Robert Jacques Turgot and Adam Smith independently derived a four-stage economic model: from hunting and gathering, to herding, to farming, to commerce.[5] And during the second quarter of the nineteenth century, Auguste Comte elaborated a model of intellectual development, from the theological to the metaphysical to the scientific. (See below, Chapter 7.)

Each model assumes that since cultures mature at unequal rates, the "primitive" cultures of modern times provide a fairly accurate picture of earlier historical stages. The most "primitive" cultures reveal the most distant past. Turgot, writing in 1750, said this explicitly:

> The inequality of nations increases; in one place the arts begin to emerge, while in another they will advance at a rapid rate toward perfection. In some nations they are brought to a standstill in the midst of their mediocrity, while in others the original darkness is not dissipated at all. Thus the present state of the world, marked as it is by these infinite variations in inequality, spreads out before us at one and the same time all the gradations from barbarism to refinement, thereby revealing to us at a single glance, as it were, the records and remains of all the steps taken by the human mind, a reflection of all the stages through which it has passed, and the history of all the ages.[6]

E. B. Tylor, one of the founders of modern anthropology, made this principle a cornerstone of his *Primitive Culture* (1873). Thanks in particular to Tylor's work, and to that of Frazer a generation later, the idea that "primitive" peoples perpetuate an early stage in the development of culture became deeply rooted. It survives today as an influential received idea, despite the efforts of anthropologists to move beyond it.[7]

The idea that cultures evolve in the same direction, but at different rates, presumes that human beings are, and have been, more or less equal in ability. The stimulus to progress comes from the environment in the broadest sense, and as Turgot said, "progress leads to further progress."[8] But even if the model is ostensibly neutral, it presupposes a hierarchy. The culture that invents the model, and applies it to other cultures, is by its own definition the most mature. There is good reason, then, to believe that the connection between display and cultural immaturity would have had strong meaning for Western culture during the century preceding the rejection of ornament.

There are examples nearer to hand than the Persian Wars. From the fifteenth to the nineteenth century, as European exploration of the world gathered speed, so did European encounters with previously unknown or little-known cultures. A few of these—Persia, India, and China—had long evoked a grudging and selective respect for their antiquity, their traditions of law and government, sometimes even their intellectual and artistic achievements. But never, with the possible exception of China, were they regarded as unqualified equals in civilization, and even China failed utterly by the standards of technological progress which dominated the modernizing West in the late eighteenth and nineteenth centuries.

With other cultures, especially those we would now call tribal, the sense of difference was far greater. A stereotype evolved which I call the trade-bead syndrome. We are all familiar with it, even if we give it no credence. The "savage," with a childlike love of display, rushes to purchase shiny beads or lengths of bright cloth from the white man, adding them higgledy-piggledy to whatever adornment the native culture has provided. The white explorer or trader, in his turn, offers the natives what they obviously want. In doing so he establishes, mentally and economically, an invidious multiple equation: non-Western culture equals love of display, equals lack of taste, equals acceptance of garish, inferior goods, equals immature culture.

Beads and cloth were standard items of trade with tribal societies, but in what spirit were they given, or received? The journals of Captain James Cook, the greatest English explorer of the eighteenth century, often refer to beads and cloth (as well as iron nails) given to Pacific Islanders in exchange for fresh food: pigs, fish, baskets of fruit. In other words, this was very low-level trading. There was no question of obtaining treasures in return for trinkets, and the islanders had every reason to trade easily renewable resources for attractive novelties. (Nails, especially the largest ones, were taken more seriously as status symbols, presumably because of their value as carving tools in what had been neolithic cultures.) More interesting still, this sort of exchange was a two-way street. Cook's men were every bit as eager to buy "curiosities" (including local cloth) from the islanders as the islanders were to obtain European goods. On his visit to Tonga in 1773, Cook recorded the following:

> The different tradeing parties were so successfull to day as to procure for both Sloops a tollerable supply of refreshments in consequence of which I gave the next morning every one leave to purchase what curiosities and other things they pleased, after this it was astonishing to see with what eagerness every one catched at every thing they saw, it even went so far as to become the ridicule of the Natives by offering pieces of sticks stones and what not to exchange, one waggish Boy took a piece of human excrement on the end of a stick and hild it out to every one of our people he met with.[9]

The perception of trade and trade-goods was not always so lighthearted. A Major Denham, who wrote an account of his journey to Bornu (in what is now eastern Nigeria) in the 1820s, had this to say about the implications of trade for an African society:

> Already the desire of exchanging whatever their country produces, for the manufactures of the more enlightened nations of the North, exists in no small degree amongst them: a taste for luxury, and a desire of imitating such strangers as visit them, are very observable; and the man of rank is ever distinguished by some part of his dress being of foreign materials, even though sometimes of the most trifling kind. It is true that these propensities are not yet fully developed; but they exist, and give unequivocal proof of a tendency to civilization, and the desire of cultivating an intercourse with foreigners.[10]

How easily the idea of cultural progress, itself biased in favor of the West, becomes indistinguishable from an assumption of racial inequality. This mindset is widely recognized and deplored. There would be no need even to raise the point here, except that Denham's unthinking arrogance has a large if unacknowledged aesthetic component. He depicted a society wholly lacking in whatever constitutes civilization, a society capable only of reaching out to "more enlightened nations" and taking whatever scraps they offer. (Denham credited the Arabs with "every approach which the African has made toward civilization" before Europeans appeared on the scene.) Their still inchoate "tendency to civilization" shows itself in luxury and imitation, the former presumably because only the material tokens of prosperity mark their emergence from an even more primitive state (a distant echo of Thucydides!), the latter because virtually any addition to their culture must be an improvement. Such reasoning is circular. Assumption A, that African culture is backward, makes possible assumption B, that for the people of Bornu every European item, no matter how inconsequential, is both a luxury and a sign of improvement. But to anyone holding this view, the supposed eagerness of the Africans to adopt such items as *luxuries* is a practical and recurring proof of their backwardness.

What are the items in question? Denham appends a list of "articles most in request among the Negro nations." It includes writing paper, plain cloth of various kinds, and objects of daily use such as cups and razors. Nevertheless, articles of display predominate: "imitation coral; Printed cottons of all kinds, with a great deal of red and yellow in the pattern; Coloured silks . . . of the most gaudy patterns; Ornamented cheap pistols"—and ten different kinds of beads.[11] The list emphasizes and caters to the Africans' love of display, while making it clear that in Western terms this means garish colors and inferior goods.

This is the trade-bead syndrome full-blown. For the nineteenth century it embodies the age-old equation of display, excess, and cultural backwardness. In the twentieth, it underlies Adolf Loos's equation of ornament and crime. The idea of crime as a survival of humanity's "savage" past comes straight out of Tylor,[12] thus indirectly from Comte and Turgot. The same ideas of progress made it possible to dismiss ornament as an anachronism. But in choosing to make the connection explicit and call for a world without ornament, Loos reached back much further than the eighteenth century. His polemic is the ideology of the Persian Wars, distilled at last into aesthetic dogma.

These responses to luxury and primitivism begin to fill in the background of the modernist rebellion against ornament, but they are far from its only cause. Paradoxically, at exactly the same time—the late eighteenth and nineteenth centuries—there grew up an attitude toward "primitive" cultures that is diametrically opposed to the one we have just traced. By a double paradox, the opposing views contributed to the same goal. We have already met with Owen Jones, who devised the color scheme for the Crystal Palace. His best-known work, *The Grammar of Ornament* (1856), is a compendium of styles and motifs according to their culture of origin, with a short commentary on each style. Since the arrangement is roughly chronological, we should not be surprised that it begins with the "Ornament of Savage Tribes": the art of earliest humanity, if not in absolute age at least in the stage of development it supposedly represents.

There is condescension in Jones's account, but it is not aesthetic condescension. Rather, it is implicit in the idea of tribal cultures as primitive cultures. Jones's respect for tribal ornament is bound up with assumptions we find both inaccurate and patronizing, but there is no doubt of his sincerity when he insists that this art has much to teach the modern West:

> The ornament of a savage tribe, being the result of a natural instinct, is necessarily always true to its purpose; whilst in much of the ornament of civilized nations, the first impulse which generated received forms being enfeebled by constant repetition, the ornament is often-times misapplied, and instead of first seeking the most convenient form and adding beauty, all beauty is destroyed, because all fitness, by superadding ornament to ill-contrived form. If we would return to a more healthy condition, we must even be as little children or as savages; we must get rid of the acquired and artificial, and return to and develope [*sic*] natural instincts.[13]

Jones's vision of an ornament based directly on impulse, unmediated by convention, reflects the Victorian longing for an authentic style in the midst of a wealth of borrowed ones. The irony probably did not escape him, that he was contributing to the problem even as he tried to solve it. Artists in a complex society cannot "be as little children or as savages," however much they admire impulse and instinct. The most they can do is imitate works embodying those qualities. In doing so they expand the eclectic repertory still further, without changing their own nature. Be that as it may, a larger question remains. Granted that artists or designers of mid-nineteenth-century England might wish to change their way of seeing, or their relation to the creative process, in the hope of escaping from the trap of eclecticism, why should they want to change in this particular way? How could a thoroughly mainstream designer like Jones suggest, however unrealistically, the emulation of savages as a means to aesthetic salvation?

The answer lies in the ideal of the "noble savage," which flourished especially during the eighteenth century alongside the opposing vision of an ascent from savagery. Its essence is appropriately simple. Humanity once lived (and in some places still lives) in freedom and virtue, untroubled by the struggles and deceits which beset more complex societies. The so-called progress of civilization has been a movement away from our earlier happiness, and its supposed achievements are worthless compared with the simple virtues of the primitive. The ideal had a double origin: in Greco-Roman images of the Golden Age, and in favorable accounts of contemporary tribal societies, especially those of the Americas.

The image of the noble savage is linked, above all, to the name of Jean-Jacques Rousseau (1712–1778). This is unfortunate, since Rousseau himself never used the term, and his writings express different and sometimes contradictory views on primitive humanity and the value of progress.[14] It is not necessary to sum up Rousseau's entire contribution here, or to debate the consistency of his thought. The essay that brought him fame is unambiguous in its contempt for civilization. But this is not all. Its implications for the fate of ornament go far beyond setting the stage for pronouncements like those of Owen Jones. Rousseau's argument draws strength from a deep-seated Western mistrust of ornament, as though ornament symbolized the dangers of civilization itself.

The work in question is the *Discourse on the Sciences and Arts* (often called simply the *First Discourse*), written and published in 1750.[15] Rousseau wrote it for a competition sponsored by the Academy of Dijon, on the question: "Has the restoration of the sciences and arts tended to purify morals?" The members of the Academy, in a remarkable display of broad-mindedness, fed the mouth that bit them, and awarded him the prize. Rousseau's entry is the very opposite of what they must have had in mind. It is a condemnation of progress itself, and thus undermines that cornerstone of the Enlightenment, the idea that intellectual and social progress go hand in hand.

In a sense, the *First Discourse* only carries the familiar distrust of luxury to its logical conclusion. It exemplifies the extremism that results when simplicity replaces moderation as the opposite of excess. (Excess usually means excessive luxury, but simplicity can easily become asceticism, itself a form of excess.) The ideal of simplicity allows Rousseau to judge the cultural achievements of Greece and Rome—a fortiori, the achievements of civilization as a whole—by the same standards Greece once applied to the "barbarian." For Rousseau, excessive luxury was a vice the Greeks had *not* managed to avoid or put behind them (*First Discourse*, p. 43):

Athens became the abode of civility and good taste, the country of orators and philosophers. The elegance of buildings there corresponded to that of the language. Marble and canvas, animated by the hands of the most skillful masters, were seen everywhere. From Athens came those astonishing works that will serve as models in all corrupt ages.

It is not that cultural pursuits can sometimes lead to vanity or luxury. They are bound up with it from the start: "Behold how luxury, licentiousness and slavery have in all periods been punishment for the arrogant attempts we have made to emerge from the happy ignorance in which eternal wisdom had placed us" (p. 46). Or again (pp. 50–51):

Luxury rarely develops without the sciences and the arts, and they never develop without it. I know that our philosophy . . . holds contrary to the experience of all centuries that luxury produces the splendor of States; but having forgotten the necessity for sumptuary laws, will our philosophy still dare deny that good morals are essential to the stability of empires, and that luxury is diametrically opposed to good morals?

Only a few societies, according to Rousseau, have managed to avoid the pitfall of luxury by training their citizens in virtue alone, rejecting all forms of refinement. Ancient Sparta, the archetype of an ascetic society and nemesis of culturally brilliant Athens, is the prime example, but Rousseau also praised the Scythians and Germans of antiquity, and the Romans and Persians—before vanity brought them low.

To justify such pessimism about the proudest achievements of Western secular culture, it is not enough to assert that luxury (by which Rousseau meant all the refinements and aspirations that distinguish civilization from mere subsistence) destroys first morals then empires; one must have a clear idea of how it does this. On one level the explanation is obvious. Luxury makes people "soft." They neglect military discipline and become less and less able to bear hardship. Eventually a simpler, tougher people conquer them. This is the ideology of the Persian Wars all over again, the historical baggage of the "gold-laden Medes," though Rousseau cited many other examples to support his case (pp. 51–52). But beneath this simple answer lies a network of more complex assumptions. Refinement is not just harmful because it softens. Or rather, it is far more harmful than it first appears, because it softens in other ways than the physical (p. 36):

The needs of the body are the foundations of society, those of the mind make it pleasant. While government and laws provide for the safety and well-being of assembled men, the sciences, letters, and arts, less despotic and perhaps more powerful, spread garlands of flowers over the iron chains with which men are burdened, stifle in them the sense of that original liberty for which they seem to have been born, make them love their slavery, and turn them into what is called civilized peoples.

In other words, if civilization means the pleasurable elements in human societies, then civilization is inherently evil because it reconciles people to political oppression. Not only this, but the game is not worth the candle. The refinement for which people trade their innate sense of liberty is "the semblance of all virtues without the possession of any."

The issue is no longer toughness or love of freedom, at least not directly. Civilization may subvert both, but this does not make it the *semblance* of anything. Inference must move the other way, with the idea of semblance as Rousseau's starting point. Military considerations aside, why should civilization be a semblance of virtue, and not virtue itself? The answer, for Rousseau, is that civilization conceals and deceives. Not only does it mask the oppressive power of the state, but it constrains us daily to mask ourselves from one another: "No more sincere friendship; no more well-based confidence. Suspicions, offenses, coldness, reserve, hate, betrayal will hide constantly under that uniform and false veil of politeness, under that much vaunted urbanity which we owe to the enlightenment of our century" (p. 58).

Ornament is thus identified from the beginning with deception and concealment. We have already seen it implicitly in the image of chains adorned with garlands. Only a page later, Rousseau made a far more explicit connection (p. 37):

> It is in the rustic clothes of a farmer and not beneath the gilt of a courtier that strength and vigor of the body will be found. Ornamentation is no less foreign to virtue, which is the strength and vigor of the soul. The good man is an athlete who likes to compete in the nude. He disdains all those vile ornaments which would hamper the use of his strength, most of which were intended to hide some deformity.

Rousseau used the term "ornamentation" in the most general sense, but this does not diminish its relevance. Visual ornament is only a special case of the far larger phenomenon. Whether we cover chains with garlands or a courtier's languid body with gold, the assumption is that ornament hides something bad. If civilization is the ornament of society, then by definition it conceals every "deformity" of society under an attractive exterior: hence "the semblance of all the virtues without the possession of any." It follows, too, that if ornament has no purpose but to conceal the bad, it must itself be bad. This assumption survives in the modernist doctrine that good design needs no ornament, but that may be the least of its influences. In equating civilization, ornament, and falsehood, Rousseau tapped into a current of Western thought uniting art and morality on the most basic level. This is the ancient and deep-seated fear of artifice.

A MISTRUST OF art as something both powerful and false is intrinsic to our culture. It comes to us from both the Judeo-Christian and the Greco-Roman traditions. On the one hand, we have the Second Commandment, against graven images, to warn us against substituting human work for the Ineffable. On the other, we have Plato's admonitions, of which the parable of the cave is only the most dramatic, against mistaking semblances for reality.[16] We cannot understand the fear of artifice without this background, but I have in mind something more specific. As words or concepts, "art" and "artifice" are closely related, but artifice has negative connotations which art, in today's culture at least, does not have. It implies something contrived and very possibly deceptive. The adjectival form makes this explicit. If something is artificial it is inauthentic, by definition.

Artifice can mean many things, but a working definition is "human creativity added to nature or substituted for nature." It can appear in any realm of expression, and appeal to any combination of senses and sensibilities. If it substitutes for nature, this may be because it plausibly imitates nature, or because it provides an aesthetic alternative to nature. By implication it is carefully thought out and carefully executed, otherwise it could not succeed as imitation. It is unspontaneous, because of the amount of planning and work it entails, but also because of the unshakable convention that claims spontaneity as an attribute of nature.

Artifice is a far broader term than ornament, and ornament is one of its many subsets. Within limits, we should expect a society well-disposed toward artifice to favor ornament, while a dislike of artifice should carry over into the visual arts as cosmophobia. The reality is more complex. Artifice is suspect from the start, and rarely evokes unqualified praise, even from those most intent on practicing it.

In the tenth century, the palace of the Byzantine emperors featured a gilded metal tree, its branches filled with mechanical songbirds.[17] We do not know what this object looked or sounded like, but almost a thousand years later in the poem "Sailing to Byzantium," it served Yeats as a symbol of the "artifice of eternity," an old man's refuge from the rush of life toward death. As an alternative to nature, artifice is an alternative to death, but only at the cost of being an alternative to life. The West has come no closer to an embrace of artifice than this tragic ambivalence.

The English poet and dramatist Ben Jonson (1573–1637) exemplifies the disdain for artifice as perverse novelty and extravagance run wild:

> But now nothing is good that is naturall: Right and naturall language seeme to have least of the wit in it; that which is writh'd and tortur'd, is counted the more exquisite. Cloath of Bodkin, or Tissue, must be imbrodered; as if no face were faire, that were not pouldered, or painted? No beauty to be had, but in wresting, and writhing our owne tongue? Nothing is fashionable, till it bee deform'd; and this is to write like a *Gentleman*. All must bee as affected, and preposterous as our Gallants cloaths, sweet bags, and night-dressings: in which you would think our men lay in; like *Ladies:* it is so curious.[18]

Jonson took for granted the opposition of nature and artifice. Nature is not only superior, it is also simpler. It follows that even a thoroughly human creation like language is most natural (whatever that means) when least elaborate. To love artifice is to reject nature. What Jonson perceived as the ascendancy of artifice, and corresponding disdain for "naturall language," signals a decline from the standards of an unspecified earlier time. Artifice in writing, like artifice in dress, is a plaything of fashion; and for fashion's sake, each commits torture and deformation. (There is no question of *concealing* deformities here: artifice itself deforms, and openly!) Finally, in the same way that Jonson compared the fops of his day to women for their indulgence in cosmetics and outlandish dress, so by implication an "artificial" literary style is not just frivolous but unmanly.[19]

It is an irony worth savoring, the care Jonson took to break up his elegant cadences with sudden jolts of good English talk. Nothing effeminate here! The title of his book is writhed and wrested from two languages. *Silva* in Latin means a forest, by extension an abundance of something, and by further extension a miscellany. By calling his collection of short pieces *Timber*, Jonson combined a learned pun with an impeccably English word, signifying not just standing trees but wood as a building material, full of rustic solidity. And this is to write like nature!

Jonson was not one to *fear* artifice, however much he might ridicule it. Neverthe-less, there is a darker undercurrent which he acknowledged obliquely. The chief dan-ger of an ornate style was not frivolity but deception. To understand this, we must remember the enormous importance Greek and Roman society gave to rhetoric, the art of verbal persuasion. It was *the* art of public life, and the focus of education. Since the goal of rhetoric was success in politics or law, it was always a pragmatic art. The point was to win. Therefore clarity and truth mattered less than emotional impact and the *appearance* of truth. It was also an "artificial" art: self-conscious, elaborate, and governed by many rules. These rules and their interpretation—the relation of means and ends, the scope of language, how to exploit and by implication deflect its power—are among the foundations of Western literary criticism. Our linguistic self-awareness is inseparable from our awareness of the power of language to mislead. For the writ-ers of antiquity, and their successors in the Renaissance, it was the ornate style, the style furthest removed from "naturall language," which most seriously threatened to conceal or distort the truth. Ostensibly, Jonson condemned artifice as frivolity in lit-erature and daily life. His real target was deception and the society that nurtures it.[20]

If linguistic deception is the only truly threatening facet of artifice, it is because we have remained within secular limits. Physical artifice, particularly, is suspect in Chris-tianity. The stricture "it is easier for a camel to go through the eye of a needle than for a rich man to enter the kingdom of God" (Matt. 19.24) is not directed at artifice per se, but at the entire set of worldly assumptions and ambitions that surround it. More directly relevant is Christ's admonition in the Sermon on the Mount: "Consider the lilies of the field, how they grow; they neither toil nor spin; yet I tell you, even Solomon in all his glory was not arrayed like one of these" (Matt. 6.28–29). This is a dismissal not just of luxury but of artifice itself, a reminder that no human effort can match the least of the splendors of nature.

If artifice lost any of its allure as a result, we would not know it from the pomp of Christendom. This refusal to renounce artifice in practice, whatever lip-service was paid to the ideal, is the source and essence of its spiritual danger. Artifice, whether phys-ical or verbal, conjures up a substitute reality, with the accompanying risk that we will prefer the substitute to the real thing, or lose the ability to distinguish between them. This concern echoes in Jonson's complaint that "nothing is good that is naturall," but only in the religious sphere does it become a matter of life or death. To reject nature in favor of artifice is to lose touch with God as he manifests himself in the physical world; at worst, it is to set oneself above God as a creator.

These concerns translate directly into the debate on ornament. We can now understand why Ruskin insisted so passionately that even the most abstract ornament should be based on natural forms, and that ornament must *never* represent human artifacts. For the same reasons he fought with equal passion against any architectural or decorative technique that disguised its own operation.[21] In principle, his insistence on technical honesty was absolute. He would have outlawed even the use of metal clamps in stone construction; only the utility and universality of the practice forced his grudging acceptance.

To Ruskin, the secular and religious effects of artifice were inseparable. Unchecked artifice progressively excludes nature. Deceptive building techniques and ornament based on artifacts—artifice within artifice—threaten to create a man-made visual environment requiring no reference outside itself. Not only is such an environment literally godless, it is also self-perpetuating. Surrounded by falsehood, we lose our ability to recognize truth, including the truth of nature as the manifestation of God. Ruskin sought the reform, not the elimination of ornament. Artifice, for him, was not just something that must be controlled, it was something that *could* be controlled. (I mean, of course, morally controlled. Technical control is intrinsic to artifice.) His mission, and his great achievement, was to show people how.

Ruskin lived in a Protestant society, and Protestantism has always been wary of artifice, over and above the basic Western ambivalence. Puritanism, with its violent rejection of luxury, is the obvious example, but it is an extreme example, therefore a poor guide to the pervasive role of religious belief in everyday aesthetics. The Protestant revulsion from artifice is sharply and practically focused on the environment of worship. It has but one goal: to do away with anything that might interfere with the worshipper's direct and personal relation to God. This includes devotional images (by far the most threatening category, since they raised the double specter of idolatry and unnecessary mediation); any architectural feature that breaks up the congregation, interferes with the clear reading of Scripture, or blocks free movement in the church, especially in a way that privileges the clergy (e.g., chancel screens and raised altars); elaborate clerical vestments (symbolic of priestly hierarchy); and any kind of elaboration suggesting a reliance on good works—donations—instead of faith as a means to salvation.

It should not surprise us that the literature on Protestantism and art says little about the relative (and sometimes absolute) austerity of Protestant churches, especially church interiors, as an *artistic* achievement.[22] It is a religious ideal, and the artistic effect is incidental. But incidental does not mean negligible. Indirectly, the simplification of worship generates a powerful aesthetic of simplicity. In religious terms, the physical paraphernalia of worship which the Protestants have discarded represent everything that is wrong with Catholicism. In purely visual terms, without reference to any doctrine, these same paraphernalia represent artifice, visual richness, multiple foci, and multiple opportunities for ornament. Religious conviction rarely makes such a dispassionate appraisal. The more attractive the visual environment, the greater the temptation to accept and enjoy it, and thus to readmit on artistic grounds what had just been banished on religious ones. Visual beauty, insofar as it derives from lavishness and artifice, becomes synonymous with temptation. There is a difference between rejecting the conditions in which ornament can flourish, and rejecting ornament itself, but it is easy to dislike what endangers your immortal soul, even when you meet it in a less threatening context.

All these factors, and more, were at work in Ruskin's England. Since the sixteenth century the Anglican Church had been Protestant in that it rejected the authority of Rome, but that rejection had come by royal fiat rather than by a groundswell of religious reform. The seizure of church treasures following the suppression of the monasteries was official confiscation and unofficial pillage, with hardly a veneer of religious justification.[23] Yet the radical current in English Protestantism was strong enough to fuel—and survive—the Puritan Revolution of the seventeenth century. The Church of England itself remained divided between those who saw it as fundamentally Catholic and those who saw it as fundamentally Protestant.[24] By the nineteenth century, it comprised not only these opposing movements (High and Low Church, respectively, with many gradations between them) but also Evangelical sects that sought to recapture the fervor and simplicity of the earliest Christians.

Outside the Church of England there were denominations as old as the Reformation itself, such as Congregationalism, and others more recent, of which the most influential was Methodism, founded in the first half of the eighteenth century. Each sect, whether Anglican or Dissenting, had its own regional, social and economic base, and each made a different accommodation of religious values to a culture whose combination of formal eclecticism with an explosion of new technologies is arguably the high-water mark of artifice.[25] It is no surprise that Owen Jones could complain, "Ever since the Reformation, when a separation took place between religion and art, England has not had anything like a [decorative] style of her own."[26] There was never a full separation of religion and art, but their relation was always problematic. Both the style and the amount of ornament took on specific, often divisive connotations.

Ruskin's insistence on absolute rules for morality and art seems arbitrarily restrictive today, but in the ferment of his time he stands out as a genius of moderation. The Gothic style, which he championed, is both ornate and historically inseparable from Catholicism. This combination led other theorists toward extreme views, or appealed to those who already held them. A. W. Pugin, Ruskin's older contemporary and the most eloquent spokesman for a revived Gothic architecture as the ideal setting for Christian worship, was a convert to Catholicism. The so-called ecclesiologists, ideologues of the Gothic revival in English church architecture, remained Anglican, but their romantic attachment to a medieval (i.e., Catholic) past, and to the visual panoply of worship, alienated large segments of their church.[27] In contrast, Ruskin defined and defended a middle ground. By subjecting Gothic architecture, including its ornament, to strict rules based on the relation of art and nature, and by ruthlessly excluding its most ornate phases as a violation of these rules, he reinvented the Gothic style as an organic and therefore "natural" style. This does not mean a style without artifice, but one which keeps artifice within strict bounds, as a tribute instead of an alternative to nature. By this strategy, Ruskin did more than any other thinker or designer to make the Gothic an acceptable setting for Protestant as well as Catholic worship. Whatever we may feel about the result—a century's equation of church architecture with Gothic architecture—it was a remarkable piece of artistic diplomacy.[28]

UP TO THIS point, we have been looking at forms of aesthetic puritanism which apply to ornament only indirectly or as a manifestation of something else: excess, primitivism, luxury, artifice. There is, however, a cultural prejudice that touches ornament more directly—the prejudice against transformation and monstrosity. By transformation I mean the changing of one type of being into another in violation of the observed laws of nature: a person into a stone, an animal into a plant. Monstrosity is the image or embodiment of transformation. It combines features of two or more types of beings in a single entity, which we call a monster.

Transformation is the essence of ornament. Ornament transforms materials by concealing them—the difference between clay and lusterware—or by virtuoso handling that ignores their "intrinsic" character. It transforms two dimensions into three, by any combination of illusionism and actual relief. It turns an object into something that is no longer just that object, most obviously when recognizable images are added, but to some extent by the addition of any pattern. Above all, ornament takes transformation as its subject matter. It revels in the creation of monsters. Animals emerge from plants, flowers shade into geometric shapes, with an ease that belies their unnaturalness. The crest of a helmet becomes a woman's body (fig. 56), and as though that were not enough, she is transformed in turn, from the waist down, into a plant, from each of whose spiraling tendrils a winged Cupid half emerges.

These changes are whimsical rather than terrifying, but the loss of intrinsic shape is a deep-seated fear. If ornament sometimes disarms this fear through playfulness, familiarity, and the assertion of human control, the popularity of transformation as a theme attests to a fascination we cannot appreciate unless we recognize its more sinister aspects. These are to be found in myth, literature, and popular belief, rather than in responses to ornament per se. Monsters can be imaginary, like the Minotaur, which had the body of a man and the head of a bull, or they can be real. The same word was used for freaks of nature, such as a two-headed calf, or extreme deformities suggestive of another species: the "elephant man."

It is revealing that the word "monster," which today might conjure up a destructive creature of fantasy from the depths of the earth or from outer space, originally meant a portent. Extreme natural abnormalities signified disruption in the world, or in the relations between humans and the divine. They were a source of fear to the populace, and of urgent concern to religious authorities. It is easy for us to separate the concept of monstrosity into its natural and supernatural components, but to do so here would be missing the point. A monster is a being that terrifies because it has no precedent in nature, and therefore should not exist. It may portend the disruption of human existence, or it may be the agent of that disruption. Symbolically there is no difference.

Unlike monstrosity, transformation has no basis in fact. Nevertheless, its hold on the Western imagination has been enormous, thanks to the influence of Greek mythology. Already in Homer's *Odyssey* we find that shadowy yet archetypal figure, the enchantress Circe, who turns men into animals. Transformation is a recurring theme in Greek and Latin literature, culminating in Ovid's *Metamorphoses*, a retelling of all the major transformation myths.

Like monstrosity, transformation is the expression of extremity. It marks where the boundaries separating human and nonhuman, or even animate and inanimate, nature break down. Transformation at the hands of a god—a god is nearly always the agent in these myths—may come when a lesser being offends the gods by arrogance, or by intruding, even unwittingly, on their secrets or their privacy. Actaeon, who chanced on Artemis bathing in a forest pool, was turned into a stag and killed by his own dogs.

Transformation could also be the price of resisting (or not resisting!) a god's amorous advances. The nymph Daphne fled Apollo, calling on her father, a river god, to save her from rape. Unable to contend against Apollo, he turned his daughter into a laurel tree. Or transformation could come as an end to unbearable fear or suffering. But whether it functions as a punishment or a kind of refuge, transformation is always a disruption of the human order, memorialized in a disruption of the natural order. It is a crossing of boundaries that should not be crossed.[29]

With the rise of Christianity this perspective changed. Christianity utterly rejected the old Greek and Roman gods, and the body of myth that defined their relation to the human world. Yet in the art, literature, and commonplace of the huge Late Roman Empire, they were far too deeply rooted to eradicate, however much the sternest Christian thinkers may have wished to do so. In *The City of God*, St. Augustine granted the myths of transformation a basis in fact, but with several provisos.[30] Clearly he was uncomfortable with the whole matter, and would have dismissed it out of hand were it not for reliable contemporary accounts of what we would call out-of-body experiences involving transformation. Comparing these accounts with the myths, Augustine offered this explanation: God, who is just but inscrutable, sometimes allows the demons—invisible, immortal beings wracked by ungovernable passions—to punish or torment humans. Transformation is one of the ways in which they do this. Because demons have no power to create, they cannot change a human being into something fundamentally different: not the body, and certainly not the soul. Therefore all transformation, however plausibly attested, is an illusion worked upon both the victim and the observer. In extreme cases the victim may be spirited away and killed, to be replaced by another creature, but the victim's substance is never changed.

This attempt at debunking leaves the myths of transformation as unsettling as before, though in a different way. No less than under paganism, humans are at the mercy of an inscrutable god, though now it is supernatural riffraff who do the dirty work. Transformation has lost its exemplary value: it no longer helps us chart the extremities of the human condition. Deceit has become the crucial element, an apparent trivialization of the theme. Most important, Augustine's interpretation breaks down the distinction between past and present. Classical myths are firmly situated in the past. Often they explain how some aspect of the natural or human world came to be as it is: a monument, a ritual, the behavior of an animal. If transformation is instead the work of demons, under implicit license from God, it is a present danger from which no one is ever completely safe.

This danger, and the identification of transformation with illusion and deceit, implies a new level of human responsibility: to foil the demons by distinguishing illusion from reality. Throughout Christian antiquity and the Middle Ages, demons work their mischief under the guise of illusion. It does not matter whether that mischief is torment or temptation, since there is finally no difference between them. Temptation need not be subtle or voluptuous; terrifying demonic assaults are a temptation to abandon faith in God.

Ornament is deeply implicated here. Even when it does not deal directly in illusion, it is by definition artificial, and artifice is always a kind of illusion. Like transformation, artifice interferes with nature; both can tempt and deceive by offering an alternative to reality. Nowhere in Christian thought is the link between transformation and artifice more clearly illustrated than in Book II of Edmund Spenser's *The Faerie Queene* (1596), where Sir Guyon, the personification of temperance, destroys the Bower of Bliss, home of the enchantress Acrasia. Her name, by an ingenious pun, means intemperance in the double sense of excess and lack of control. She is a Circe-like figure, transforming her lovers into animals, but where Circe's victims were transformed in body alone, Acrasia transforms both body and soul. Or rather, she transforms the body while leading the soul into a trap of its own making. The equation of human passions with animals is a classical and medieval commonplace, and Acrasia has no need to remake her victims in any radical sense. She merely gives physical form to the animal that is latent in each man's nature.

Acrasia is physically seductive in the highest degree, but relies on more than her beauty to strip away men's self-control. The Bower in which she lives is a creation of lavish artifice, enhancing, imitating, and finally replacing nature. Its gate is of ivory, recalling the gate of false dreams in Vergil's *Aeneid*, and the pleasure garden within is designed to make anyone who enters forget the outside world. It is in the most literal sense a substitute reality, complete with an arbor in which real grapes and grapes made of gold share the same vines. The message is clear. Artifice tempts, deceives, and ultimately cuts us off from reality. Without reality to sustain us, we cast aside temperance, and passion transforms us into animals.

A century later, in an intellectual climate changed almost beyond recognition from Spenser's day, the imagery of magic and deception conveyed a related anxiety: that the world as humans perceived it had little in common with its "true" nature as revealed by science. In 1712 the critic and essayist Joseph Addison wrote:

Things would make but a poor appearance to the Eye, if we saw them only in their proper Figures and Motions: And what Reason can we assign for their exciting in us many of those Ideas which are different from any thing that exists in the Objects themselves (for such are Light and Colours) were it not to add Supernumerary Ornaments to the Universe, and make it more agreeable to the Imagination? We are every where entertained with pleasing Shows and Apparitions, we discover imaginary Glories in the Heavens, and in the Earth, and see some of this Visionary Beauty poured out upon the whole Creation; but what a rough unsightly Sketch of Nature should we be entertained with, did all her Colouring disappear, and the several Distinctions of Light and Shade vanish? In short, our souls are at present delightfully lost and bewildered in a pleasing Delusion, and walk about like the Enchanted Hero of a Romance, who sees beautiful Castles, Woods and Meadows; and at the same time hears the warbling of Birds, and the purling of Streams; but upon the finishing of some secret Spell, the fantastick scene breaks up, and the disconsolate Knight finds himself on a barren Heath, or in a solitary Desart.[31]

To understand what Addison is talking about, we must know that a revolution in thought had just taken place. Sir Isaac Newton's *Opticks*, published in 1704, dispelled the assumption that color was an essential property of objects or substances. Rays of light have, in Newton's words, the "Power and Disposition to stir up a Sensation of this or that Colour," but this is very different from color being a property of light, or of the objects that reflect light. Color is the product of our own perceptive mechanisms. Elsewhere in the *Opticks*, Newton points out that a burning coal moved rapidly in a circle leaves the image of a circle of fire, and that pressure on a closed eye produces a burst of colored light. In the former case, perception lingers after its object has moved on; in the latter a visual impression is created even though there is nothing to see. Newton's conclusions about color thus extend to visual phenomena in general. We see because of the way certain stimuli affect our eyes, nerves, and brain. But since this process takes place within ourselves, and depends on our own physiology, it has nothing to do with the intrinsic character of the stimuli. It follows that we may no longer assume that what we see corresponds to physical reality.[32]

Addison gives an unsettling double view of the revolution's outcome. On the one hand, the world of the senses is divinely ordained for our pleasure. On the other, our perceptions still deceive, and the agent of deception is ornament. Not, of course, ornament in the art historical sense, but in a more general sense which certainly includes it, that of anything "supernumerary," added for the sake of pleasure alone. What we see around us, the ornament of the universe, may be a gift of God and a source of boundless delight, but it is not real. With the breaking of the spell, it ends. Addison yoked together the old tradition of romance and the new tradition of scientific rigor. However improbable the pairing, there is one thing on which they agree absolutely. As a precondition for reaching a higher knowledge, the spell and the illusion must end.

The cultural associations of transformation provide a foil to the popularity of monstrous themes in Western ornament. But although there are texts from as long ago as the first century b.c. which condemn monstrosity in ornament, they do not acknowledge its darker side. Instead, the attack comes in the name of a literal-minded artistic puritanism. Horace, in his *Ars Poetica*, mocked the painter who might depict a creature with the head of a woman, feathers like a bird, and a fish's tail. Monstrosity is a flagrant violation of consistency and good taste, but it is laughable, not frightening. Vitruvius, author of the only treatise on architecture to survive from antiquity, directed his attention specifically to architectural ornament:

> We now have fresco paintings of monstrosities, rather than truthful representations of definite things. For instance, reeds are put in the place of columns, fluted appendages with curly leaves and volutes, instead of pediments, candelabra supporting representations of shrines, and on top of their pediments numerous tender stalks and volutes growing up from the roots and having human figures senselessly seated upon them; sometimes stalks having only half-length figures, some with human heads, others with the heads of animals.
>
> Such things do not exist and cannot exist and never have existed. Hence, it is the new taste that has caused bad judges of poor art to prevail over true artistic excellence.[33]

Vitruvius condemned these motifs because they depict things that are biologically or architecturally impossible. If something does not exist, there is no reason to make an image of it, and only a jaded striving after novelty can account for the fashion. Not surprisingly, Vitruvius was helpless in the face of human nature. No amount of preaching could change the Roman taste for monstrous ornament. "Inhabited scrolls" combining plant, animal, and human forms became more, not less fantastic (and popular) with the passage of centuries. The incongruities that provoked Vitruvius continued to flourish in the ornamental idiom known as the grotesque. Fantastic animals remained a pillar of the repertory. In other words, there was a serious inconsistency between the ornament enjoyed by the Romans and the ornament which they (or some of their spokesmen, whether official or self-appointed) said they should enjoy.

This inconsistency came back to haunt the artists and theorists of the Renaissance. Vitruvius was a bible to those bent on emulating the Roman achievement, for the simple reason that nothing else of its kind was available, but the surviving examples of Roman decorative art sent a very different message. One, in particular, stands out as the catalyst of a new ornamental style: the so-called Golden House in Rome, a palace of the emperor Nero, whose discovery in the fifteenth century gave artists their first direct access to Roman ornamental painting in general and the grotesque in particular.[34] Theory and practice were not invariably at odds: Michelangelo himself is said to have embraced the grotesque as a symbol of artistic freedom, explicitly distinguishing monstrosity from falsehood.[35] But the contradiction was never finally resolved. Some of the strongest prejudice against monstrosity was built into the Western awareness of ornament at the very time when designers began raising the grotesque to a complexity and strangeness beyond anything the Romans knew (fig. 72).

The next two hundred and fifty years, approximately from 1500 to 1750, are unique in the history of ornament. No comparable period, in Europe or perhaps anywhere else, has seen so much experimentation, or so many forms and variations added to the ornamental repertory. One theme above all gave the movement its life: transformation. Throughout the sixteenth and seventeenth centuries artists made images of change whose ingenuity, exuberance, and assurance surpassed anything in pagan antiquity or the Christian Middle Ages. Yet this was no more than a prelude. The real culmination came in the first half of the eighteenth century, in the style known as the rococo. Then, as never before or since, the genius of design and the virtuosity of craft were focused on the pervasive, promiscuous transformation of one form of being into another. By forms of being I do not just mean forms of life. Rocks become plants, plants become animals, buildings emerge from shapeless concretions of matter, and objects open suddenly onto limitless vistas (fig. 73).

Artists of the Renaissance and baroque eras may have delighted in monsters, but their techniques for creating them, derived from the Greco-Roman tradition, were relatively literal-minded. They simply combined parts of humans, animals, and plants to produce a "new" creature. The rococo treatment of monsters was significantly different. Monstrosity was no longer just the incongruous juxtaposition of forms, but

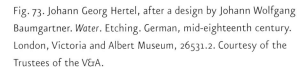

Fig. 72. Platter. Ceramic. Italian, 1508. New York, The Metropolitan Museum of Art, 1975.1.1024, Robert Lehman Collection, 1975.

Fig. 73. Johann Georg Hertel, after a design by Johann Wolfgang Baumgartner. *Water.* Etching. German, mid-eighteenth century. London, Victoria and Albert Museum, 26531.2. Courtesy of the Trustees of the V&A.

the threatened dissolution of form itself. This was not a matter of carelessness or declining skill. Anything but. Rococo designers were for the most part brilliant draftsmen, but even their most precise creations have a labile quality that can leave us uncertain of what is being depicted, or where one substance ends and another begins. To combine precision and lability requires a less literal, more intuitive sense of the monstrous than we find in typical Renaissance and baroque ornament.

I believe that this unique development paved the way for the revolt against ornament. The rococo dealt Western visual culture a blow even neoclassicism could not heal. By threatening to dissolve reality itself, rococo ornament fed the deep-seated fears of excess, artifice, and transformation, and focused them on a single target. But why was the threat taken so seriously? An ornamental style, no matter how vertiginous, is after all only an ornamental style. To appreciate the danger, we must recognize that it was much more than an artistic caprice. European thought, and the history of science in particular, display just as strong a fascination with transformation and weird composites. If rococo ornament seems to mock the idea of consistency in nature, so did the intellectual climate in which it evolved.

In the late seventeenth century, the Dutch anatomist Frederik Ruysch (1638–1731) assembled and displayed a collection of anatomical specimens that illustrates this correspondence. Ruysch was famous for his skill in injecting even the most delicate specimens with dyes and preservatives, and his museum provided a stage on which to display this virtuosity. The most prominent exhibits, captured on paper in his multivolume *Thesaurus Anatomicus*, were tableaux of infant human skeletons in postures of lamentation, in landscapes whose rocks and trees were ingeniously mounted bladders, bronchial tubes, kidney stones, and so forth.[36] In scientific guise, this is the old tradition of memento mori and the dance of death, a special kind of bravado that revels in the macabre. It draws equally on the love of transformation, of visual puns, and of the grotesque (in both its general and technical senses), which flourished in the Renaissance and which appeared most flamboyantly in the work of the late sixteenth-century painter Giuseppe Arcimboldo. The only surprise is that we should find this vision flourishing in so late a period.

But more survives of Ruysch's work than these tableaux. Other illustrations in the *Thesaurus Anatomicus* reveal a very different sense of organic form,

Fig. 74. Juste-Aurèle Meissonnier. Design for a monstrance. Engraving. France, published c. 1750 (the object dates from 1727). Art & Architecture Collection, Miriam and Ira D. Wallach Division of Art, Prints and Photographs, The New York Public Library, Astor, Lenox, and Tilden Foundations.

more in tune with its time and much more disturbing. One of them depicts a human fetal abnormality of the most extreme sort, a collection of infant body parts emerging at random from an amorphous mass that is presumably the placenta.[37] In the same decade, the goldsmith and designer Juste-Aurèle Meissonnier, one of the pioneers of rococo ornament, drew cherubs—disembodied infant heads—emerging from a cloudlike matrix (fig. 74).[38] The visual resemblance is too strong to be coincidental. I do not mean that rococo ornament took its inspiration directly from the scientific depiction of abnormalities. More likely, both art and science reflected a mindset in which the instability of form played a central role.

The same mindset fueled a new debate about the nature of monstrosity. During the seventeenth and eighteenth centuries it was widely believed that a pregnant woman's fantasies and desires, even the things she looked at, could cause her child to be born deformed. As an increasing number of scientists contested this view, the debate reached far beyond the medical arena, to the legal issue of determining paternity, and the legal and religious question of what constituted a human being.[39] Although scientific reason eventually prevailed, the controversy helped establish two modern perceptions relating directly to ornament. The first, which goes back to Aristotle, is of the monster (in the biological sense) as a falsehood or deception because it resembles a species other than its own. The second perception is of monstrosity in its other sense, a sentient destructive power beyond our understanding or control.

Although the original conflict centered on the destructive effects of *female* imagination, it was symptomatic of a much more basic conviction: that imagination itself is a potent force for evil, capable of inflicting even physical harm. The original issue may be long forgotten, but the conviction is still with us. It echoes through Goya's etching entitled *The Sleep of Reason Produces Monsters;* through Joseph Conrad's *Heart of Darkness;* through Freud; and through popular psychology in its moment of glory, the 1956 science-fiction film *Forbidden Planet,* and the dying science officer's warning: "Monsters! Monsters from the id!"[40]

This is not the only point of correspondence between the lability of form in ornament and natural philosophy in the eighteenth century. The central issue in eighteenth-century biology was the nature of species. For some thinkers, species were distinct and immutable. For others, adherents of the theory called *gradation,* there was no absolute distinction between the plant and animal kingdoms, or even between what we would call living and nonliving matter. Life is an unbroken continuum. Between any two forms there is, or once was, an intermediate form, ad infinitum. What appear to be fundamental differences between species are accidental: they are gaps in the "chain of being" caused by extinction or simply by the fact that not all forms are to be found in the same place.[41]

Although the doctrine of distinct (though *not* immutable) species eventually prevailed, gradation enjoyed enormous popularity in the eighteenth century and beyond. Even Linnaeus, the founder of modern biological classification, with its emphasis on distinction, began by assuming a continuum. The first edition of his seminal work *The System of Nature* (1735) made no greater distinction between rocks and what we would call primitive life-forms than between plants and animals. In 1741, Abraham Tremblay's description of the "polyp," a microorganism better known today as the hydra, caused great excitement, not only because of the organism's regenerative powers, but because it apparently supplied the crucial link between plants and animals. Tremblay's discovery held out hope that similar discoveries near the bottom of the scale of life would eventually bridge the gap between minerals and plants.[42]

In the eighteenth century, in both science and ornament, forms "flowed into" one another, softening or obliterating qualitative differences. There is good reason to suspect a historical link between the two phenomena, though not necessarily a conscious one. By the 1730s a generation of thinkers had grown from childhood to maturity amid images of transformation and flux, while at the same time the public interest in scientific debate made it inconceivable that designers and their patrons were ignorant of current theories. Nevertheless, gradation is not transformation. The belief that rocks, plants, and animals (not to mention human beings) occupy a theoretically unbroken continuum is not enough to turn a rock into a plant, or a plant into an animal. The same cultural trends may have nourished science and ornament, but there is nothing overtly sinister in this interaction, nothing comparable to the association of ornament with monstrosity. Yet a new scientific movement was about to create just such a threat, making the lability of form an image of social and spiritual uncertainty. This movement was *transformism*.

Transformism is gradation, but no longer as a static continuum. By what Arthur Lovejoy called the temporalization of the chain of being, it becomes a dynamic process going on through time, all the time.[43] Every species, from the simplest to the most complex, is constantly evolving. By arranging species in ascending order of complexity, we can see not just an abstract hierarchy but a progression through time.

The definitive statement of transformism is the *Zoological Philosophy* of Jean-Baptiste Lamarck, published in 1809.[44] Lamarck is remembered as the scientist who got evolution wrong, half a century before Darwin got it right. His name is also virtually synonymous with one of the most famous wrong ideas in biology, the inheritance of acquired characteristics. As a result, history tends to treat him as a straw man, rather than as the culmination of a daring intellectual movement without which the later developments would have been impossible. Like many of his predecessors,

Lamarck believed in the spontaneous generation of life, but not in the gross sense of complex organisms leaping suddenly into existence through no perceptible mechanism. That had been disproved over a hundred years earlier.[45] Nor did he believe in the sudden transformation of species: a mouse did not turn into a horse overnight, or at all for that matter. For Lamarck, life in its most primitive undifferentiated form can and does emerge continually from nonlife, through the action of sunlight on "various fluids" circulating within the earth. From such beginnings

> every species has derived from the action of the environment in which it has long been placed the *habits* which we find in it. These habits have themselves influenced the parts of every individual in the species, to the extent of modifying those parts and bringing them into relation with the acquired habits.[46]

In other words, environment affects behavior, and behavior affects structure—but very slowly. It follows that different environments affect members of the same species in different ways. Eventually, the populations evolve along different lines and become distinct species.

Transformism flew in the face of the Aristotelian doctrine of fixed species, whose consistency with the biblical creation story had long kept it sacrosanct. The idea that life could come into existence by purely natural means, then progress onward and upward under its own power, through the effort of individual organisms, is in direct conflict with creation as the unique act of an omnipotent god. It requires no great imagination to see that these ideas would have threatened many entrenched beliefs and institutions. Transformism undermines the belief that humanity occupies a privileged and by implication permanent place in nature. As early as 1769, Diderot said of evolving animal life, "We have no more idea of what they have been in the past than of what they will become. The imperceptible worm wriggling in the mire is probably on its way to becoming a large animal." And again, "Who knows what animal species preceded us? Who knows what will follow our present ones? Everything changes and passes away."[47]

The human significance of constant evolutionary change is implicit in Diderot: he gives it no special weight. But as decades passed and the idea of evolution won ever wider acceptance, its implications were increasingly recognized and spelled out. By 1850 (still nine years before Darwin's *On the Origin of Species*) the famous "Nature, red in tooth and claw" passage from Tennyson's *In Memoriam* (LV–LVI) makes it clear that the idea of an impersonal, evolving Nature strikes at the very heart of religious faith, or at least of *optimistic* religious faith:

> Are God and Nature then at strife,
>   That Nature lends such evil dreams?
>   So careful of the type she seems,
> So careless of the single life. . . .
>
> 'So careful of the type?' but no.
>   From scarped cliff and quarried stone
>   She cries 'A thousand types are gone:
> I care for nothing, all shall go.
>
> 'Thou makest thine appeal to me:
>   I bring to life, I bring to death:
>   The spirit does but mean the breath:
> I know no more.' And he, shall he,
>
> Man, her last work, who seem'd so fair,
>   Such splendid purpose in his eyes,
>   Who roll'd the psalm to wintry skies,
> Who built him fanes of fruitless prayer,
>
> Who trusted God was love indeed
>   And love, Creation's final law—
>   Tho' Nature, red in tooth and claw
> With ravine, shrieked against his creed—
>
> Who loved, who suffer'd countless ills,
>   Who battled for the True, the Just,
>   Be blown about the desert dust,
> Or seal'd within the iron hills?

By this time the threat was not just emotional but social and political. The atheist journal *The Oracle of Reason*, published in England in the early 1840s, made transformist evolution a weapon in its no-holds-barred campaign against all forms of religion. The third in a long series of articles it printed on the "Theory of Regular Gradation" (here the term includes the transformation of species through time) contains a sort of *credo* for advocates of evolution-as-subversion: "There are no fixed modes (laws as they are styled) for each species and each part, there being nothing *fixed* in the parts of nature, which are in a state of continual flux and change."[48] This plays directly on the fear that nature lacks an eternal, divinely instituted order; and indirectly on the fear that without the paradigm of an unchanging nature to shore them up, the "fixed modes" of society would crumble.

At almost exactly the same time we find Marx insisting that "spontaneous generation is the only practical refutation of the theory of creation" (by which he means divine creation). His point is that we are unfree so long as we regard ourselves as created by some outside force. To be free, we must be self-created. "But since," he writes, "for socialist man what is called world history is nothing but the creation of man by human labour . . . he has the observable and irrefutable proof of his self-creation and the process of his origin."[49] We have all heard of social Darwinism, the once powerful belief that natural selection and "survival of the fittest" were laws of social as well as biological evolution. What we have here is its counterpart, social Lamarckism: a vision of human progress modeled on the belief that species evolve by their individual members' *will* to evolve, and that every successful adaptation contributes to the further success of the group.[50]

The "transformist" ornament of the rococo reflected and affirmed a view of nature cut loose from divine purpose or human prediction. The ornament of the mid-nineteenth century retains this character, although in general it avoids the most blatant displays of formal dissolution. Where the eighteenth century delighted in forms flowing effortlessly yet impossibly into one another, nineteenth-century ornament gives us a jumble of historically incompatible *styles*. This too is a heritage of the rococo. Eighteenth-century designers felt perfectly free to combine Gothic and "Chinese" forms.[51] The nineteenth century carried that tendency much further, mixing Egyptian, Greek, Etruscan, Renaissance, Islamic, and more in a single setting, even a single object.

As with styles, so with materials and techniques. Writing in 1852, on the occasion of the Great Exhibition's closing, Gottfried Semper warned of the danger of an "*abundance of means*."[52] The implication is that new materials and techniques were becoming available faster than the culture could assimilate them. To use Semper's example, designers faced with the innovation of gaslight, and lacking the decades or even centuries needed to evolve an appropriate form, were reduced to imitating candles. By this standard, the "sham materials and sham techniques" against which Pevsner fulminated more than eighty years later are only the signs of a culture caught off guard and struggling to catch up. Yet materials and techniques can and do transform, and in transforming, deceive. In the technological hothouse of the nineteenth century, innovation often began as imitation.

Excessive naturalism troubled the ornamental reformers of the mid-nineteenth century at least as much as excessive fantasy. This is not so paradoxical as it seems. On the one hand, naturalism implies a *convincing* imitation: it is inherently deceptive. On the other hand, the greater the degree of naturalism in ornament, the more *unnatural* the combinations of object and decoration to which it leads. Naturalism in ornament is the very essence of transformation. It is the closest that two dimensions can come to three, or one object to becoming another object altogether. Naturalistic flowers on a carpet or wallpaper are as much a subversion of physical reality as a flower transforming itself into a three-headed dog. The reformers attacked this problem in a novel and dramatic way. The Great Exhibition had turned a substantial profit, and the money was used to found a Museum of Ornamental Art, which would ultimately become the Victoria and Albert Museum. Among its exhibits was a group of objects embodying "false principles of design," and the worst of these principles, in the words of the reformer Richard Redgrave, was "the tendency toward the direct imitation of nature."[53]

Behind these abstract and symbolic fears lay a frightening reality. With the Industrial Revolution, Western civilization was in the throes of the most radical disruption in its recorded history. Over and above the social dislocation—the transformed and often ruined lives—the explosion of science and technology was bringing nature increasingly under human control. Once again *The Oracle of Reason*, ever on the alert for new weapons against religion, is the litmus test of a scientific idea's subversive power. Admitting it was not yet possible to shape the complexities of life from chemical elements alone, the 1842 journal nonetheless assumed that science was on the verge of this ultimate achievement:

> It is only our imperfect knowledge which prevents us from producing organic *forms*, with all their vital energies, precisely as we find them in nature, and of course, if it be our ignorance only which presents a barrier to our forming wheat from the simple elements of which it is known to be composed . . . it follows that an incapacity to make man, also, must result from the same cause. . . . May not the rising generation see a monument erected in Westminster, or St. Paul's to the memory of Frankenstein?[54]

Once we accept the emergence of life from nonlife, not only have we no need for a God, it is only a matter of time until we ourselves usurp the highest of God's creative functions. Mary Shelley's *Frankenstein* (1816), which *The Oracle of Reason* so bravely invoked, owes its status as the only modern myth worthy of the name to its anticipation of a uniquely modern fear: power without wisdom, control without understanding. The monster in *Frankenstein* is the product of a technically brilliant but fatally ignorant attempt to manipulate the laws of nature, transforming dead into living matter. Frankenstein does not create his android *ex nihilo*, or from undifferentiated protoplasm, but by assembling and reanimating a collection of body parts. He does so with no thought to the whole, selecting each feature for its individual beauty. In a powerful though possibly unintentional foray into art criticism, Shelley makes it clear that the result of this eclectic approach is not just discordant but so unendurably ugly that it condemns the android as a monster in the eyes of all who encounter him—his own creator included.

By the mid-nineteenth century a unique pattern of elisions was in place. Transformation and monstrosity were linked with evolution and eclecticism, and all of these with unrestrained imagination, overconfidence, deception, the collapse of "fixed modes," and the threatened dissolution of cherished social and spiritual institutions. When such concerns exist side by side with a mainstream culture besotted with novelty and eclecticism, we should not be surprised to find a society at war with itself. Nor should we be surprised that ornament, directly or symbolically involved in all these issues, was the battleground on which the armies converged.

Anxieties of Industry

SOCIAL AND ECONOMIC OBJECTIONS TO ORNAMENT

HOW CLOSELY THE rhetoric of modernism echoes the anxieties of the nineteenth century. Ruskin's strongest theme, the appeal to honesty in the design and making of objects, lives on in the insistence on functional form and truth to materials. As for style mixing, that most mainstream of twentieth-century art historians, Kenneth Clark, seems torn between laughter and tears at the failure of Chippendale and other eighteenth-century designers to separate the various styles from which they took their inspiration. He actually calls the stylistic hybrids "monsters," and comforts himself that "In the history of taste true understanding of an unfamiliar style is very often preceded by a period of ill-formed and uncritical enthusiasm."[1]

The idea that successful assimilation of an unfamiliar style depends on "true understanding," rather than on selection and reinterpretation according to the tastes of one's own culture, seems limiting if not downright naive today. But Clark, like many critics before and after him, had a higher agenda: to expose the dazzling, eclectic whirl of styles as the sleep of reason. Kenneth Clark is not most people's idea of a modernist ideologue, but *The Gothic Revival* is almost exactly contemporary with Pevsner's first jeremiads against the art of the Great Exhibition, and the correspondence is striking. It was Pevsner, after all, who wrote, "The insensibility of the artist towards the beauty of pure shape, pure material, pure decorative pattern, is monstrous." Shape, material, and pattern—each has its own nature, clearly defined and clearly visible. When they do not, when one thing blurs into another, the result goes beyond mere ugliness. Consciously or not, Pevsner combined the most ominous meanings of monstrosity: a deformity and a portent of chaos.

Even the "abundance of means" problem continues almost unchanged to the present day. Recently I was given two small trays. They differ in size but have almost the same shape, and the same decoration imitating red-veined marble. The idea behind the gift was that I should have a matched set, but the matching is fortuitous. The trays come from different manufacturers, and are made of different materials. The smaller one is porcelain, the larger one, plastic. My first response was to consider the plastic tray a cheap imitation of the porcelain. But why? They are for all practical purposes identical, and both were mass produced, so it cannot be a question of superior versus inferior craftsmanship. The difference must lie in the materials themselves. Yet plastic and porcelain are very similar. Each is man-made and homogeneous, a tabula rasa to which the maker gives shape, color, and pattern. Granted, porcelain has a satisfying heaviness that plastic generally lacks, but a tray is not something one handles constantly, and that is just as well, for the fragility of porcelain would be a liability. The only explanation remaining is that porcelain is the "superior" material because it is older and more traditional. It is also more expensive. The association with an older and supposedly more luxurious way of life justifies its higher price, and price in turn preserves its luxury value.

This reciprocity, which affects so much of what we buy and use, played an important if equivocal role in the change of attitude toward ornament in the early twentieth century. For the moment it is enough to note that the difference in status between porcelain and plastic is a matter of pedigree. At the time of the Great Exhibition, when the ancestors of today's plastics stood for all that was newest in industrial technology, they already bore the stigma of imitation. In Semper's words, "Rubber and gutta-percha are vulcanized and utilized in a thousand imitations of wood, metal and stone carvings exceeding by far the natural limitations of the material they purport to represent."[2] This prejudice has not changed. So long as the new material imitates the old, it is inauthentic. At best, its artistic and monetary value are less; at worst it is a deception to be shunned.

This seems a virtual axiom where materials are concerned, but what about decoration? Returning to the example of my trays, both are decorated in imitation of marble. To call the porcelain tray the original or authentic piece is meaningless when it imitates still another material with even older connotations of luxury. Are we then to imagine a slowly evolving hierarchy of materials and techniques, with new ones coming into being as technology permits and economic necessity demands, starting out as lowly imitations and gradually winning acceptance as luxury arts in their own right? This has happened in the past, and it will certainly happen again. In a few decades, or a few centuries, plastic will doubtless evoke no more contempt than ceramics do today.

More is involved than imitation versus authenticity. The decoration on the porcelain tray is confined to a border less than an inch wide. The rest of the tray is white. In other words, the decoration was not intended as a convincing imitation of marble. This is because decoration imitating marble has a long history in Western art, long enough for the characteristic veining of marble to become an ornamental motif in its own right. At least as far back as classical antiquity, marble was copied in painted stucco, which may sometimes have been intended to deceive, and in mosaic, which certainly was not. As with purple cloth in the Roman world, its effect is problematic. If it did not deceive, did it—does it—still imply luxury? Or has even the hint of deception given way to a comfortable familiarity, no different in its effect from any number of well-known, unchallenging patterns, which no one thinks of as imitations?

Imitative decoration raises yet another issue of authenticity. One of Loos's early essays is "The Principle of Cladding."[3] The archaic and little-used English word "cladding" translates the German *Bekleidung*. The root meaning is clothing; as an architectural term it means a facing or revetment, one surface that masks another. Concerned as he was with honesty in building, yet recognizing that cladding was a fact of life in architecture and the decorative arts generally, Loos proposed the following "law": "we must work in such a way that a confusion of the material clad with its cladding is impossible. That means, for example, that wood may be painted any color except one—the color of wood." He continued:

> Applied to stuccowork, the principle of cladding would run like this: stucco can take any ornament with just one exception—[the imitation of] rough brickwork. One would think the declaration of such a self-evident fact to be unnecessary, but

just recently someone drew my attention to a building whose plaster walls were painted red and then seamed with white lines.

What Loos means is that ornament may do anything but deceive. This is an arbitrary stand but a relatively liberal one, and easy to sympathize with: the quixotic morality of a Ruskin, much tempered by Loos's characteristic pragmatism. Still, it leaves many questions unanswered. If Loos forbids stucco painted red and seamed with white lines, would he admit stucco painted green and seamed with red lines in the same pattern? It is only by convention, after all, that we associate certain colors with bricks and mortar. Are the trays that imitate marble acceptable only because they do not imitate it closely? Again, Loos insists that the cladding material must not match the original surface, except by happenstance—for example wood veneer on wood—yet he never really explains why a wooden surface may be covered with a wood veneer but not with the painted semblance of one.

Those two small trays have led us from one conundrum of authenticity to another. A hundred years ago they would have been signposts for serious debate. Today, with their baggage of ambiguities, they make an elaborate if unintended postmodern joke, whose punch line is that none of the issues matter any more. The trays were designed and made without regard to their "higher" implications, in the simple expectation that people would buy and enjoy them. This, for the most part, is how such objects have always been made, and how they will continue to be made. The intense ideological struggles of the past century and a half are an exception, an interlude.

Although we can still recognize the issues, I suspect that even this will not be true much longer. It is not just that attitudes and styles can change a great deal in much less than the hundred years since Loos wrote about cladding. Even seemingly incidental details can cut us off irrevocably from the past. Small tiles, such as we are accustomed to see on bathroom floors, are now rarely laid individually by hand. One buys them in panels one or two feet square, held together by a plastic mesh backing, with spaces in between for the grout. To lay them neatly still requires experience and skill, but that is not the point. Is a tile floor simply a floor covered with tile, or is "tile" an art form encompassing the process as well as the product? And if we agree that tiles are tiles, whether laid one by one or in panels, where do we stop? What about larger tiles, each simulating an arrangement of smaller ones; or, for that matter, a substitute like linoleum or vinyl that makes it possible to cut out a seamless "tile" floor from a single huge sheet? We are back to Loos's stucco painted red and seamed with white lines. At what point does a labor-saving device become an imitation—and why should it matter? We rarely think to ask these questions, because they presuppose materials and techniques that have largely been supplanted.

There is another, more immediate explanation for our losing touch so completely with the old debate and the concerns that fuelled it. For a century and a half these concerns have given us not only styles but rules, first for the making of ornament, then for its rejection. Modernism has been in the saddle long enough that many of its dictates have become second nature. Postmodernism lets us turn our backs on those dictates: the only rule is that there are no rules. The result is a pale shadow of 1851, the eclecticism without the exuberance or the sense of history. More than any other culture before or since, the Victorians knew what ornament looked like, and they had a vast repertory of old and new techniques at their command for making it. We do not. Modernism has stripped away our historical awareness of ornament and broken the tradition of craft that once kept ornament alive. Not since the artists and connoisseurs of fifteenth-century Italy set out to rediscover classical antiquity has a culture been so completely on its own in exploring the past. This is one irony that postmodernism, with all its love of irony, has not recognized: to move forward under the banner of eclecticism, we must first reinvent the wheel.

REGARDLESS OF ITS contributory causes, the rejection of ornament was a direct consequence of the Industrial Revolution. Industrialization gave us more than new methods of production, however much they may have reshaped our material culture. Mechanical industry set a new standard of efficiency, and the growing dependence on machines in virtually every branch of the economy created a new *awareness* of efficiency. Out of this came functionalism, the aesthetic of the machine and eventually the central tenet or doctrine of modern design: efficient function has a beauty of its own, hence an object reduced to its functional essence is ipso facto beautiful. Since simplicity is the outward sign and guarantee of efficiency, it is also considered the key to beauty. The reality is different. Virtually any object, even a machine, can be adorned without compromising its usefulness, while visual simplicity is no guarantee of efficient function. Far from being a self-evident truth, functionalism is only one of many possible accommodations between aesthetics and industry. If the history of ideas had followed even a slightly different path, we might still see electric generators in the likeness of Egyptian temples.

There is another accommodation, equally important, in the design of goods for industrial production. We take it for granted not only that machines should be unadorned but that they should not be used to make ornament. The two principles are equally products of circumstance. Neither is self-evident or inevitable, and there is no logical connection between them. Even if we accept the functional aesthetic for machines, why must a product reflect the same artistic standards as the apparatus used to make it? Yet hindsight and habit have forged an intuitive link in defiance of logic. Looking back on almost a century of implacable hostility to ornament, it is hard not to see the two ideas as two sides of the same coin.

All the more startling, then, to realize how separate they were in the nineteenth century. Historically, the aesthetics of machines and of machine-made goods are no more than distant cousins. Both started as responses to industrialization, but to very different aspects of industrialization. They did not start as artistic principles, but as speculations about industrial society in the broadest sense: politics, economics, social welfare, science, and technology, each in its practical and moral dimensions—everything, in short, but art! This goes far toward explaining the enormous power of these ideas once they converged on the issue of ornament. The ornament question took on a life-or-death urgency as it became the microcosm of a society in turmoil. Why ornament? At first glance nothing could be stranger than this dubious honor. A closer look, and nothing could be more obvious. Ornament is the area in which industry impinged most directly on our capacity for creation and delight. Ornament stood for everything that made life worth living, and that was under siege. The ornament question was a test of our ability to weather the upheavals of the modern world with our humanity intact.

A good deal has been written about the development of functionalism as the discovery and attainment of an ideal.[4] If we approach it, instead, as an aesthetic attitude whose connection with actual function is incidental or secondary, the terms of inquiry will be very different. We do not have to ask what constitutes efficient function, or even how our understanding of it evolved, but only what it stood for in the nineteenth century that made it such a crucial legacy for the twentieth. Why did it matter so much? Industrialization per se does not provide an answer. People have always had an intuitive grasp of efficiency, and have always had labor-saving devices of one sort or another. The increasing number and complexity of such devices during the eighteenth and nineteenth centuries produced a qualitative change in Western society, but the change did not have to extend to the veneration of mechanical efficiency as the source and symbol of beauty.

Functionalism has two components: efficiency and simplicity. If people had venerated efficiency alone, they would not have rejected ornament so long as it did not interfere with function. We must therefore assume that simplicity played a crucial role, but an irrational or symbolic one, which had to be masked by equating it with efficiency. The nineteenth century had many reasons to long for simplicity, reasons which designers and the public might have felt uncomfortable stating openly, as matters of mere preference, and thus have sought to conceal behind so obviously "good" an imperative as efficient function. Perhaps the most obvious of all, in visual terms, was that the radical simplification of design would have offered a release from the eclecticism in which so many designers felt themselves trapped.

William Morris suggested more than once that the general weakening and confusion of art in the nineteenth century (he specifically included ornament) might go so far that society would "one day wipe the slate, and be clean rid in her impatience of the whole matter."[5] His utopian novel *News from Nowhere* depicts a future society that has renounced mechanical industry and the commercialism of which it is a symptom, and whose members devote their ample leisure to making beautiful things. After the devastating civil war which destroys the old order, the rebirth of ornament is a sign that the best of human nature has begun to reassert itself.

The clean slate is not just a fictional device, but a powerful idea that has been part of Western civilization since late antiquity. Christianity is the prototype, and the ideal reappears in more restricted form in the Reformation. An ostensibly secular version came into its own in the eighteenth and nineteenth centuries. In *Common Sense*, the book that did so much to inspire the American Revolution, Thomas Paine asserted: "We have it in our power to begin the world over again. A situation, similar to the present, hath not happened since the days of Noah until now."[6] This is a revolutionary statement in every way. Not only does it implicitly sanction violent political revolution, but it declares for the first time that we have the right and power to shape our own future: we need not be slaves to our own history, any more than to a tyrant.

The idea of liberation as, or by means of, a break with the past runs through nineteenth-century revolutionary thought.[7] Marx's insistence that Communist man be self-created is a vivid example. But it also applies, on a subtler level, to calls for intellectual revolution. History, from this standpoint, is not so much the legacy of past events as it is a way of thinking about the past. Nietzsche, in his essay "History in the Service and Disservice of Life," neatly encompassed both meanings:

Man . . . struggles under the great and ever-growing burden of the past, which weighs him down and distorts him, obstructing his movement like a dark, invisible load. . . . And so the sight of a grazing herd or, closer to him, a child who does not yet have a past to disavow . . . shakes him as though he remembered a lost paradise."[8]

Here, the burden of the past is a self-imposed burden of memory. Great passion and great action only can exist outside history, in the intensity of an all-consuming present. Too much knowledge ceases to be power and becomes weakness. Allowing for the far greater power of Nietzsche's rhetoric, we might almost be reading one of the Victorian critics of eclecticism in ornament: Owen Jones, for instance, with his urging that we recapture the innocence of children or savages. But where Jones reached out wistfully toward an ideal, Nietzsche brought an established tradition of revolutionary thought to the intellectual arena. No stranger to the clean slate, he wrote from the conviction that it was possible simply to erase the greater part of our historical awareness. And history—cultural if not political—has proved him right.

These speculations seem far removed from the problem of function, but ideologically it is no distance at all. Art and design provide a symbolic remedy for the more general cultural malaise. To shed the burden of history, simply do away with historically based ornament; that is to say, all ornament. Function is the pretext, to all appearances an unassailably rational one. In retrospect this is a naive approach to the problem of "too much history," but it was a radical step in its time. Even to see it as a possibility required long preparation and a major shift in cultural priorities.

Credit for this shift belongs, above all, to *positivism*, the first major intellectual movement to break with the past and identify with a specifically technological future. Its shaping mind was Auguste Comte (1798–1857), whom we met briefly in the previous chapter in connection with the idea of distinct stages in human social and cultural evolution. This "law of the three stages" is at the heart of both his analysis of the past and his program for the future. Comte called his third and final stage the positive stage. The term is not intuitively clear, but what he meant is the stage of scientific reason, in which human inquiry is focused on the "invariable natural laws" by which the universe operates.[9]

Each mental stage has a characteristic mode of life. For the positive stage it is industry. There is more to this than saying that the future belongs to industry, something which lesser minds than Comte's could have deduced by looking around them. Comte is saying that the positive or scientific stage is the culmination of our intellectual growth, and that industry is the natural expression of the new outlook. The future belongs to industry by right and in perpetuity, as the outward sign of the reign of reason. Since Comte believed that the growth of industry was a product not just of human reason but of human emancipation, it is easy to see how his ideas fostered a general connection of industry with "progress."[10]

Not content with analyzing the past, Comte sought to shape the future as well, promoting science as the way to control nature for the benefit of humanity.[11] The vision of a future humanity raised by its own effort to an almost godlike condition is still seductive. We see it in the expectation that science will give us a better world, and in the readiness to blame science when it fails to deliver. As the thinker most directly responsible for this vision, Comte was under no illusion that science by itself—in our sense of the natural sciences—was enough to transfigure humanity. He therefore proposed applying the most rigorous scientific or "positive" methods to the study of human society, with the aim of predicting and ultimately directing its growth: "From Science comes Prevision: from Prevision comes Action."[12] His goal was order, political as well as intellectual, and to this end he envisioned a hierarchical society under the leadership of a scientific elite.

It is rarely possible to give the bare bones of a utopian system without making it sound naive, and Comte's is no exception. Comte was anything but naive about the difficulty of restructuring a complex society. Social and economic function, he saw, depend on a balance between individuality and interdependence, and this balance becomes more difficult to maintain as society becomes more complex and occupations more specialized. The division of labor in industry is an extreme case. For Comte, its danger did not lie in the division itself but in the tendency of specialization to impose ever narrower horizons, so that self-interest and small-scale political haggling replaced a concern for the public good. Comte saw a further danger in unrestricted economic competition, since the pursuit of efficiency implied the increasing use of machinery and consequent loss of employment.[13]

Comte often used the old image of society as an organism, but in proposing to regulate its complex interdependencies he did not speak as a doctor. The harmonious interaction of parts was not an end in itself, but the means to a desired result. In this respect Comte was above all a theorist of industry, a technologist. His real model for society was not the body but the machine, which must continually be adjusted to eliminate friction and redesigned for ever greater efficiency. But where the pursuit of efficiency in the modernizing world around him was fueled by ruthless and unregulated competition, so that the victory of one meant the downfall of many, Comte saw first Europe and ultimately the entire world drawn into a unity in which innovation led only to further progress, to the benefit of all.

This is the real origin of functionalism. What made Comte's vision so compelling was not just that it gave the future to science and industry, but that it made their fundamental principles, reason and efficiency, the means of realizing all that is best in humanity. In the face of the often catastrophic effects of industrialization, only this radical aspiration could turn the machine into an icon, and an ultimately humanistic icon at that. If simplicity became a symbol of function, function itself was already a symbol of the future. A clean slate in design was not just a negative gesture, a last-ditch attempt to shake off the weight of the past. It was an act of faith that the innovations which seemed poised to crush humanity could instead be a path to salvation.

There is an irony here which helps explain the appeal of functionalism. Modernism may have turned against ornament, but it never abandoned historical eclecticism.[14] It merely substituted a historicism of the future for the historicism of the past. The future is, of course, unknowable. Even leaving aside environmental factors like plagues or climatic change, we cannot predict the occurrence or outcome of large-scale social, political, and religious movements. We cannot predict scientific discoveries and their implications, either for subsequent discoveries or for society at large. This has always been true, but it mattered much less in premodern societies than it has since the beginning of modernization, because fundamental change happened more slowly. Skills for work and rules for conduct, once handed down through generations, are now obsolete within a single generation if not sooner. Education for an unknown future is a fact of life in the modernized world.[15]

One way of coping with this uncertainty is by imagining a *predetermined* future. In this scheme of things, we do not simply pass into the future by imperceptible stages, along with the rest of the universe. The future is already waiting, fully formed, around the next turn where we cannot see it. We do not so much pass into it, as move toward it. An advertisement for the Champion International Corporation, which appeared in *Time* and *Newsweek* in the fall of 1979, bears the caption, "The Future is Coming. Are You Ready?" (fig. 75). The outward message is that if we do not prepare for the future it will catch us unprepared. This could be a reminder of the need for flexibility in the face of an unknown future, but the picture contradicts this. It shows a cityscape of the kind the 1939 World's Fair did so much to popularize, one that has long been a staple

Fig. 75. David Schleinkofer. Advertisement for the Champion International Corporation. 1979.

of science fiction: free-form skyscrapers, a streamlined monorail train, unrecognizable flying machines.

The image suggests a future transformed by science and technology along the lines Comte first laid down, though without reference to his proposed restructuring of society. But to be meaningful, the image must be recognizable. We must be able to look at the designs of the individual buildings, the train, and so on, and immediately think "city of the future." What makes this possible is the convention linking certain kinds of simplicity—lack of ornament is the lowest common denominator—with the life-enhancing aspects of technology. Once this equation is established, we "know" what the future looks like. It looks like modernism, only more so.

In this paradigm, we create the future by reaching forward and "copying" it. The advent of the future demands not flexibility but conformity. No less than the Gothic revival, the arts of design under modernism take their inspiration from the style of another time.

SO POWERFUL were the associations of functionalism, we should not be surprised that it spread beyond the domain of function. If the Crystal Palace of 1851 was the first modern building in its reliance on industrial techniques and materials, the Eiffel Tower of 1889 may be the first *modernist* building. The difference is that the Crystal Palace had features calculated to soften the industrial effect. In the Eiffel Tower, the industrial features are the building's raison d'être. It has been called styleless and functionless.[16] Far from it. The building's function is to proclaim a style, and that style in turn symbolizes function. The belief that even nonfunctional objects (in the mechanical sense) should serve the functional ideal helps explain the compulsion to reject all ornament, not just ornament that interfered with efficiency. But this belief only accounts for the positive aspects of the movement, in both the popular and the Comtean sense. It explains how industry could be seen in a favorable light, and how this vision led to a consensus about the "right" style for the machine age. There is a reverse side which it does not address: the conviction that making ornament by machine was a betrayal, not of the machine, but of ornament!

Pevsner, with his "sham materials and sham techniques," was eloquent on this issue, but the nineteenth century had far more eloquent voices of its own. As early as 1840 we read this, by Sir Francis Palgrave:

All the higher modes of intellect, all that cleverness and sensibility of hand, quite as essential as inventive genius, were called into action, elicited, taught, by the calling in which [the artisan] gained his daily bread. These are advantages which we have lost, and for ever, by the vast improvements which modern days have effected in machinery.

The means of multiplying elegant forms by punches, squeezes, moulds, types, dies, casts, and like contrivances, enables us to produce objects with a sufficient degree of beauty to satisfy the general fancy for art or ornament, but so as to kill all life and freedom. A permanent glut of pseudo-art is created; the multitudes are overfed with a superabundance of trashy food, and their appetite will never desire any better nutriment.

. . . All ornamentation, out line, design, form or figure produced by machinery, whether the medium be block, mould, type or die, may be compared to music ground by a barrel-organ:—good tones, time well observed, not a false note or a blunder, but a total absence of the qualities without which harmony palls upon the ear. You never hear the soul of the performer, the expression and feeling, speaking in the melody.[17]

To all appearances, Palgrave's diatribe leaves machine-made ornament defenseless, and indefensible. If industry has wiped out craftsmanship, so completely that we can no longer hope for real ornament in our daily lives, surely it is better to have no ornament at all than the "glut of pseudo-art," the aesthetic junk food that industry offers in its place.

Yet this view was by no means universal in the nineteenth century. Machine-made ornament did not force itself on a resisting public, or even a resisting elite, by brute economic force. It had its defenders. Ornament gave pleasure, the argument ran; why not make this pleasure available to as many people as possible? Industry had already brought heat, light, and travel within the reach of the many, in ways that a century earlier were beyond the reach of the few. It should be the same with ornament. Efficient manufacture meant lower prices and greater availability, and this is the glory of industry: virtually universal access to what had once been luxuries.[18]

One version of this argument even gives it a moral dimension. The philosopher of science and sometime art historian William Whewell, in his review of the Great Exhibition, conceded that when it came to quality in decorative art, British industry could not surpass the craftsmanship of Persia and India. That being so, what could justify such a huge cultural and financial investment in technology? His answer: "That in all those countries [of Asia] the arts are mainly exercised to gratify the tastes of the few; with us, to supply the wants of the many. There, the wealth of a province is absorbed in the dress of a mighty warrior; here, the gigantic weapons of the peaceful potentate are used to provide clothing for the world."[19] Pleasure moves outward to the masses, and in return wealth moves inward to the industrialist—a fair exchange. Whewell contrasted it with the system in which a privileged few hold a monopoly on wealth *and* pleasure, exploiting the workers as virtual slaves. Industrial production implies not just the greatest amount of pleasure for the greatest number of people, but an adjustment of society in the direction of greater equity.

It is the second clause that opens Whewell's argument to ridicule. Anyone who could suggest, in 1851, that industry was an economic as well as an aesthetic leveler, was either disingenuous or blind. Yet this should not be allowed to invalidate the rest of his argument. If we put aside its social implications, both real and fanciful, there is nothing wrong *in principle* with Whewell's economy of pleasure. That does not mean we must accept it, but we should at least ask why so many outspoken and influential critics have fought, for the most part successfully, to make sure we do not.

The first obstacle to its acceptance is quality. The opposition of good handwork and bad machine work has been with us for almost two hundred years. Whewell himself admitted that even in England, the home of industry, the best work was done by hand. But for half its life at least, that opposition has incorporated a double standard. Machine-made objects can be beautiful provided they are simple. Is this no more than an extension of functionalism, or is there some property of ornament that makes it aesthetically as well as ideologically unfit for machine production?

Palgrave to the contrary, in machine production too *little* precision is a far greater danger than too much. Often the technique itself is to blame. Not every technique does justice to every style, and some styles may not lend themselves to industrial production at all. Only constant experimentation and rigorous quality control, artistic as well as technical, can determine which combinations work and which do not. In many cases industry carried out just such a program, but the major critics and tastemakers of ornament, with the partial exception of William Morris, would have none of it.

On the dangers of too much precision, Palgrave's remarks are devastating but parochial. He assumed that perfect repetition is exclusive to machine work, and that it inevitably robs a pattern of its human touch, its soul. Neither assumption is true. Since long before the beginning of modern industry, some kinds of ornament have required the precise translation of a drawn pattern into some other medium. Deviation from the pattern is not the imprint of the maker's "soul," it is a sign of sloppy work. This is especially true in weaving. Successive innovations in Western loom technology over the last fifteen hundred years have been aimed at increasing control and uniformity in the production of repeating patterns. I am not talking about production for a mass market. Textiles made in this way were often lavish and detailed in their patterns, precious in their materials—silk, exotic dyes, silver and gold thread—and conspicuous as symbols of rank (figs. 4, 24, 28, etc.). The power-driven looms of the nineteenth century are the culmination, not the rejection, of that history.

The desire for perfect regularity in ornament does not demand a complex or evolving technology. In the monumental architecture of Mughal India, the characteristic method of exterior surface decoration is colored stone inlay. This is a handcraft in every possible sense, though the original makers doubtless used treadle-driven polishing wheels, as did the artisans I saw in 1973, replacing lost or damaged inlays and making copies for sale. The level of craftsmanship in the old work (and much of the new) is extremely high; so is the level of regularity. Visiting the sixteenth- and seventeenth-century palaces and tombs at Delhi, Agra, Fatehpur Sikri, and Sikandra, I came to recognize—unwillingly, since it went against all my preconceptions about "good" handmade ornament—that variation had a very small role to play. Mughal architecture delights in contrasts of color and material, in bizarre and arbitrary forms, and in free borrowings from cultures as far afield as France and China. What it does not countenance is arbitrary deviation from a plan. Individual forms such as plants are either perfectly symmetrical or belong to simple repeating or alternating series, or both. The decoration on one side of a niche or doorway, whether simple or complex, will almost always be found in exact mirror-image on the other side (fig. 76).

It follows that similar qualities in machine-made ornament do not in themselves signal the death of ornament. They embody a current of taste among many possible currents, but this particular one has been out of critical favor since at least the mid-nineteenth century. Just how far out of favor is clear from Ruskin:

> Always look for invention first, and after that, for such execution as will help the invention, and as the inventor is capable of without painful effort, and *no more*. Above all, demand no refinement of execution where there is no thought, for that is slaves' work, unredeemed. Rather choose rough work than smooth work, so only that the practical purpose be answered, and never imagine there is reason to be proud of anything that may be accomplished by patience and sand paper.

Fig. 76. Monumental gateway. Indian, 1605–13. Sikandra, Tomb of the Emperor Akbar. Author's photo.

This suggests that there is nothing wrong with refinement so long as it does not become an end in itself. But Ruskin went further:

> If the workman is thinking about his edges, he cannot be thinking of his design; if of his design, he cannot think of his edges. Choose whether you will pay for the lovely form or the perfect finish, and choose at the same moment whether you will make the worker a man or a grindstone.[20]

Perfect finish is not just the enemy of invention, it is the enemy of humanity. It turns the worker into a machine.

The eclipse of perfection in ornament continues an older tradition, not confined to ornament, equating visual spontaneity and boldness with authenticity, originality, inspiration. The equation goes back to the Renaissance, when the enormous aesthetic and monetary value placed on both antiquities and contemporary paintings fueled the search for a reliable way of distinguishing originals from copies. As early as the sixteenth century, spontaneity and boldness were considered the qualities most resistant to copying. Therefore, not only did their presence indicate an original, but they became the measure of its superiority to a copy. Precision of detail, which lent itself to the unspontaneous skills of the copyist, was devalued accordingly.[21]

To exalt spontaneity and denigrate precision is a romantic stance even more than a Renaissance one, but as the nineteenth century progressed it took on a special significance which looks back to its Renaissance origin. The Industrial Revolution brought a crisis of authenticity in the visual arts. Copies proliferated on every level, in every medium. Gutta-percha imitated wood. Photography threatened, in the eyes of some, to make painting obsolete. Electrotyping made a masterpiece like Morel-Ladeuil's Milton shield (fig. 77) accessible not just through illustrations or fragile plaster casts, but in "scientifically accurate" metal facsimiles. Imported Kashmir shawls, handwoven by a technique so laborious that hand embroidery was sometimes resorted to as a quick, cheap substitute, competed on the market with copies and adaptations from European power looms.[22]

What ensued were more copies, sometimes better copies, and a general explosion of *multiples:* works which are not necessarily copies of something else, but can be produced in large numbers with no apparent variation. Such a climate not only increased the possibility of mistakes and deception, but could drown the very idea of an original by eliminating the visual qualities that defined originality. This is what Palgrave meant by his image of a public satisfied with "trashy food." The solution is simple. Discredit the love of perfect finish, abolish the taste for ornament that *can* be reproduced by machine, and machine-made ornament ceases to be a problem. The remarkable thing is not that this solution was proposed but that it was adopted, and it worked.

We know that a rebellion against ornament was building, like an ocean wave that is scarcely visible until it approaches shore. The mechanization of ornament was the shoal that brought the wave into full view, in all its power. But this could not have happened if the rebellion against mechanization were confined to moral and aesthetic pleas, however impassioned. Instead, it drew its strength from forces that had little to do with ornament but everything to do with industry.

In 1899, the economist Thorstein Veblen pointed out that our appreciation of hand-work is inseparable from its "honorific value"—its value as a status symbol.[23] Hand-work is much more expensive than machine work; therefore it confers status and machine work does not. Even assuming it possible to make an object by machine that was for all practical and aesthetic purposes identical to an object of the same type (such as a spoon) made by hand, Veblen argued that the machine-made object would lose its hon-orific value as soon as its real origin became known. He went so far as to suggest that small but perceptible imperfections are essential to the honorific value of an object, because they guarantee that the object was made—expensively—by hand.

This puts the whole issue of reproducibility in a new light. Ornament is a special case of handwork. Not only is it labor intensive and therefore expensive, but it is non-functional and therefore unnecessary: the embodiment of what Veblen called con-spicuous consumption. In this model, machine-made ornament is still nonfunctional, but it is no longer labor intensive. To own it gives none of the satisfaction of patron-age or acquisition. To display it is a false claim to status, doomed to exposure and ridicule.

If that is so, we must take another look at the continuity between craft and indus-try. I have implied that in making ornament the ends have always justified the means. If (*pace* Ruskin) the goal is perfect finish, then any technical innovation is justified. What matters is the product. The manufacturing process is not an end in itself, but a path from the designer's brain to the finished work. Mechanization is a way of mak-ing that path as short and straight as possible. But if perfect finish becomes undesir-able for reasons of status, being equated with machine work and low cost, this no longer holds true. Suddenly it is the *process* that matters, not the product. Handwork is the high status process, not because it gives a better product, but because it costs more. The product is important only as physical evidence of the amount of work done and paid for.

In theory, technology applied to the production of ornament is an extension of hand-work. And so it was in practice, until the technological explosion of the nineteenth century. By sheer volume, the new technology of multiples destroyed an extremely delicate symbiosis of technology and craft. When perfect finish (or perfect symmetry or perfect repetition) became a mark of cheapness, a gulf opened between hand and machine work that no amount of quality control could close. Let industry struggle for even greater precision, and it advertises its inferiority. Let it imitate the tiny flaws of handwork, and it compounds inferiority with deception, and transparent deception at that, since the "human" touches are themselves predictable.

Fig. 77. Léonard Morel-Ladeuil. Shield with scenes from *Paradise Lost* (the "Milton Shield"). Silver, iron, and gold. French (active in England), 1864–67. London, Victoria and Albert Museum, 546–1868. Courtesy of the Trustees of the V&A.

In very different ways, both Veblen and Ruskin recognized that since the mechanization of what had once been handicrafts, true handwork has a new meaning. The process is what matters now—the *fact* of handwork—and the product is above all an emblem of that fact. Ruskin went so far as to define art itself in these terms:

> All art which is worth its room in this world . . . is *art which proceeds from an individual mind, working through instruments which assist, but do not supersede, the muscular action of the human hand.*[24]

This definition shapes our response to art and craft to this day. Its enormous influence, and above all its crucial role in the modernist rejection of ornament, goes beyond questions of authenticity or status. To understand it, we must look at how the Industrial Revolution changed the economic, political, and moral meaning of work.

The Greeks and the Romans despised manual labor as the portion of slaves. In the Old Testament it is a punishment for original sin. Early Christianity, with its promise of redemption and insistence on the equality of masters and slaves in the sight of God, rehabilitated work on both counts, and saw it as a way of glorifying God, but only in humility, by submitting to monotonous tasks with cheerful patience. Protestantism saw work as a performance of one's duty to God, and success in work as a sign of divine favor. In each of these stages, what mattered was the place that work, and by implication the worker, held in the human or divine scheme of things. Only with the Industrial Revolution did a new focus emerge, no longer emphasizing what work *is* but what it should be to achieve the maximum benefit and self-realization *for the worker.*[25]

Few subjects in history remain as pertinent, and therefore as controversial, as the Industrial Revolution. Modernization shapes our lives in every conceivable way.[26] Marxism, the central political movement of the twentieth century, was a direct response to the sudden transformation of society by industry. And the turbulent history of organized labor has its beginnings in the new alignment (or misalignment) of economic forces resulting from the growth of the factory system. It is no surprise that the enormous literature of industry is tinged with partisanship, open or hidden. Was the Industrial Revolution "bad" or "good"? In more sophisticated terms, this means sorting out the intertwined yet opposing myths of glorious progress and terrible suffering, and asking how much they reflect reality. What were the evils and the benefits of industry? How did it start, and once it started, were its effects controllable? Could the outcome have been different? And since modernization is a continuing process, have we the power to make it different now? Even scrupulously impartial studies may be fueled by a desire to know which side to take.[27]

Any attempt at a full account would be out of place here, and in any case I am not qualified to give one. But there is an aspect of industrialization that relates directly to the conflict over ornament. This is the division of labor. I shall not try to assess its full economic and social effects, but to show how those effects have been perceived, and how the perception, above all the tendency to demonize the division of labor and blame it for the downfall of handicraft, has become a historical force in its own right. This, for example, is from a recent study of British textile production:

> By the beginning of the nineteenth century this division of labor had created seri-
> ous defects in the production of design. . . . There seem to have been two main
> problems: first, the artist or designer had no knowledge of the mechanism of pro-
> duction. They produced inapplicable and impractical designs. Secondly, workmen
> lacked the drawing skills and the idea of design, leading to failures in execution.
> Having once lost their artistic training and intimate contact with artists, workmen
> were no longer capable of combining their skill with artistic taste and they spoiled
> the design."[28]

Such assertions preserve a stereotype which grew in strength throughout the nineteenth century, and which did as much as any failing of industry to seal the fate of ornament in the industrial age.

Division of labor is nothing new. It is the same as specialization, and as such it has long been recognized as a prerequisite of social organization.[29] Among the first to see its negative aspect was Comte, who recognized that interdependence and specialization were inseparable. In the measure that interdependence led to social integration, specialization led to social *disintegration* by cutting individuals off from general awareness of the public good. The more complex the society, the greater the interdependence; hence the greater the danger of specialization.

In Comte's view, this danger has nothing to do with industry per se. Mechanical and intellectual specialization are equally harmful:

> If we have been accustomed to deplore the spectacle, among the artisan class, of a
> workman occupied during his whole life in nothing else but making knife-handles
> or pins' heads, we may find something quite as lamentable in the intellectual class,

in the exclusive employment of a human brain in resolving some equations, or in classifying insects. The moral effect is, unhappily, analogous in the two cases. It occasions a miserable indifference about the general course of human affairs, as long as there are equations to resolve and pins to manufacture.[30]

The danger that Comte described is abstract, a centrifugal tendency in society, to be weighed against and controlled by other tendencies. For Marx, a generation later, the danger was anything but abstract. Division of labor was inextricably bound up with the growth of industry. That bond made it a blight on individual lives, and on society as the sum of those lives. Marx spelled this out in the first volume of his culminating work, *Das Kapital*.[31] There is a continuum between the division of labor in its most basic forms—such as farmer, herdsman, fisherman—and the extreme specialization of modern industry, but Marx did not emphasize this. Rather, he found the origin of the modern division of labor in cooperation, specifically in manufacture. By manufacture he meant the systematic production of goods involving several different processes, and therefore (to be practical) several workers applying their individual skills and tools. Marx used the example of a carriage, which requires not only carpentry but the services of the wheelwright, harness maker, upholsterer, and so on (*Das Kapital*, p. 456).

It is impractical for a single worker, however versatile, to build a carriage unassisted. This is obviously not true of all crafts, but Marx reminds us that even in simpler ones, such as papermaking, division of labor can turn craft into manufacture. This happens when artisans who have traditionally worked side by side, each separately carrying out the entire process from start to finish, discover the greater efficiency of a system in which each performs a single operation. For Marx this implied a diminution of the individual worker's achievement. He quoted with great approval the remark that "Each labourer produces only some part of a whole, and each part, having no value or utility in itself, there is nothing on which the labourer can seize, and say: It is my product, this I will keep to myself" (p. 475, n. 34).

His real concern, however, was that the specialized tasks and talents of many workers add up to a "collective worker." Since each individual worker has a task assigned on the basis of ability, the collective worker has no weaknesses, being in theory equally and maximally skilled in all areas. This collective strength has serious repercussions for the workers as individuals. "The one-sidedness and even the deficiencies of the specialized individual worker become perfections when he is part of the collective worker. The habit of doing only one thing converts him into an organ which operates with the certainty of a force of nature, while his connection with the whole mechanism compels him to work with the regularity of a machine" (p. 469).

On the one hand, what results is efficient production and full use of each worker's greatest ability. On the other, specialization can become so extreme that it leads (in Marx's view) to physical deformity. The worker no longer controls the process; it controls him. And most serious in the long run, workers are "appropriated and annexed for life by a limited function." Since manufacture reduces production into its many component processes, it inevitably distinguishes between those requiring skill and those that do not. A permanent force of cheap, unskilled labor is created: "If [manufacture] develops a one-sided specialty to perfection, at the expense of the whole of a man's working capacity, it also begins to make a specialty of the absence of all development" (p. 470).

Remember that Marx was still talking about manufacture, which is essentially coordinated handicraft. With the introduction of machinery the division of labor is even more pernicious. Since individual crafts are no longer involved, the traditional hierarchy of skill disappears. Manufacture had analyzed production into *unequal* parts, thereby institutionalizing the gap between skilled and unskilled labor. As both strength and skill became embodied in the machine, it was possible to analyze production into *equal* parts. All labor was now unskilled labor. "The lifelong specialty of handling the same tool now becomes the lifelong specialty of serving the same machine. Machinery is misused in order to transform the worker, from his very childhood, into a part of a specialized machine. In this way . . . his helpless dependence upon the factory as a whole, and therefore upon the capitalist, is rendered complete" (p. 547).

Marx never suggested that the malevolent forces of capital invented the system for the specific purpose of stripping workers of their skill, independence, and self-esteem. Nevertheless, he left no doubt that it has had this effect, which capitalists have ruthlessly exploited (p. 562). Since technological change is directed not just toward greater efficiency, but actually *against* the workers, capital need not provide the kind of training that would help labor adapt to new kinds of machinery. The end result in human terms is a "disposable working population held in reserve, in misery, for the changing requirements of capitalist exploitation" (p. 618).

The step-by-step progression from division of labor to ruthless exploitation and mass unemployment is indictment enough, or so it would seem. But I do not think I am belittling the physical plight of industrial workers, or Marx's sympathy for it, if I say that the main factor in that sympathy is an abstract, even mystical concern with the nature of work. We can see this in his unpublished early writings, especially in the unfinished essay "Alienated Labor."[32]

The crucial idea is in the title. Workers have no control over their work, in the sense of the act of working *or* the product. Most of us would agree that this is an undesirable state of things, but a fact of life nonetheless. For Marx it was so desperately bad that a way must be found to correct it at all costs. To understand why, we must look back past Marx to his most influential predecessor, Hegel. In *The Phenomenology of Mind* (1807), Hegel identified labor as a means of self-realization.[33] His account is abstruse to say the least, more myth than argument, but it is clear that he did not mean self-realization in any relative sense, as an improvement in the quality of life. It is through labor that one becomes a self in the first place.

Marx, too, understood that depriving workers of their work meant depriving them of their humanity. But in what sense did he mean this deprivation? "The product of labor," he wrote, "is labor embodied and made objective in a thing."[34] This *thing*, the product and embodiment of labor, is a commodity. Hence labor is a commodity, and so is the worker who performs it. The worker embodies himself in something that is not himself, and which he is forced to sell to stay alive.

The disastrous result is that

the worker is related to the *product of his labor* as to an *alien* object. . . . The more the worker exerts himself, the more powerful becomes the alien objective world which he fashions against himself, the poorer he and his inner world become, the less there is that belongs to him. . . . What the product of his work is, he is not. The greater this product is, the smaller he is himself.

As with the product, so with the process:

How could the worker stand in an alien relationship to the product of his activity if he did not alienate himself from himself in the very act of production? After all, the product is only the résumé of activity, of production. If the product of work is externalization, production itself must be active externalization.[35]

If the product does not belong to the worker, it must belong to someone else. The same holds for the act of labor. Labor is alienated because it is unfree; it is under the control of another.

Elsewhere in the early manuscripts, Marx said: "The division of labor is a true division only from the moment a division of material and mental labor appears." And a little later, "the *division of labor* implies the possibility, indeed the necessity, that intellectual and material activity . . . —enjoyment and labor, production and consumption—are given to different individuals, and the only possibility of their not coming into conflict lies in again transcending the division of labor."[36] From this we must understand that the division of labor into mental and physical is not just the crucial, paradigmatic division of labor, it is also the essence of alienation. This is the subtext for Marx's systematic attack on industrial capitalism more than twenty years later. By imposing an ever greater division of labor, with loss of skill at every stage, industry erects an impassible barrier between the physical and mental aspects of work. It robs the workers not only of their health and even their lives, but of their *selves*.

Ruskin never read these early writings of Marx: they were not published until 1932. Yet we might suppose he had read them, so directly does he address the same issues. I have in mind, above all, the chapter from *The Stones of Venice* called "The Nature of Gothic." I believe it to be the greatest piece of writing about art in English, and possibly in the whole Western tradition, for the power and music of its prose, for its ability not just to define but to evoke a style, and for its depth of human sympathy. It is also Ruskin's answer to the problem of alienated labor. For Marx the only practical remedy was an almost unimaginable social change, the abolition of private property. For Ruskin the solution was literally aesthetic, involving a change in our perceptions. It must begin with our defining what kinds of labor are and, more important, are *not* alienated, and learning to recognize them in and by their products.

Here, Ruskin and Marx are in strange accord. Both saw the product of labor as the embodiment of labor, and ultimately of the worker. Beyond this, Marx would certainly have dismissed Ruskin's approach as quixotic. How, after all, can there be *any* unalienated labor when people are forced to work and forced to sell the product of their work? Ruskin has an answer, but we must read between the lines to see it. If the work is done right, it does not matter under what conditions it is done, or what happens to the product. The *process* is not alienated; it belongs inalienably to the worker. This gives him spiritual title to the product as well, regardless of who holds the physical title. This outcome depends on more than the worker's state of mind. As viewers and consumers, we are responsible for giving the worker his due. By learning to recognize the process in the product, we confirm the worker's title to it.

Like Marx, Ruskin utterly condemned the separation of mental and physical labor.

In ornament, that separation gives rise to "slavish" styles, in which the artisan mind-lessly copies someone else's design, and perfect finish substitutes for imagination. Among these styles Ruskin unhesitatingly placed that of his own nineteenth-century England, and that of ancient Greece as well. In contrast, he extols the Gothic style as a giver of freedom.

The key to this freedom is what Ruskin calls the "savageness" of Gothic. Today, we consider the Gothic style the epitome of refinement; if anything, it can seem too refined (fig. 54). It is hard to remember that critics once dismissed Gothic art as uncouth and barbarous. This prejudice was overpowering in the Renaissance, and still a living mem-ory in Ruskin's day. Ruskin stood it on its head. Yes, he said, there is much in Gothic architecture and ornament that looks clumsy, undisciplined, unfinished, but that is its glory. He did not just mean that these features can be visually exciting—"creations of ungainly shape and rigid limb, but full of wolfish life"—but that they embody the inclu-siveness, generosity, and humanity of the style.

Every worker, he insisted, no matter how dull, has some spark of creative imagina-tion. We—the employer or supervisor, but also the public as the maker of its own taste—have a choice. We can train the worker thoroughly in a purely mechanical skill, and tell him precisely what to do, thereby assuring a high standard of work but suppress-ing that small creative spark. Or we can encourage the spark, setting imagination above precision, and value the result because it is human, even when it is a very small spark indeed, even when it means sacrificing a great deal of finish for very little originality. For Ruskin the greatness of Gothic architecture, and its lesson for his own time, are in this above all, that it nurtures the humanity of every worker and integrates the best and the worst in "a stately and unaccusable whole."

Gothic, for Ruskin, was not just a style but an attitude toward work. It is the antithe-sis of the pernicious division of labor, especially in the root sense of the split between mind and hand. Ruskin's disdain for the "slavish" ornament of Greece makes it clear that the split existed long before industry, but industry has made it far worse:

> We have much studied and much perfected, of late, the great civilized invention
> of the division of labour; only we give it a false name. It is not, truly speaking, the
> labour that is divided; but the men:—Divided into mere segments of men—broken
> into small fragments and crumbs of life; so that all the little piece of intelligence
> that is left in a man is not enough to make a pin, or a nail, but exhausts itself in
> making the point of a pin, or the head of a nail.[37]

For Comte, the pin was a symbol of cultural myopia. For Ruskin, it was a symbol of something far worse, the utter, stupid waste of the most precious of all resources, human individuality.

The ideal of craft as free expression, limited only by the imagination and skill of the worker, but embracing every level of imagination and skill, looks back to a preindustrial golden age when society allowed its artisans to live and work by the dictates of their craft alone. Such a golden age has almost certainly never existed. Even before industrialization as we know it, craft was regulated, and often highly industrialized by the standards of the day. The conditions of life for artisans could be very poor. Nevertheless, the myth of the happy artisan was powerful. Engels invokes it at the beginning of *The Condition of the Working Class in England* (1845). Only William Morris, himself an artisan, was hardheaded enough to place it not in the past but in the future, and then only after a violent revolution had changed the very nature of society.[38]

To some degree, the myth crystallized out of "the generalization that because . . . conditions were very bad, they could not have been worse and therefore must once have been better."[39] Yet it had a more personal component. To nineteenth-century workers and their sympathizers, the opportunity to find fulfillment in their work was something they or their parents or grandparents had once enjoyed, then lost. The nostalgia was real enough, but we must take it with a grain of salt. Artisans, there can be no doubt, hated and feared the regimentation of factory work. By this we imagine the skill-destroying division of labor and the mind-destroying routine of machine operation. In fact, artisans hated and feared the factory *before* it was mechanized. Merely bringing a number of looms or other traditional apparatus together under a single roof and a single management was seen as an affront to the workers' jealously guarded independence.[40]

When industry prevailed, it did not simply drive out craft. Unable to compete with power looms, handloom weavers did go out of work in very large numbers, and their plight has colored our view of society in that period. In other trades, those best able to make the transition from hand to machine work continued to regard themselves as craftsmen. Best known in this regard were the mule spinners—the operators of the device called a mule, which was a mainstay of the cotton industry between about 1780 and the late nineteenth century. A mule could spin hundreds of threads simultaneously. The earlier models were powered by the operator himself, who pushed the entire apparatus forward and back, thereby drawing out the threads. This required both physical strength and very precise control. Thanks to their special abilities, mule spinners in

England and America achieved not only high wages but considerable bargaining power with their employers.[41] The invention of a practical power-driven mule in the 1790s did not put an end to their high status. They transferred their skill and training, in particular their powers of long-term concentration, to the new device with conspicuous success. Only in the eighteen-thirties and forties, with the development of a "self-acting" mule, were the mule spinners reduced to the position of "minders," with a consequent loss of bargaining power. Yet for another half-century their authority in the workplace was more in keeping with their past glory than with their current diminished role.

Even true mass production, the making of fully interchangeable parts for other mechanisms, offered scope for creative intervention. This would seem a contradiction in terms. Since interchangeable parts must be for all practical purposes identical, creative intervention should approach zero. It is hard to imagine a circumstance better calculated to dehumanize both the worker and the work. Yet a study of the manufacture of military firearms at the Springfield Armory around the beginning of the twentieth century reveals that it provided ample scope for innovation and improvisation, not by the designers and builders of machinery, but by the machine operators themselves.[42]

Although the mindset of craft made at least a partial accommodation with industry, there is no denying it had to do so on radically new terms. The machine was the unquestioned center. Success, pride, and even pleasure came from mastery of its processes, no longer from what Veblen called the "forceful and dexterous use of an implement."[43] The autobiography of Joseph Gutteridge says much about this new approach to work. Gutteridge (1816–1899) was a weaver in Coventry, England. Like others in his trade, he had a precarious existence, at the mercy of a fluctuating market and of industrial relations punctuated by strikes, lockouts, and violent confrontations, up to and including arson. In periods of prosperity he could own a loom; in bad times he had to sell it to feed his family, and sought work in factories. He nevertheless found the time to become a serious amateur scientist, and to assemble a nationally known collection of fossils.

These interests may explain why he never achieved financial security, but he might not have managed it in any case. Few weavers did. In no way does he fit the stereotype of the dehumanized industrial worker. Exhausted, uncertain of the future, sometimes near death from starvation, he was never a mere slave to the machine. The fact that he kept his intellectual interests alive in such conditions says much for his character, and reminds us that there were resources available even to hard-pressed workers—

sometimes. But for our purposes the most significant fact in his career is that he regarded machinery as a friend, not an enemy.

While still an apprentice, Gutteridge witnessed a riot over the installation of steam-powered looms in a nearby factory. Outraged weavers captured the inventor of the new loom (he was also the owner of the factory), set him backwards on a donkey, and paraded him through the streets of Coventry—a traditional punishment for violating the customs of trade—while another mob trashed his house, broke into the factory, and smashed and burned the looms. At the risk of his life, Gutteridge made his way to the factory, where he stood enraptured by the "beauty and simplicity" of the new machines, almost fainting with rage and disgust as he watched them destroyed.[44] In later life his greatest successes and satisfactions (none of them very lucrative) were in repairing and improving looms, and in demonstrating the latest advances in technology to his employers and co-workers. That Gutteridge was a craftsman there is no doubt, but his true craft was not weaving cloth. Gutteridge was an artisan *of the machine*.

In part, I have cited these cases to set the record straight, to show that there was more to the industrial nineteenth century than the unrelieved gloom that Marx depicted in such stunning detail. But still more, I have done it to show how strong the idea of a preindustrial golden age remains, even today. For what matters, ultimately, about these exceptions to the gloomy rule is how little they matter. Not because they are statistically insignificant, which I am quite prepared to believe they are, but because they are the wrong kind of exceptions. If these tiny islands of craft are all that survive in the sea of industry, it is small comfort. Perhaps no comfort at all, if they remind us of the wealth of craft that has been swept away, and of the compromises that kept even a remnant alive.[45] Reading Gutteridge, I felt an uneasiness I could not place, until I recognized it as what I might have felt on reading the memoir of a wartime collaborator: the taint of capitulation, a broken spirit, however well concealed. Have I Marx or Ruskin to thank for my response?

It is one thing for Ruskin to offer us Gothic architecture as a model and a myth, a lesson in the human dignity of work. To put that lesson into practice in the face of nineteenth-century industry is something else altogether. Ruskin certainly idealized the Middle Ages, but he was no romantic dreamer, urging a return to the past. Rightly fearing a violent escalation of workers' grievances, he proposed a revolution of his own:

> It [the threat to society] can be met only by a right understanding, on the part of all classes, of what kinds of labour are good for men, raising them, and making

them happy; by a determined sacrifice of such convenience, or beauty, or cheapness as is to be got only by the degradation of the workman; and by equally determined demand for the products and results of healthy and ennobling labour.[46]

This program has in part been carried out. Failing of its true goal, to change the impact of machine-based industry on workers' lives, it has still achieved a lasting symbolic success. By the late nineteenth century, there was no realistic hope of a general return to handwork and the old traditions of craft. Increasingly, to reject machine-made ornament meant rejecting ornament itself. In this sense the rejection of ornament was neither more nor less than a boycott. As a "determined sacrifice of such convenience, or beauty, or cheapness as is to be got only by the degradation of the workman," it was and perhaps still is a way of saying: If we cannot have *real* ornament, then let us be proud to have *no* ornament.

Ruskin's plan survives, too, in our highly selective reverence for handicraft. We do not feel reverence for tourist souvenirs and other things that are essentially "mass produced" by hand. We feel it when some intangible quality in the finished object bespeaks a freedom and dignity of work which industry denies. We have learned, on a small scale and by a path that Ruskin never imagined, to see the process in the product, and to find beauty in the "results of healthy and ennobling labor." Seen in this light, the silk scarf in figure 3, with which I introduced the whole problem of the modern world's relation to ornament, becomes far more than the last wretched survival of an uprooted tradition. Nor is it just a defiant affirmation of craft in a world that has forgotten craft. It is not a relic but a solution, to a problem that barely existed two hundred years ago, and one hundred years ago seemed to have no solution. By disguising neither materials nor technique, the artist has done as much as humanly possible to reveal the process in the product. To say it is "about" weaving, as some critics used to insist that painting must be "about" paint, misses the point. What it is about is abolishing the division between the work of the mind and the work of the hand. The identity of means and ends, perhaps the most powerful unifying theme in the modern craft movement, is an affirmation of work as freedom, against the enveloping, historically unprecedented fear of work as slavery.

In 1938 the philosopher R. G. Collingwood published a book called *The Principles of Art*, intended to free its readers from the "rags and tags of moribund theory" which might hamper their appreciation of modern art.[47] Collingwood was at pains to distinguish between art and craft. The core of his argument is that craft is always directed toward a specific goal. A craftsman knows what he or she wants to make, and makes it. Art relies on craft to varying degrees, but always goes beyond craft, and the measure of its superiority is its unpredictability. Unlike the craftsman, the artist never knows in advance what the finished work will be like, because imagination and experience act upon the creative process in ways not under the artist's conscious control.

This hierarchical view depends on the aesthetic of process, and at the same time rationalizes it. If craft is predictable and art is not, then a work which suggests that its creation was not under the maker's full control will be judged as art, not as craft. By implication, Collingwood carried the attack on division of labor to its logical conclusion. If craft implies a predictable result, it must also imply a splitting of the maker into two halves, mental and physical, with the former dictating and the latter "mindlessly" obeying: the most invidious division of labor in microcosm! The exaltation of art over craft puts an end to this degrading situation, at a price. In terms of ornament and the skills that sustain it, Collingwood threw out the baby with the bathwater—not that he would have cared.

Given the choice, would any maker choose the subordinate role of craftsman over the exalted role of artist? No one had to. The same ideology that imposed the choice offered an easy means of escape, available to all. To choose between craft and art, one had only to identify oneself with a specific style of decoration. Traditional ornament, insofar as it emphasized precision, was the embodiment of craft, and the fact that it could be reproduced by machines was further proof, if proof were needed, of its inferiority. But merely by renouncing "ornament" and at the same time embracing process, it was possible to align oneself with the highest levels of artistic creativity, regardless of the medium in which one worked. Unpredictability was not just a decorative mode, but a shorthand for inspiration. The emphasis on process over product was an affirmation of status. Small wonder, then, that generations of makers have kept modernist ornament a secret, even from themselves.

Modernism and the Rebirth of Ornament

WE ALL KNOW what modern design looks like. Functionalism is a reality, whatever its relation to actual function. Yet however much the twentieth century learned to disdain ornament, ornament has survived. In the most obvious sense this is due to the very techniques of production that helped spark the revolution against ornament. Floor coverings, wallpapers, dishes, furnishing and apparel fabrics throughout the century have offered a spectrum of choice from the harsh geometries of functionalism to an eclectic lavishness the Victorians might have envied. What permits ornament to flourish on this scale is not just the widespread dissemination of patterns through multiple production and mass retailing, but also the conviction that we have no ornament. Since mass-produced ornament is beyond the pale by definition, we do not have to think of it as ornament. The old debates and strictures no longer apply.

When we pick out wallpaper or wedding china or neckties we are selecting products, patterns, but never *ornament;* at least not consciously. Our choices thus reflect our regional, ethnic, educational, economic, and even professional backgrounds, but not our sense of history. Taste is personal, but the rules of taste are social. Too great a divergence from the standards of the group can provoke censure in terms like old-fashioned, pretentious, or vulgar. Consider decorated cowboy boots, a good example of the survival of traditional ornament in modern times. In the American West they are a standard item of luxury dress for both men and women. The choice of a particular style reflects a fairly subtle interaction of personal taste and local convention. Someone from Boston who buys a pair of boots on a week's visit to Dallas is unlikely to understand the nuances, and could easily end up looking foolish—in Dallas. Back in Boston those nuances disappear, leaving only a general "western look." Depending on the wearer and the context, this look might be fashionable, eccentric, or ridiculous. The one thing that is almost certain not to happen, in Boston or Dallas, is for the ornament to attract attention for its own sake.

A more dramatic example is tattooing. For several years the so-called tattoo renaissance in Europe and America has been producing some of the finest traditional ornament of our time (plate 8). Traditional, that is, in its reliance on recognizable, historically based patterns executed with the greatest possible finesse. The patterns themselves come from sources as diverse as Borneo and Japan, psychedelic and "biker" art, and careful study of medieval interlace, and they represent a radical break with the cliché of the sailor's tattoo parlor.

The perceived association of tattooing with a criminal and, more recently, a sexual underworld still suppresses those distinctions for much of mainstream society. An extensively tattooed person automatically sets him or herself apart from the mainstream, and that social message is likely to drown out the aesthetic message of the tattoo as ornament. What comes through, at most, is the intensity of the wearer's involvement with a particular pattern, enough to make it a part of his or her own body, permanently, at the cost of much physical pain. We will probably notice whether that pattern is a skull, a flower, or a powerful abstraction from Borneo, and perhaps go on to wonder what aspect of the wearer's personality it expresses, but in most situations, sheer social awkwardness will keep us from looking more closely.[1]

In this area at least, modern Western society has achieved something like the innocent intensity it has often envied in premodern cultures' relation to ornament, the sense that ornament matters on a visceral level, far removed from analysis and debate. Whether this ideal corresponds to any real premodern culture is irrelevant. It is, after all, a distinctively modern ideal. That it was not achieved until long after we supposedly renounced ornament is ironic but hardly surprising. Endless ideological marching and countermarching in pursuit of the "right" style and the "right" significance for ornament placed Western culture in the same position as the king whose salvation depended on *not* thinking of a camel. No end to this predicament was possible until fashion replaced ideology.

We talk about the tyranny of fashion, but it is not so simple. Absolute freedom in taste is a chimera. At the very least, our choices and even our imagination are constrained by what is available. In a cosmopolitan society like ours, "everything" is theoretically available, and the possibilities should be almost infinite. In practice, society limits the range considerably. As in the example of the cowboy boots, too much eccentricity appears as *nothing but* eccentricity. Too free a choice can cancel out the individuality it was meant to express.

Fashion, in the general sense of prevailing tastes, and the restricted sense of this year's stylish wardrobe, is society's way of simultaneously permitting and restricting choice. For both creator and consumer, it defines the sphere in which the interaction of personal taste and social convention is likely to be most fully recognized and therefore most successful. Since fashion changes constantly, not only with time but from place to place and from one segment of society to another, it is by nature pluralistic, innovative, antidogmatic. Seen close up, on a year-to-year basis, fashion is trivial and evanescent, shining bubbles on a cultural wave. Historically, over decades of evolving design, fashion *is* the wave. At once a unifying and a diversifying force, it is the way in which "big" cultural and artistic trends are translated into the innumerable small details of everyday life.

Although traditional ornament survived in the popular sphere of fashion, the truly radical development took place elsewhere, in the elite, ideologically scrutinized arts of architecture and luxury handicraft. In the guise of a revolution *against* ornament, these arts gave us a revolution *in* ornament, the sudden birth of a new style. It must seem at times that the so-called rejection of ornament belongs entirely to the history of ideas. But ideas alone cannot make a style, and they cannot destroy one. Styles come out of other styles; ideas are the catalyst. The so-called rejection of ornament was a rejection of ornament *as practiced in the nineteenth and early twentieth centuries*. Something must have been wrong with it, to make the rejection possible. People do not readily give up something that works well. They must be persuaded that it does not work, or offered something that works even better.

What makes nineteenth-century ornament inadequate to the needs of the twenti-

Fig. 78. Ceramic vase. English (Rockingham), 1826. London, Victoria and Albert Museum, 47–1869. Courtesy of the Trustees of the V&A.

Fig. 79. John Hunt and Robert Roskell. Salver from the Hawksley Testimonial. Silver-gilt. English, 1880. London, Victoria and Albert Museum, M. 4–j-1974. Courtesy of the Trustees of the V&A.

eth century? Clutter is the least of its problems. More damaging is what we today would call inconsistency, the combination of different aesthetic principles in the same work with no apparent concern for the harmony of parts (fig. 78). There is also a strong naturalistic strain (fig. 18). Earlier, we looked at the transforming power of naturalism in ornament, and the ambiguity that an illusory third dimension imparts to a two-dimensional surface. Equally important, naturalistic ornament implies a lack of subordination: of the parts to the whole, and of the ornament to the object. Naturalism implies minutely differentiated detail, which in turn demands the kind of close examination that keeps us from seeing the pattern or the object as a whole. Often it eliminates the need for a pattern as such. Spatial ambiguity contributes to this effect: it is hard to look *at* an object if you are also looking *into* it.

Even this brief glance yields a substantial list of symptoms: clutter, eclecticism, inconsistency, naturalism, minuteness, lack of subordination, spatial ambiguity. Not one of

Fig. 80. Sir Alfred Gilbert. Centerpiece honoring the Golden Jubilee of Queen Victoria. Silver, rock crystal, and other materials. English, 1887–90. Royal Collection, Great Britain (on loan to the Victoria and Albert Museum).

these is unique to the nineteenth century, but the combination is. We can see its full effect in the gilded silver tray which the Nottingham Waterworks Company presented to the engineer Thomas Hawksley in 1880 (fig. 79). It has a raised rim, lavishly decorated with leaves in relief and flowers in very high relief. The flat surface of the tray is divided into six compartments. Each contains a panoramic landscape featuring some aspect of

Hawksley's specialty, city water supply. A starlike figure with six points occupies the rest of the surface, its six arms bordered by narrow interlacing bands. They enclose six different kinds of aquatic plants, another reference to Hawksley's work.

No one work can sum up an era, but for the second half of the nineteenth century the Hawksley tray comes close. It is almost an anthology of trends—past, present, and future. The irruption of landscape into ornament, calling both space and pattern into question, is a legacy of the rococo. The floral rim, naturalistic yet repetitive, and the sentimental literalness of the plant symbolism and the landscapes, are reassuringly close to popular stereotypes of the Victorian age. The interlace and the plants look forward with remarkable clarity to the full development of Art Nouveau in the 1890s. But most telling of all is the way these elements coexist without interacting. Despite the high level of craft, there is neither harmony nor tension, only uncertainty.

It is not a matter of incompatible styles, as though the artist were trying to combine Greek, Moorish, and Aztec. Rather, on every level from a single flower to the whole composition, we miss the unpredictable, impulsive, even awkward stroke, the difference between perfect competence and inspired confidence. From beginning to end of the nineteenth century, the confidence to make such a stroke is hardly to be found in all the eclectic ornament of Europe and America, in any medium on any scale. No wonder Ruskin longed for the "wolfish life" of medieval ornament. The ornament of his own time did not have a wolfish bone in its body! Its besetting faults are weakness and tentativeness, so deeply ingrained that no artist could fight free of them within the bounds of traditional ornament: not Pugin, not Morris, not Sullivan, Tiffany, Mackmurdo, Voysey, Dresser, Guimard, Lalique, Hoffmann, Van de Velde; not even the dark-minded visionary Sir Alfred Gilbert, too long neglected as a designer, whose fusion of ornament and monumental scupture came closest to a breakthrough (fig. 80).[2]

These names span the development from Victorian eclecticism and the Gothic revival through Art Nouveau to incipient modernism. Art Nouveau is no stronger, more decisive, or more spontaneous than the styles that preceded it. This is not always clear to see, because two achievements set it apart from the nineteenth-century mainstream: an emotional explicitness that is probably unsurpassed in the history of ornament, and the near total integration of figure, ornament, and design (fig. 81). Both innovations have their source in the most abstract and labile forms of the rococo, and this pedigree also defines their failings. What lifts the rococo above mere whimsy is its passionate strength of line. Reinterpreted by a later generation of artists for whom that strength was unattainable, the same forms radiate exoticism and febrile sensuality. Art Nouveau embodies the self-consciously worldly yet hopeful mindset of the *fin-de-siècle*, reaching for innocence and renewal yet refusing to leave the embrace of decadence.

Historically, Art Nouveau was a thing of the moment. It did not become the basis of twentieth-century ornament. The obvious explanation is that it was tied to a mindset that probably could not last; it was too specialized, and above all too sexual. This is true as far as it goes, but the limits of Art Nouveau are stylistic as well as cultural. If the tone is the same whether the form is innocent or lubricious, it is because the style, not the content, is limited. Art Nouveau achieves its intensity at the cost of what little formal strength nineteenth-century designers could muster; but the difference from its predecessors is not just a matter of degree. Art Nouveau exploits its congenital weakness as a source of emotional strength. There is a saying: "Be careful what you wish for, you might get

Fig. 81. Gorham Silver Company. Ewer with plateau. Silver. American, c. 1901. New York, The Metropolitan Museum of Art, 1974.214.26ab. Gift of Hugh Grant, 1974.

it." The most influential designers of the late nineteenth century wished for a style that could express emotion directly, without invoking the connotations of historic styles. They got their wish, but only for emotions that could be expressed in weak and languid (albeit graceful) forms.

From the implicit to the explicit dissolution of form may be a logical step, but it is still an unprecedented one. In all probability the revolution in ornament would not have come when it did, with the force it did, without the stimulus of painting. The generation that rejected nineteenth-century ornament was the same one that rejected the conventional forms of pictorial representation, and sometimes the idea of representation itself. In 1908, when Loos first presented "Ornament and Crime," the first great experiments in formal dissolution were decades past. Turner died in 1851; the Impressionists began their innovative work with color in the 1870s; and it was in 1877 that Whistler's *Nocturne in Black and Gold: The Falling Rocket* (fig. 82) provoked Ruskin's notorious outburst about "flinging a pot of paint in the public's face."[3] In none of these is vagueness or dissolution an end in itself, but a sacrifice to achieve a particular quality of light or movement.

The history of Western art testifies to the evocative power of paint, through color, texture, and the captured movement of the brush. In itself, paint evokes nothing. Only when it is made the embodiment of a particular fact or feeling does its evocative force cease to be potential and become actual. In the process, a gap inevitably opens between the physical reality of a painting—the color and texture of paint on canvas, plaster, or whatever—and the pictorial illusion it is supposed to create. Single units of paint, of which the brushstroke is only the most basic, rarely correspond precisely to the objects or substances they evoke. Depending on the degree of detail the artist wishes to convey, the unit may correspond to a leaf, a tree, or a wooded hillside at dusk. This correspondence is a matter of convention. Whatever the subject, its actual size, shape and texture are most unlikely to match the size, shape, and texture of the unit of paint that comes closest to representing it. Illusion comes from the interaction of many such units, viewed at an agreed-on distance by an eye that has learned to ignore the parts except as a means to the whole.

When the illusion is of something fleeting or intangible, like the firework in Whistler's *Nocturne*, the gap between paint as reality and paint as illusion can be very wide. With only the most tenuous relation to concrete or even identifiable forms, brushwork vanishes into the illusion it helps create. In effect, it reverts from actual to potential evocation, becoming once again "mere paint." This is neither bad nor good, simply a fact of painting that happens to be much more pronounced in some styles than others. One painter, Cézanne, saw it as a problem to be met head-on, and thereby set the course of modern art for more than half a century. Especially in his last years, from approximately 1900 to his death in 1906, he sought and often achieved a synthesis of the physical and representational aspects of paint.

What his predecessors had done for the transient qualities of light, Cézanne did also for the solidity of form. Light and form are translated equally into arbitrary units of paint, and neither light, nor form, nor brushwork is sacrificed. Cézanne's brushwork cannot disappear into the illusion: it is too bold. The result is a dynamic abstract surface that coexists with the illusion on equal terms (fig. 83). Every representational form is charged with the variety, spontaneity, and movement of individual brushstrokes. Multiplied hundreds of times across the canvas, this effect gives Cézanne's images a per-

Fig. 82. James Abbott McNeill Whistler. *Nocturne in Black and Gold: The Falling Rocket*. Oil on Canvas. American, 1875. The Detroit Institute of Arts, 46.309. Photograph © 1989 The Detroit Institute of Arts. Gift of Dexter M. Ferry Jr.

Fig. 83. Paul Cézanne. *Mont Sainte-Victoire Seen from the Bibémus Quarry*. Oil on canvas. French, c. 1897. Baltimore Museum of Art, BMA 1950.196, the Cone Collection, formed by Dr. Claribel Cone and Miss Etta Cone of Baltimore, Maryland.

manence that enhances the solidity of his subjects, and a dynamism that transfigures their stillness.

If there is a way to carry this development further in the same direction, no one has found it. Any change must upset the balance. Within a very few years of Cézanne's death, the cubism of Picasso and Braque, and the futurism of Boccioni, had shifted the emphasis to paint and the life of the surface. Areas of paint no longer reinforced the subject by transmuting it into something at once more spontaneous and more physically real. They became an end in themselves, and subject matter survived chiefly as a point of reference, a way to gauge the artist's virtuoso powers of dissolution. The elimination of subject matter, usually credited to Kandinsky, now seems the inevitable final step.

The formal legacy of these crucial years is a seductive yet defiant indeterminacy. Brushstrokes and areas of color continue to create form, sometimes even three-dimensional form, but the forms themselves are arbitrary. Therefore the relations of color and form, form and space, must also be arbitrary. Nothing is defined, nothing is predictable. Shapes end abruptly, or dissolve into one another. Sometimes they come together in a fragment of mass or a hint of perspective, even something as specific as a human face, but the illusion is no sooner offered than withdrawn. No less than the comfort of solidity, that of unity is beyond our reach. Surfaces are in constant flux, a denial of system. The only constant is paint: not so much mastery *of* paint as mastery *by* paint, an imperious claim to every inch, every level of the picture as the domain of personal expression. Where an older generation of artists might have sacrificed clarity for the sake of light or movement, the founders of modernism were glad to sacrifice the image itself to this abstract, passionate, self-centered goal.

We are now ready for Loos, not the Loos of "Ornament and Crime" but of the Villa Karma, the Kärntner Bar, and the Michaelerplatz (fig. 71). Ignoring both his insistence that what he was doing in these works was not ornament, and the fact that instead of designing his ornament he exploited the natural variations of wood and stone, we can see that the forms he chose—labile, ambiguous, unpredictable—belong precisely to the repertory of his time. *The modernist ornament that is Loos's great achievement bears the same relation to modernist painting as the ornament of any earlier period bears to the period's representational art.* In this light, "Ornament and Crime" is neither more nor less than a piece of showmanship—cultural hokum of the very highest order.

Loos's ornament springs directly from the materials. This makes it not only an ornament without predetermined motifs and patterns, but without "artifice." For the first time in Western art, an ornamental style is safe from the taint of falsehood and deception which has haunted ornament for millennia. Doubly so, for the absence of ornament implies both naturalness and spontaneity. These are quite different concepts, but in matters of style they are effectively synonyms. Loos's ornament is "natural" in the sense that it highlights the beauty of natural forms, but since it does this with the minimum of human intervention, it is also natural in the sense of spontaneous.

I am not just playing with words here. A rock is natural, but we do not usually think of it as spontaneous. If we do, that is because some quality of its form reminds us of human work. Yet we do talk of spontaneous combustion, meaning combustion that happens by itself, without anyone striking a light. The "patterns" in stone and wood are spontaneous in both senses. They happen by themselves: cutting and polishing only reveal what is already there. And they *look* spontaneous, if by spontaneity we mean a lively unpredictability resulting from the absence of calculation. What, after all, could be less calculated than a pattern that is not even human work?[4]

But Loos's choice of ornament was overdetermined. Even without the influence of painting, the decorative arts were moving toward the same goal, though on a somewhat fainter path. That path began not in Europe or America but in Japan. The sudden meeting of Japanese and Western art in the second half of the nineteenth century was wrenching and enormously fruitful for both traditions. For the West, the most significant Japanese influence was in the decorative arts. Not only did the contact bring a wealth of new motifs, but the Japanese love of figural as well as abstract decoration reinforced the Western tendency to blur image and ornament. At the same time there was a different, even contrary influence. More than any other culture before our own century, Japan embraced (as it still does) natural, spontaneous, and even random effects as an aspect of "high" art.

These effects are not evenly distributed. We find them in building, where plain wood is used for some of the most revered structures, sacred or secular. We find them even more in cabinetry; the coarse, flamelike grain of zelkova (*keyaki*) makes it the wood of choice. Ink painting and calligraphy, especially where they have come under the influence of Zen Buddhism, have a long tradition of wild, almost anarchic brushwork, its spontaneity channeled through years of rigorous training.[5]

Most directly influential in the West are Japanese ceramics (fig. 84). Their shapes, patterns, and finishes reflect a diversity of origins, from cosmopolitan workshops to isolated village potteries. Village ceramics entered the mainstream by way of the tea cermony, a somewhat improbable fusion of the simplicity, spontaneity, and discipline of Zen with an aristocratic love of collecting, connoisseurship, and display. Beginning in the sixteenth century, rustic utensils, chosen for their strong, imperfect shapes and minimal decoration (often just irregularities in the clay or glaze) were included alongside more refined works. It was not long before sophisticated potters deliberately emulated the spontaneity of folk art.

We can appreciate this phenomenon by remembering how eagerly the pioneers of modernism in the West imitated African or Cycladic sculpture, then turned around and praised it for being so "modern." The difference is that in Japan the interaction of refined, rustic, and pseudo-rustic traditions within the spiritually charged, multisen-

Fig. 84. Tea storage jar. Glazed stoneware. Japanese (Shigaraki), 1573–1615. The Cleveland Museum of Art, Sundry Purchase Fund by Exchange, 1969.227.

Fig. 85. Christopher Dresser. Pitcher. Earthenware. English, c. 1879–82. New York, The Metropolitan Museum of Art, 1988.423.1. Gift of Cynthia Hazen Polsky, 1988.

sory experience of the tea ceremony gave rise to one of the subtlest systems of connoisseurship ever evolved.[6] Even today it is little understood outside Japan; certainly foreign artists had no opportunity to explore it in the first decades of contact. Equally certain, a glimpse beyond the banality of export wares would have shown that openly and even flamboyantly "crude" ceramics had a place of honor in Japan. For Western designers and artisans of the late nineteenth century, under subtle but increasing pressure to put more of themselves into their work by emphasizing process over product, the assurance with which Japanese potters handled rugged, even lopsided shapes, and took advantage of seemingly uncontrolled technical processes, was a revelation.

The West has always had folk art of its own, including many local pottery styles. These played some part in the movement toward greater spontaneity, but they never inspired a breakthrough in design on an international scale. Japanese pottery did. Japan offered the thrill of novelty, the cachet of acknowledged mastery in decorative art, and above all, a fait accompli: a fully realized style embodying the directness of folk art, but selected, reinterpreted, and canonized by generations of connoisseurs. There was no need for Western artists to go through this process themselves; all they had to do was appropriate the results.

The first to do so was probably the English designer Christopher Dresser. In 1876 he visited Japan on a combined artistic and commercial mission, displaying examples of his own work, arranging exports and exhibits, and providing the Japanese government with a Western perspective on Japanese manufactures.[7] By 1880 the Linthorpe Art Pottery in Yorkshire, which Dresser helped to found, was producing wares of his design, with a fluid, unpredictable play of colors instead of traditional ornament (fig. 85). This was an important step. Whether it was a revolutionary step is a different question, and the answer depends on what Dresser thought he was doing.

Dresser was a protean designer, who has been claimed as a pioneer of modernism *and* a precursor of postmodernism. He was both, but the eclecticism which made this possible marks him as a man of his time, a Victorian. Dresser had a virtually inexhaustible fund of ideas, and no dogmatic scruples about realizing all of them. Much concerned with the relation of form and function, he was responsible for some of the earliest and most striking examples of functional design, but this did not stop him from creating extravagant ornament in any number of different styles. The only common factor is his awareness of the demands of multiple production. Even his most lavish decorations were created for industry, which probably explains why so many of the objects are of relatively simple form, with ornament applied to the surface in color or molded in low relief. In retrospect we can see that his life's work was to lay the foundation for a humane industrial design, far too big a task for an imagination blinkered by ideology. He recognized that a society as complex as the one he lived in had a place for elaboration as well as simplicity—and for everything in between.

Dresser's eclecticism and lack of ideological posturing make a telling contrast to Loos a generation later. Certainly he lacked Loos's flair for making his public do something under the impression that it was doing the exact opposite. We tend to associate the most radical innovations with a visionary, crusading spirit; did Dresser intend his Linthorpe ware to be revolutionary, or merely attractive? Attractive it certainly was. Dresser worked hard to perfect his colors and glazes, and was rewarded with immediate critical and commercial success. From our point of view the colors of Linthorpe pottery bear some relation to Japanese glazes, but not a very close one. Some of the shapes are

Japanese or Chinese; often, as in figure 85, they are distinctly not. But again, that is from our point of view. People saw things differently in Dresser's time. Japanese were among the Linthorpe Pottery's biggest customers, and it was rumored that some of the ware was being sold back to the English as Japanese pottery.[8] Whether the rumor was true does not matter. The point is that contemporaries thought Dresser's work far more "Japanese" than we can easily imagine.

By his own account, Dresser visited sixty-eight potteries during his four months' stay in Japan. Attending a tea ceremony, he understood that it was an occasion for the display and enjoyment of treasured objects. He recognized both the distinctive artistic character of tea wares and the enormous value the Japanese placed on them. Describing the prestige of *raku*, "a common black earthenware with lead glaze," he recounts how feudal lords had once gone to war for possession of a single tea bowl.[9]

Dresser tended to accept cultural differences as he found them. He neither extolled nor ridiculed the unevenness of tea ware, and acknowledged that its value had nothing to do with Western ideas of luxury or beauty. Elsewhere, he noted that "many of the things most esteemed by the Japanese would be unappreciated in Europe." Among them he specifically cited the "little round stone-ware jars" much favored for the tea ceremony.[10] This is not a value judgment but a statement of fact, based on European tastes, which Dresser knew as well as anyone alive. Even if he had personally admired Japanese pottery at its most alien and demanding—and there is no proof that he did—he would hardly have made something that his clients were likely to reject.

What he made instead was a compromise—objects new enough to be convincingly, refreshingly exotic, but fundamentally European and therefore familiar enough to catch on without difficulty. No revolutionary, Dresser was nonetheless an innovator. As one of the first Western artists, perhaps the very first, to make fully decorated studio pottery using neither representation nor predictable patterns, he cannot have been insensitive to its impact. Specifically, he must have understood that genuine indeterminacy and unpredictability in surface effects (as distinct from mechanically produced "irregularities") were among the few ways of countering the impersonal precision of machine production. The introduction of "spontaneous" effects, while not a dominant feature of Dresser's art, is consistent with his lifelong attempt to close the gap between industry and craft.

Other artists followed Dresser's lead, with an increasing awareness of Japanese and to some extent Chinese pottery as a treasure-trove of unpredictable surface effects—drips, splashes, color changes, and crackle—not to mention deliberate irregularities of shape. By the early 1900s these devices had entered the mainstream of European and American art pottery, where they remain to this day. Just as the classical architecture of so many schools, courthouses, and state capitols is a tribute to Greece and Rome as the source of our ideas of civic virtue, so in pottery the irregularity of form and surface evokes Japan as the wellspring of spontaneity in craft.

The most spectacular expressions of this trend are not in pottery but in glass, the one craft medium that is even more labile than clay. Between the late 1890s and 1910, Louis Comfort Tiffany, already a leader in more traditional decorative art, pioneered the manufacture of what he called favrile glass. This was his trade name for several techniques, each intended to produce dramatic, apparently random changes of color and texture (plate 9). Despite Tiffany's unprecedented mastery of the complicated chemical reactions needed to produce each color, the processes were never completely controllable. Many of the changes were genuinely random, and the interplay of skill and chance ensured spontaneity. No two works could be the same, and even within a single work precise repetition was impossible.

There is a remarkable similarity in the surface effects of Dresser's pottery, Tiffany's glass, and Loos's marble. They define a fashion, a "look," but not what most of us would call an ornamental style. This is most understandable with Loos: he was ornament's first sworn enemy. But on a much more general level, we associate ornament with patterns and images, order and system. A surface that has none of these may still be beautiful, but calling it ornament threatens to rob the word of its meaning. If this is ornament, prejudice seems to say, then anything can be ornament.

Critical ideas are never exactly in step with artistic practice, but here the time lag is startling. While our sense of what constitutes painting has kept pace with the development of painting itself, our ideas of ornament are almost a century out of date. Part of the explanation lies in the ambiguity of the word "abstract" as applied to twentieth-century art. Abstraction in its original sense is not the absence of subject matter, but the disregard for sensuous reality.[11] Art can be highly abstract and still represent something. This is often the case in traditional ornament. A Roman vine scroll is a simplified, unnaturally regular image of a grapevine, but we can still recognize it. In certain Ottoman Turkish textiles, there is no attempt to suggest a specific kind of plant, but the form is still recognizable as a plant. Elsewhere, the form may not even be recognizable as an image, but it is still recognizable as a form, and if several forms come together to make a pattern, it will be recognizable as a pattern.

What makes some twentieth-century art radically new is the willingness to do away with form itself. This may simply be another level of abstraction, or it may be something else altogether. The common use of "abstract" to mean either non-representational or indeterminate glosses over this uncertainty and its implications. The distinction between twentieth-century art and what came before has nothing to do with abstraction in the strict sense. The crucial difference is not even between representational and nonrepresentational, but between determinate and indeterminate.

Historically, Western art is determinate. A culture whose dominant arts are determinate is overwhelmingly likely to have determinate ornament. Some rococo ornament uses indeterminate effects, but we should not confuse indeterminacy with incomprehensibility. Many eighteenth-century textiles have such intricate patterns that it is difficult to see what is going on, but this is because they are so subtly organized, not because they lack organization. The same is true of medieval interlace. Two good but highly restricted examples of true indeterminacy are Damascus steel and marbled paper.[12]

In the first decade of the twentieth century, Western art, including ornament, crossed over into indeterminacy. The revolution in ornament was clear to see, but no one noticed it at the time because the effacement of subject matter in painting, the mimetic art par excellence, set the tone for the entire process. Ornament has always been abstract, or at least capable of abstraction. Once painting, too, became "abstract," it was obvious that the two kinds of "abstraction" had nothing in common. Whatever the new indeterminate painting might be, the old abstract but still determinate ornament clearly was not. Neither inspired the other, and neither offered any help in appreciating the other. In the heady climate of those years, such incompatibility only could mean that ornament had proved its inadequacy by failing to keep pace.

There were two possible solutions. One was to redefine ornament so that it could keep pace with perceived advances in painting: in other words, to make it indeterminate. The other was to do away with ornament. The modernist answer was to do both at once, and it was Loos's genius that made this possible. Loos never explicitly called his wood or marble facings ornament. That would have given the game away. Nevertheless, he came very close to a visual confession. Remember that in "Ornament and Crime" his aesthetic case against ornament is weak and half-hearted; the real argument is that ornament is anachronistic, an obstacle to progress, and above all a waste of time and money. Only a year later, in 1909, he began work on his most important commission, a combined retail and residential building on the Michaelerplatz in Vienna, now widely known as the Looshaus (fig. 71). It is the first practical expression of his ideas on ornament. Far from contradicting the views he had just committed to paper, it complements them.

Design and construction took more than two years. The civic authorities rebelled against the austerity of the facade, and repeatedly demanded compromises (including the notorious window boxes) or tried to have the whole exterior redesigned.[13] Loos had already begun to use veined marble on facades, but the practice is especially significant here. Situated on a large open square among traditionally ornamented buildings—notably the Imperial Palace!—the Looshaus is *very* public architecture. When Loos accepted the commission, he made himself responsible not just to his clients (the tailoring firm of Goldman and Salatsch, for whom he had worked before), but to the city of Vienna and its collective, ornate self-image.

His solution was elegant, not only visually but as a way of reconciling the demands of public architecture and his own repudiation of ornament. The marble facing and columns call attention to the building, divide the facade into visually manageable units, and introduce a wealth of surface effects with no other goal than pleasure. In short, they do everything that ornament could be expected to do. For such a direct substitution to work, the veining of the marble would have to be recognized, at least subliminally, as the equivalent of traditional ornament. And it did work. The authorities gave Loos no trouble over the lower part of the facade. What they rejected was the austerity of the next four stories, between the zone of marble and the roof. They failed to see the need for this austerity, but Loos saw it clearly. Any ornament in the old sense would have competed with the veining of the marble, and given the strength of convention, would probably have overshadowed it. To function as ornament in its own right, the marble had to be unequivocally the only embellishment on the building.

This is why Loos kept his detailing to a minimum, even in the lowest, decorated zone. Smooth unbroken surfaces, two-dimensional wherever possible, let the marble speak for itself, and remind us that nothing else is needed. Finding our ornament ready-made does not simply free us to elaborate in other areas. This constraint has an economic as well as an aesthetic force. Loos did not just offer an ornament without motifs, artifice, or history, he offered an ornament without anachronism or unnecessary labor.

Loos did not always practice what he preached. The four columns of the Looshaus facade are nonfunctional—they carry no weight—yet they are made of solid marble. This is hardly a model of economy, but Loos was not being capricious. He needed uninterrupted surface effects. Flat surfaces could be clad in a thin layer of marble, but a round column could not. For the ornament to be continuous, the column had to be cut from a single piece of stone. Doubtless the occasion justified the extravagance in Loos's eyes, and since the design as a whole was assertively economical he may have been at pains to avoid seeming cheap. But beyond any technical or financial consideration, the lower part of the facade is a tour de force of classicism, capturing the strength and balance of early Greek temples in purely modern form. By this means, Loos defined himself as a classical architect, and claimed the high ground against anyone rash enough to accuse him of ignoring or subverting history. Physically, the columns carry no weight; symbolically, as the only direct classical allusion, they support the entire building. There was good reason for this posture of defense. For all its elegance, the lower facade was daringly austere. And this, remember, is the *decorated* part of the exterior. To make sure it is recognized as such, the rest must be even simpler. The stark, repetitive facade of the middle stories was Loos's answer to this challenge. Since the lower part of the building was already so simple, the choice was correspondingly limited. This should not obscure Loos's courage in taking the contrast as far as it would go. Not only does the ornamental character of the marble show to maximum effect, like an oasis in the desert, but the (intended) lack of any decorative work above the mezzanine keeps that effect undiluted. There is no blurring of themes to ease the transition. Austerity and lushness, repetition and unpredictability, determinate and indeterminate form confront each other endlessly, and endlessly enhance one another, as each creates an appetite the other satisfies.

In this reciprocity, Loos pays ironic homage to his own dismissal of ornament. The new, untrammeled architecture of which he had made himself the prophet has arrived—as what?—as a grid of windows in a blank wall. The spontaneity that gives it life, the complex, unpredictable "human" touch, is no longer the work of human hands. What art has renounced in its triumph over the past, nature must provide.

If Dresser was the first to sense the value of indeterminacy as an alternative to traditional ornament (though he never explored it systematically), Loos was the most complex, artistically self-aware exponent of the new style. For both, it was an admission that industry had irrevocably changed the nature of decorative art. It was also a way of limiting or controlling that change by capturing the essence of ornament in a form that was economically and technically viable in a modernized society, yet immune to the repetition that industrial production imposed on traditional ornament. Given the pressure—social and economic as well as technical—which the Industrial Revolution brought to bear on the decorative arts, it is no surprise that the quality to be preserved at all costs was spontaneity. The unpredictable flow of shapes and col-

Fig. 86. Textile. Italian, c. 1960. New York, Cooper-Hewitt, National Design Museum, Smithsonian Institution/Art Resource, 1991–90–10. Photo: Dennis Cowley.

ors was a guarantee of artistic and technical uniqueness. At a single stroke, the new style solved two great problems of nineteenth-century ornament—historical eclecticism and mechanization.

It has been a long time since modernist ornament had to rely directly on materials and processes. For decades, it has been a full-blown style capable of being interpreted in the most traditional techniques without apparent contradiction. What matters is not that the ornament be natural, the way marble veining is natural, but that it appear unpremeditated. It must give the impression of being outside human control, insofar as human control means organization, precision, or predictability. Early in 1992, in the Cooper-Hewitt Museum in New York, I saw a display that summed up this principle. Two textiles were hanging side by side. One was a length of camouflage material from the Persian Gulf War. Even those of us who have never been soldiers or hunters know what camouflage looks like.

It is the essence of indeterminacy, a shifting, unpredictable play of forms and colors designed to make anything from a person to a battleship disappear.

Camouflage as we know it is a relatively recent invention. It dates from the very end of the nineteenth century, when the American painter and naturalist Abbott H. Thayer, by analyzing the interaction of colors in birds' feathers, first reduced indeterminacy to scientific principles.[14] As an artist, Thayer was competent but undistinguished. He was no innovator, certainly no modernist, and had no influence on the "advanced" painting of his time. His contribution to the art of war was far greater, though it was years before the military took his discoveries seriously. Still, the timing of those discoveries is significant: indeterminacy was in the air.

Juxtaposed suggestively with the military fabric was a length of Italian dress fabric made around 1960 (fig. 86). I do not think it would make anyone disappear, yet its blotchy and seemingly unpredictable forms bear more than a passing resemblance to camouflage. Three techniques combine to produce this effect: jacquard weaving, which can incorporate enormously complex patterns into the cloth itself; discharge printing (printing on colored fabric with a bleach instead of the more usual practice of printing on plain fabric with a dye); and machine embroidery. All three processes are well understood and highly controllable, even in large-scale production. If they give every appearance of disorder, we must assume the designer sought precisely that effect.

Once we recognize that indeterminacy is the distinctive force in twentieth-century ornament, similarities appear where none had been before. At one extreme, a 1991 ceramic vase by Lee Segal (fig. 87) repre-

Fig. 87. Lee Segal. Vase. Stoneware. American, 1991. Private collection. Author's photo.

sents the pursuit of spontaneity in one of its most freewheeling forms. Japanese influence, both direct and indirect, is strong. The basic technique is a version of *raku*, cited by Dresser more than a century ago and widely recognized today. In Segal's vase, the matte black surface typical of *raku* is only partly glazed. The alternation of rough and smooth, the apparently random color changes, and the deep crackle all belong to the "iconography" of spontaneity which is Japan's great gift to Western ceramics. At the same time, the brash energy of the decoration, with its deep surface grooves and passages of color laid on like paint with a broad brush, comes out of Western "abstract" painting. The organization of light and dark areas around the whole vase is especially reminiscent of Motherwell. Remarkably, instead of calling attention to themselves as decoration, these effects retain a strong association with materials and techniques. Juxtaposed with Tiffany's favrile glass, the vase is a reminder that the first ideal of modernist ornament, to embody the process in the product, retains much of its original power.

In this connection it is worth looking yet again at the silk scarf which I have adopted, despite or perhaps because of its simplicity, as this book's emblem of modern handicraft (fig. 3). It has passed through several incarnations already: pitiful vestige of ornament in a postornament world; defiant assertion of craft for its own sake; symbol of the honesty of labor. There is one more incarnation: as a typical if unglamourous piece of modernist ornament.

I have called modernist ornament an ornament without motifs. Since it is based on indeterminacy, especially the unpredictable "patterns" found in nature, this should be true by definition. Certainly it was true at the beginning, but as the style became established, the grain of wood, the veining of marble, and the texture of handspun yarn and handwoven cloth became cultural clichés. They lost their uniqueness and spontaneity by becoming symbols of uniqueness and spontaneity. Once this happened, the stage was set for their use as motifs in the traditional sense. The architect Louis Kahn pioneered a now-familiar device: concrete poured into wooden molds, so that when dry it preserves the outline of the boards and the highlights of their grain. On one level this is concrete being true to itself, product as the record of process. On another level, Kahn accepts modernist ornament as a set of forms that can be transferred from one substance to another. Wood grain in concrete is still indeterminate, but it is not spontaneous.

In all these works there is a distorted Ruskinianism, a dim echo of Ruskin's insistence that variety and perfect finish are incompatible. Yet at the other end of the craft spectrum, where the finish *is* perfect and precision could scoff at indeterminacy if it chose, the modernist strain in ornament remains strong. Instead of evoking spontaneity through indeterminate surface effects, artists breathe lability and randomness into the most carefully delineated forms. Each, in its way, is a refusal to do anything that might be pinned down to a pattern or an image. Whether we are looking at the aggressively scuptural jewelry of Albert Paley (fig. 88) or the innovative needle-lace of Virginia Churchill Bath (fig. 89), the mastery of form is never in doubt, yet the forms themselves elude our grasp. Shapes seem frozen on the way to something recognizable. Expected symmetries vanish in a dazzling show of disconnection and caprice.

The forms come from Art Nouveau, with its sensual evocation of organic growth and movement, but the calculated indifference to visual necessity is new. In a sense,

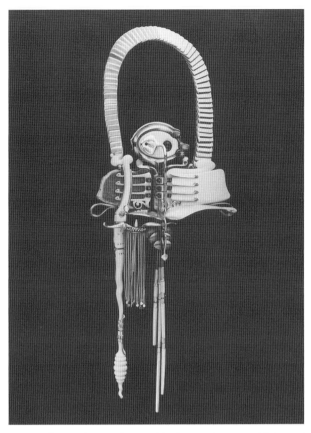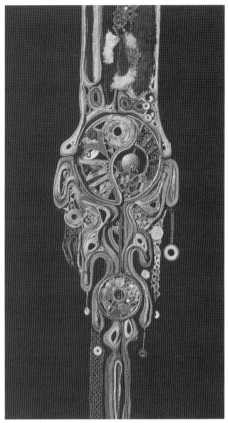

Fig. 88. Albert Paley. Pendant. Gold, silver, and copper with ivory, labradorite, moonstone, jade, and glass. American, 1973. Washington, D.C., Smithsonian American Art Museum, Gift of the James Renwick Alliance and museum purchase through the Smithsonian Collections Acquisition Program, COPR. 1973, Albert Paley.

Fig. 89. Virginia Churchill Bath. *Long Construction I* (detail). Needle lace: linen and other fibers, with suede, mica, wood, and metal. American, before 1987. Possession of the artist. Artist's photo.

they reflect a more sophisticated idea of growth, whose symbol is no longer a plant or flower seen whole and graceful, but a bone, shaped by too many needs and stresses to be merely graceful.[15] But these ornamental forms were never shaped by stress. They are as alien to functional as to visual necessity. In this light, their affinity is no longer with Art Nouveau or modern science, but with the rococo at its most radical, or with those astonishing precursors of the rococo, the van Vianen family of silversmiths in seventeenth-century Utrecht, whose challenge to determinacy is one of the turning points of Western art (fig. 7).

Modernist ornament has succeeded across a broad range of materials and applications—the mark of a historically important style—but its success has come at a price. Eclecticism and mechanization were two of the great problems that ornament faced in the nineteenth century; weakness was the third. Modernist ornament is a temporary escape from weakness, not a remedy for it. Historically, the abolition of recognizable form in ornament is not just a response to similar developments in painting. It is the final stage in the progressive weakening and dissolution that afflicted ornament throughout the nineteenth century. If we do not recognize the forms of modernist ornament as weak, it is because there are so few *forms* left to recognize.

In the ornament of our century, only one artist stood firm against the current of dissolution. This was Matisse, in the paper cut-outs he made with increasing frequency between the 1930s and his death in 1954 (plate 1). Matisse first adopted the technique as an alternative to sketching, but increasingly he came to regard it as an art form in its own right, especially when illness made it difficult for him to paint.[16] The cut-outs share the unpredictability of modernist ornament, but this may be only half of their genealogy. The multilobed plant forms, especially, bear an extraordinary resemblance to wood carvings and felt and leather appliqués of the fifth and fourth centuries B.C. from Pazyryk in Siberia (fig. 10). Buried in underground tombs, then preserved by water that filled the tombs and froze, these objects were excavated by Soviet archaeologists beginning in the 1920s. Some were included in the Soviet display at the 1937 World's Fair in Paris.[17]

If Matisse actually saw the Pazyryk specimens, it might help explain his choice of shapes, but not the power of the cut-outs themselves. Only Matisse's genius can account for that. Every contour records the smallest movement of paper and shears, and vibrates with jumpy, unpredictable life. This is an important part of the effect, but we can understand Matisse's ornament only by recognizing what it is *not*. It is not "finished." The best way to see this is by comparing his forms with similar ones from Pazyryk. The Siberian examples are no more regular, but they have an internal discipline that Matisse's forms do not, as though the Pazyryk artists, once satisfied with a basic shape, would streamline it, taking away the rough edges, the tiny unpredictabilities that might distract from the unity and flow of the design.

An ornamental form is the product of a thousand different choices, intuitions, and accidents. If one of them is changed, the entire balance may shift. Matisse's cut-outs invite or even challenge us to make a change, to finish the shape in our minds. The form may thus be made stronger or weaker, more clumsy or more graceful, but one

ORNAMENT

224

thing is virtually certain. It will be made smoother, more stable, more consistent with itself—more like the examples from Pazyryk. The Pazyryk ornament is graceful, lively, and unpredictable, but it is what it is, and no more. This is what I mean by stability. It is the trap of completion, and its lure becomes stronger the more we involve ourselves in the form. Matisse ignored it.

By leaving his forms inchoate, he left them unstable—a tense, hungry instability. He did not let them seek their level, flowing down the path of least resistance toward harmonious rest. Each form demands completion; Matisse withheld it. Inchoate form is potential form. By making it permanent without releasing its tension or resolving its instability, Matisse captured not just the shape itself but the thousand possibilities it successively invokes and rejects. Had Ruskin lived to see it, he could have found no better illustration for his opposition of variety and perfect finish.

Matisse carried out this stylistic tour de force again and again, infusing each work with new delight, as though he were rediscovering the world each time. He was supremely gifted as both draftsman and colorist, and the cut-outs distill a lifetime's confidence in both facets of his art. They are a sobering reminder of what it took, in the age of modernism, to give ornament the "wolfish life" that Ruskin romantically ascribed to a passionate mind and an unskilled hand.

Epilogue

IN THE "OFFICIAL" story, which we have accepted for generations, the modernist revolt against ornament was a rite of passage to a higher understanding: the ability to see the beauty of necessity. The necessity was social as well as functional. By rejecting ornament, Western civilization acknowledged that modernization had made traditional craft obsolete. Since ornament was rooted in craft, our society could no longer support ornament on a practical scale. Only mass-produced imitations were economically viable. Modernization offered us a crucial artistic choice: allow ornament to be co-opted by mass production, or do away with it, and take pleasure in its absence. By choosing as we did, we turned a dreadful self-inflicted defeat into a victory for the human spirit.

If only the real story were so simple. Modernization was the most direct cause of the revolution in design, but it was not the only cause. The fear of ornament was many fears. Fear of excess. Fear of seeming culturally backward. Fear of being led astray by our senses. Fear of impermanence. Fear of monsters. Fear of being reduced to machinery. Fear of the magical power of our own skill. Early or late, each contributed to the reservoir of mistrust. The anxieties of ornament are older than the anxieties of industry.

Puritanism runs strong in Western culture, and ornament is an easy target. Cosmophobia may be too deeply engrained in our heritage to be argued away, but the real justification of ornament is beyond words or logic. *Ornament makes people happy.* In the early 1960s, the American photographer Clarence John Laughlin began recording ornamental details from nineteenth-century buildings (fig. 90). The project went against the spirit of the time, but Laughlin had an explanation ready: "the American Victorians had made some very important discoveries, mostly by intuition, in the highly significant field which can be called 'psychological functionalism'—which enabled them to understand the supremely important roles of fantasy and decoration in architecture—and led to many of their houses being far more human and livable than ours."[1] The fact that Laughlin had to frame his insight in terms of functionalism, and present it as a discovery about the Victorians rather than as a principle taken for granted by every age and culture but our own, reflects the power of cosmophobia to limit the historical awareness of ornament, and put its champions on the defensive. The fact that he could frame it at all reflects the power of ornament to transcend the restrictions of dogma.

In many people's eyes, modernism never made up for the pleasures it took away; hence the relative abundance of ornament produced despite the ban, in such popular but critically invisible (because mass-produced) media as wallpaper, gift paper, dress and upholstery fabric, and decorated china. The style I have called modernist ornament was an honorable attempt to close the gap, but it cannot match the appeal of traditional styles, with their recognizable forms and historical associations. Fortunately there are other ways of reconciling ornament and modernism. Matisse proved that the accessibility and discipline of ornament can join forces with the passionate subjectivity of "abstract" art. At the time, no one else seemed capable of this balancing act, but the artistic climate has changed. Ornament can be invoked more openly, and with more historical awareness, than was possible sixty years ago.

A quilt called *Adam's Boat* (plate 10), made in 1994–95 by the Canadian artist Barbara Todd, combines the new acceptance of ornament with the emotional range of classic modernism. It is a real quilt that one could use; the color blue is deeply restful, and the spiral ornament is hypnotic without being threatening. Todd's vision, however, is darker in every sense of the word. With the intrusion of the black, looming shape that she calls a boat, the quilt becomes a complex and disturbing meditation on the meaning of sleep. In the context, any large black shape would have nightmarish connotations: a cloud passing over one's dreams, the shadow that death casts over sleep. But Todd goes far beyond this simple contrast. The outline of the "boat" is copied from the coverlet depicted in a twelfth-century carving of the "Dream of the Three Wise Men" at Autun Cathedral.[2] In other words, what seems most disturbing in the quilt is itself a quilt, a shelter for sleep. In St. Matthew's Gospel, the wise men's dream is a message from God, warning them not to report back to Herod that they have seen the

Fig. 90. Clarence John Laughlin. *The Improbable Dome (No. 1)*. Photograph (silver print). American, 1964. Boston, Museum of Fine Arts, 1975.339, Polaroid Foundation Purchase Fund, 1975. Courtesy of the Museum of Fine Arts, Boston. Reproduced with permission. © Museum of Fine Arts, Boston.

infant Jesus. Since this is how Jesus was saved from Herod, who planned to kill him, the disturbing shape becomes an even more explicit token of protection. Its relevance is poignantly clear when we learn that Adam is the name of the artist's son, a small child when the quilt was made.

We know from the title that the dark shape is a boat. The association of sleep and sailing invokes Robert Louis Stevenson's poem "My Bed Is a Boat," in *A Child's Garden of Verses* (1885). The last stanza reads:

> All night across the dark we steer;
> But when the day returns at last,
> Safe in my room, beside the pier,
> I find my vessel fast.

Thanks to this connection, the "quilt within a quilt" is no longer just a shelter for the sleeper, but something more dynamic, a conveyance across the sea of sleep. By allusively layering the dark form of the boat with Stevenson's poem, and with biblical images of protection, the artist seems to be promising her child that if he can embrace the darkness and mystery of sleep, with all its intimations of mortality, he will be embarking on a momentous yet safe adventure.

This is a deeply personal message, but its significance is universal. Since Adam was also the first human, the boat and its symbolism are for all of us. *Adam's Boat* is neither more nor less than an image of the unknown, our fear of it, and the peace to be won by coming to terms with both. Whether we approach it in ignorance, or armed with the artist's verbal clues, the dark shape of the boat challenges and daunts us, covering the tranquil sea with a shadow too vast to ignore. It may be our only refuge from the unknown, but at the same time it *is* the unknown. To board the boat and set sail requires no small investment of courage, trust, or both.

In purely formal terms, *Adam's Boat* overturns the modernist hierarchy of art and craft. As a functional object that is also decorative, it is a work of craft. As an exploration of the human condition it is a work of art. As a work of nonfigural art, in which a highly personal iconography conveys a universal message, it is proudly modernist. Yet ornament and craft have the last word. Instead of stopping at the edge of the boat, the spirals continue without a break, asserting the claims of pattern and everything pattern connotes: pleasure, control, the intimacy of an object of daily use, continuity with the past, the certainties of craft to balance the uncertainties of art.

No new ornamental forms are needed for this synthesis; no new structures or techniques for the ornament to relate to; only the will to revive what was long assumed to be defunct. After a century in which art and craft, ornament and modernism, subjectivity and convention were declared irreconcilable, can the restoration of ornament be such a simple matter? If what we mean by the restoration of ornament is an updated version of the time-honored, intuitive synthesis of fine and applied art (however we define these categories), the answer appears to be yes, on one all-important condition: the restoration cannot take place within the conceptual framework of modernism. Todd has stepped outside that framework. Her debt to modernism is great, and she acknowledges it with boldness and humility, but one crucial ingredient is missing: the aesthetic of process. Although the shape of the "boat" has the spontaneity of a Matisse cut-out, the balance between it and the regularity of the spiral ornament is anything but spontaneous. By *choosing* a modernist idiom for its role in her larger plan, Todd approaches modernism historically, as one stylistic mode among many. This daring venture into historical eclecticism defines her outlook as postmodern.

The resulting fusion of seemingly incompatible styles is graceful, personal, and controlled; respectful of both the recent and the distant past; eclectic without irony or greed. It is everything that postmodernist art could have been, and may yet become. If ornament is reborn in this spirit, it will matter very little which style or styles we adopt. The modernist interregnum will have achieved its true goal: an exit from the old locked room of the ornament question.

NOTES

Notes to the Preface

1. See this volume's Bibliography of Ornament.

2. I have coined the word cosmophobia by a time-honored method, from the Greek *kosmos* (ornament) and *phobos* (fear). In addition to ornament, *kosmos* means order, in the sense of careful arrangement, decorum, or the cosmos itself, the ultimate arrangement. Cosmophobia, then, could mean either fear of ornament or fear of order. As it happens, fear of order has been a major part of the fear of ornament—but only since the nineteenth century. Before that, as I show in chapter 6, it was precisely the *dis*-orderly qualities of ornament that were suspect. The roots and connotations of words for ornament are not a reliable guide to ornament itself.

3. Modernism is an ethos, not just an artistic movement. I make no excuse for its dogmatism or its posturing. Nevertheless, after the agony of the Industrial Revolution, modernism upheld the ideals of progress, the universality of experience, and the sanctity of the individual. See J. Trilling, "A Modernist's Critique of Postmodernism," *International Journal of Politics, Culture and Society* 9.3 (Spring 1996): 353–71.

Notes to the Introduction

1. John Elderfield, *Henri Matisse: A Retrospective* (New York: Museum of Modern Art, 1992).

2. Ibid., 63.

3. Amy Goldin, "Matisse and Decoration: The Late Cut-outs," *Art in America* 63.4 (1975): 49–59. Goldin is sympathetic to Matisse's decorative aims, but her article reflects what was still a near-universal reluctance to accept ornament on its own terms.

4. Barbara G. Walker, *A Treasury of Knitting Patterns* (New York: Scribner, 1968); *A Second Treasury of Knitting Patterns* (New York: Scribner, 1970); *Charted Knitting Designs* (New York: Scribner, 1972).

5. Kaffe Fassett, *Glorious Knits* (New York: Potter, 1985); *Glorious Color* (New York: Potter, 1988); and especially *Glorious Inspirations* (New York: Potter, 1991). On the role of model or pattern books, see Margaret Abegg, *Apropos Patterns* (Bern: Abegg-Stiftung, 1978). For examples of the enormous freedom that a "codified" pattern gives the artist, see James Trilling, "Styles and Motifs of Greek Island Embroidery: A Study in Diversity," in Trilling et al., *Aegean Crossroads: Greek Island Embroideries in The Textile Museum* (Washington D.C.: The Museum, 1983).

6. Craig Engelhorn, "Birth of an Off-Axis Newtonian," *Sky and Telescope*, March 1993, 87–91.

7. John Matthews, *Frog and Toad: Behind the Scenes* (Churchill Films, 1985).

Notes to Chapter 1

1. American law uses the same test to decide what is and is not protected by copyright. Whatever is visually separable from the functional shape is "applied art," and is protected as individual expression. The functional shape, however innovative and appealing, is "industrial design." As such, it belongs to the realm of ideas and principles, which are not protected. (See Donald F. Johnston, *Copyright Handbook*, 2d ed. [New York: Bowker, 1982], 27–29.) Law is not art criticism, but the same societies make and use both. It would be interesting to know why, in the age of "less is more," it is the *inessential* that receives the sheltering designation of art!

2. Ovid *Metamorphoses* 4.625–62.

3. On bizarre tastes in sixteenth- and seventeenth-century decorative art, see J. F. Hayward, *Virtuoso Goldsmiths and the Triumph of Mannerism* (London: Rizzoli International / Sotheby Parke Bernet, 1976), and Joy Kenseth, ed., *The Age of the Marvelous* (Hanover, N.H: Hood Museum of Art, distrib. by University of Chicago Press, 1991). On the van Vianen family of silversmiths, see J. R. ter Molen, *Van Vianen, een Utrechtse familie van zilversmeden met een internationale faam* (Leiderdorp: J. R. ter Molen, 1984).

4. See, for example, N. K. Sandars, *Prehistoric Art in Europe*, 2d ed. (Harmondsworth: Penguin Books, 1985), and Randall White, *Dark Caves, Bright Visions* (New York: American Museum of Natural History, 1986).

5. Claude Lévi-Strauss, "The Concept of Archaism in Anthropology," in Lévi-Strauss, *Structural Anthropology* (New York: Basic Books, 1963). Although Lévi-Strauss is writing about social organization in the broadest sense, his conclusions are highly relevant to the study of art.

6. Fiske Kimball, *The Creation of the Rococo* (Philadelphia: Philadelphia Museum of Art, 1943); William Park, *The Idea of the Rococo* (Newark, Del.: University of Delaware Press, 1992); Alain Grubar, ed., *Classicism and the Baroque in Europe* (New York: Abbeville Press, 1996).

7. Some of the best examples come from the Amur River area of Siberia and from Kazakhstan

in Central Asia. See Berthold Laufer, *The Decorative Art of the Amur Tribes* (New York: American Museum of Natural History, 1902), and *Kazakh Decorative and Applied Art* (in Russian; Leningrad, 1970). For early Chinese examples of this decorative principle see Teng Rensheng, *Lacquer Wares of the Chu Kingdom* (Hong Kong: Woods Publishing Co., 1992), esp. pl. 71.

8. Michael Brand and Glenn D. Lowry, eds., *Fatehpur-Sikri* (Bombay: Marg Publications, 1987).

9. Bernhard Salin, *Die altgermanische Thierornamentik* (Stockholm: Wahlstrom and Widstrand, 1904, 1935), 255, fig. 566.

Notes to Chapter 2

1. On ogive and pomegranate motifs, see R. Reichelt, *Das Granatapfelmotiv in der Textilkunst* (Berlin, 1956), and R. Bonito Fanelli, "Il disegno della melagrana nei tessuti del Rinascimento in Italia," *Rassegna della Istruzione Artistica* 3.3 (1968): 27–51.

2. Alois Riegl, *Stilfragen* (Berlin, 1893). Only a century later has an English translation become available: A. Riegl, *Problems of Style: Foundations for a History of Ornament* (Princeton: Princeton University Press, 1992), trans. Evelyn Kain; introduction and notes by David Castriota, preface by Henri Zerner.

3. This view was associated with followers of the architect and theorist Gottfried Semper: "Whereas Semper did suggest that material and technique play a role in the genesis of art forms, the Semperians jumped to the conclusion that all art forms were always the direct products of materials and techniques. 'Technique' quickly emerged as a popular buzzword; in common usage, it soon became interchangeable with 'art' itself and eventually began to replace it. Only the naive talked about 'art;' experts spoke in terms of 'technique.' . . . Furthermore, the natural authority that practicing artists exert in matters of technique resulted in an environment where scholars, archaeologists and art historians swallowed their pride and beat a hasty retreat whenever the question of technique arose" (Riegl, *Problems of Style*, 4). Riegl's dissociation of Semper from the dogmatic ideas of his followers is more than just courtesy. As Semper wrote in 1860, "The denial of reality, of the material, is necessary if form is to emerge as a meaningful symbol, as an autonomous creation of man" (*Style in the Technical and Tectonic Arts*, in Gottfried Semper, *The Four Elements of Architecture and Other Writings*, trans. Harry Francis Mallgrave and Wolfgang Herrmann [Cambridge: University Press, 1989], note on 257).

4. Cf. E. J. W. Barber, "The Peplos of Athena," in Jenifer Neils, ed., *Goddess and Polis: The Panathenaic Festival in Ancient Athens* (Hanover, N.H.: Hood Museum of Art; Princeton: Princeton University Press, 1992), 103–18, esp. 111–12. The danger is not that a "wrong" interpretation will prevail over a "right" one, but that proponents of the two systems will continue to inhabit separate worlds, each one holding only half the answer.

5. Depending on whether the warp or weft is dyed, the technique and the finished textile are

known as warp or weft ikat. When both are dyed, it is double ikat. The word *ikat* is Indonesian; the technique is traditional in many other parts of the world, notably Japan, Cambodia, India, Central Asia, and Central America. The Japanese word for ikat is *kasuri;* in Gujerat, the part of India where it is a specialty, it is called *patolu* (plural, *patola*). Only the Indonesian word is in general use in the West for the technique in all its forms.

6. James Trilling, *The Medallion Style* (New York: Garland, 1985).

7. Sonia Uvezian, *Cooking from the Caucasus* (New York: Harcourt Brace Jovanovich, 1976), 93; Marimar Torres, *The Catalan Country Kitchen* (Reading, Mass.: Addison-Wesley/Aris Books, 1992), 76.

8. I have been unable to verify the source of this Beowulf tale. There is no reference to it in Stith Thompson, *European Tales Among the North American Indians* (Colorado Springs, 1919), but the incident may have occurred later. Nor does it appear in Douglas D. Short, *Beowulf Scholarship: An Annotated Bibliography* (New York: Garland, 1980). Paradoxically, the amount of circumstantial detail in the story suggests that it is fanciful: if an article called "The Beowulf Legend Among the Plains Indians" was ever published, it should be fairly easy to find, and I have not found it. However, this may mean only that it was published in an obscure journal, or a journal devoted largely to other subjects.

9. James Trilling, "Medieval Interlace Ornament: The Making of a Cross-Cultural Idiom," *Arte Medievale*, 2d ser., 9.2 (1995): 59–86.

10. The fundamental work is John Irwin, *The Kashmir Shawl* (London: H. M Stationery Office, 1973). Other studies include Elisabeth Mikosch, "The Scent of Flowers: Kashmir Shawls in the Collection of The Textile Museum," *The Textile Museum Journal* 24 (1985): 6–54 (includes a catalogue of shawls in the museum's collection); Frank Ames, *The Kashmir Shawl* (Woodbridge, Suffolk: Antique Collectors' Club, 1986); and Monique Lévi-Strauss, *The Cashmere Shawl* (New York: Abrams, 1988).

Notes to Chapter 3

1. Sally Price, *Primitive Art in Civilized Places* (Chicago: University of Chicago Press, 1989), 115–18. Some of the ornament is of extremely high quality; see Sally and Richard Price, *Afro-American Arts of the Suriname Rain Forest* (Berkeley: University of California Press, 1980).

2. Nelson H. H. Graburn, ed., *Ethnic and Tourist Arts* (Berkeley: University of California Press, 1976).

3. E. H. Gombrich, *The Sense of Order* (Ithaca: Cornell University Press, 1979), 218–19. William Morris, in his essay "The Lesser Arts" (1878), speaks of "forms that once had a serious meaning, though they are now become little more than a habit of the hand" (Morris, *News From Nowhere and Other Writings*, ed. Clive Wilmer [Harmondsworth: Penguin Books, 1993], 233–54).

4. Reprinted in Ananda Coomaraswamy, *Traditional Art and Symbolism* (Princeton: Princeton University Press, 1977), 241–53.

5. Frances Elizabeth Baldwin, *Sumptuary Legislation and Personal Regulation in England* (Baltimore: Johns Hopkins Press, 1926), 228; cf. Donald H. Shively, "Sumptuary Regulation and Status in Early Tokugawa Japan," *Harvard Journal of Asiatic Studies* 25 (1965): 123–64; Stella Mary Newton, *The Dress of the Venetians, 1495–1525* (Aldershot, England, and Brookfield, Vt.: Scolar Press, 1988).

6. Meyer Reinhold, *History of Purple as a Status Symbol in Antiquity* (Brussels: Latomus, 1970); Ehud Spanier, ed., *The Royal Purple and the Biblical Blue: Argaman and Tekhelet: The Study of Chief Rabbi Dr. Isaac Herzog on the Dye Industries in Ancient Israel and Recent Scientific Contributions* (Jerusalem: Keter, 1987).

7. Grahame Clark, *Symbols of Excellence: Precious Materials as Expressions of Status* (Cambridge: University Press, 1985). For a delightfully trenchant analysis of the assumptions linking precious materials, lavish workmanship, and social and economic prestige, see Thorstein Veblen, *The Theory of the Leisure Class* (1899), esp. chap. 6.

8. Clark, *Symbols of Excellence*, 50.

9. William Durandus, *The Symbolism of Churches and Church Ornaments* (book 1 of the *Rationale Divinorum Officiorum*), trans. J. M. Neale and B. Webb (Leeds, 1843), 60.

10. Ellert Dahl, "Dilexi decorem domus Dei. Building to the Glory of God in the Middle Ages," Institutum Romanum Norvegiae, *Acta ad Archaeologiam et Artium Historiam Pertinentia*, ser. 2, vol. 1 (1981), 157–90.

11. *The Letters of Saint Boniface*, trans. Ephraim Emerton (New York: Columbia University Press, 1940), 64–65. On the "intrinsically" transcendent quality of gold, derived from its immunity to corrosion and tarnish, see Patrik Reuterswürd, "The Significance of Gold in Funerary Art," *Konsthistorisk Tidskrift* (Stockholm) 1982, 1–3; reprinted in Reuterswürd, *The Visible and Invisible in Art* (Vienna: IRSA, 1991), 9–11. Another "incorruptible" material, jade, had the analogous place in Chinese thought.

12. St. Bernard, *Apologia* 12.28; Dahl, "Dilexi decorem domus Dei," 180; Conrad Rudolph, *The "Things of Greater Importance": Bernard of Clairvaux's Apologia and the Medieval Attitude Toward Art* (Philadelphia: University of Pennsylvania Press, 1990).

13. *Canons and Decrees of the Council of Trent*, ed. and trans. H. J. Schroeder (St. Louis and London: Herder, 1941), 147.

14. 1 Kings 5–9; 2 Chron. 2–7.

15. Justinian's famous remark does not appear in contemporary accounts of the church, only in a later, wildly fanciful account, the so-called *Narratio de Sancta Sophia*. See Rowland J. Mainstone, *Hagia Sophia* (New York: Thames and Hudson, 1988), 10.

16. Paul the Silentiary, *Description of Hagia Sophia*, 647 ff., in Cyril Mango, ed. and trans., *The Art of the Byzantine Empire, 312–1453* (Englewood Cliffs, N.J.: Prentice-Hall, 1972), 86.

Unlike Solomon's temple, which was destroyed in 586 B.C., the decoration Paul describes can still be seen.

17. John Ruskin, *The Stones of Venice* (London, 1851), vol. 1, chap. 2, sec. 14 (God's work); chap. 20, sec. 24 (ornament copies nature).

18. Ibid., chap. 20, sec. 20 (curves); chap. 20, sec. 15 (human work).

19. C. G. Jung, *Psychology and Religion*, in *Collected Works* (New York: Pantheon, 1953–), 2: 5–105; here paragraph 88.

20. Ibid., paragraphs 99–101.

21. Jung, "Concerning Mandala Symbolism," in *Collected Works*, 9:355–84; here paragraph 646.

22. *Journal of the Warburg and Courtauld Institutes* 2 (1938–39); reprinted in Rudolf Wittkower, *Allegory and the Migration of Symbols* (Boulder, Colo.: Westview Press, 1977), 15–44.

23. Jo Paoletti, "Dressing for Sexes," *Threads* 19 (1988): 98.

Notes to Chapter 4

1. Franz Boas, *Primitive Art* (1929; reprinted New York: Dover, 1955), 216.

2. Schuyler Cammann, *China's Dragon Robes* (New York: Ronald Press, 1952), 31 and passim.

3. Lisa Monnas, "Contemplate What Has Been Done: Silk Fabrics in Paintings by Jan van Eyck," *Halı* 60 (December 1991): 102–13.

4. Eleanor A. Saunders, "A Commentary on Iconoclasm in Several Print Series by Maarten van Heemskerck," *Simiolus* 10.2 (1978–79): 59–83 and fig. 21. Heemskerck's print shows a papal procession. To modern eyes the participants' expressions are so self-consciously sanctimonious that it is hard to believe the artist was not being satirical. Whether or not this is so, it is clear that the pattern on the chasuble is a central emblem of the pope's ritual power.

5. Gary Schwartz and Marten Jan Bok, *Pieter Saenredam: The Painter and His Time* (New York: Abbeville Press, 1989), 136 ff. and fig. 151. The church is the Mariakerk in Utrecht (no longer extant), known at the time as a hotbed of crypto-Catholicism.

6. Louise Hall Tharp, *Mrs. Jack* (Boston: Little, Brown, 1965), 133–35.

7. Trilling, "Medieval Interlace Ornament: The Making of a Cross-cultural Idiom."

8. Veblen, *Theory of the Leisure Class*, chap. 6.

9. Belief in the evil eye is widespread but *not* universal. See John M. Roberts, "Belief in the Evil Eye in World Perspective," in Clarence Maloney, ed., *The Evil Eye* (New York: Columbia University Press, 1976), 223–78, esp. 234 on the geographical distribution of the belief, which coincides to a remarkable extent with the distribution of interlace. Unfortunately, Roberts's survey lacks the chronological precision needed to relate them directly. Are interlace and belief in the evil eye recorded in a particular place at the same time, or a thousand years apart? Roberts

provides an extensive bibliography on the evil eye; see also Waldemar Déonna, *Le symbolisme de l'oeil* (Paris, 1965), 153 ff.

10. On the folklore of knots, see Karl-Heinz Clasen, "Die Überwindung des Bösen," in E. Fidder, ed., *Neue Beiträge deutscher Forschung: Wilhelm Worringer zum 60. Geburtstag* (Königsberg, 1943), 13–35. E. H. Gombrich makes a similar but more general argument in *The Sense of Order*, 162–63; most recently see Henry Maguire, "Garments Pleasing to God: The Significance of Domestic Textile Designs in the Early Byzantine Period," *Dumbarton Oaks Papers* 44 (1990): 215–24, esp. 216.

11. On the connection between knots and spells, see Hans Dieter Betz, *The Greek Magical Papyri in Translation* (Chicago: University of Chicago Press, 1986), 129–30; on the protective value of knots, see Mircea Eliade, "Le 'dieu lieur' et le symbolisme des noeuds," *Revue de l'histoire des religions* 134 (1947–48): 5–36, esp. 23–24; and on knots as charms in medieval Europe, see Clasen, "Die Überwindung des Bösen," 16.

12. W. W. Tarn, *Alexander the Great* (Cambridge: Cambridge University Press, 1948), 2: 262–65.

13. W. L. Hildburgh, "Indeterminability and Confusion as Apotropaic Elements in Italy and in Spain," *Folk-Lore*, 1944.

14. For the labyrinth in its broadest sense, as a convention of both art and literature, see Penelope Reed Doob's elegant study *The Idea of the Labyrinth from Classical Antiquity through the Middle Ages* (Ithaca: Cornell University Press, 1990).

15. In form, *hec arma* should be a neuter plural nominative or accusative, with *hec* a corruption of *haec*. (*Arma* in classical Latin is plural in form but singular in meaning.) However, the text makes sense only if we read *hec arma* as a feminine ablative singular, with *hec* a corruption of *hac*. It can now be partly translated: With this *arma* faith preserves the faithful from harm. As to the meaning of *arma*, it is by no means clear that a Latin so changed in form retained its classical nuances. Still, it is worth noting that while (according to Lewis and Short) *arma* could denote any kind of weapon used at close quarters, its primary meaning was a defensive weapon, especially a shield. Even if the classical sense of the word was lost, the phrasing still implies a defensive weapon. See Charlton T. Lewis and Charles Short, *A Latin Dictionary* (1879; Oxford: Clarendon Press, 1962).

16. B. Bischoff, "Kreuz und Buch im Frühmittelalter und in den ersten Jahrhunderten der spanische Reconquista," in *Bibliotheca docet: Festgabe für Carl Wehmer* (Amsterdam, 1963), 19–34; expanded version in Bischoff, *Mittelalterliche Studien*, vol. 2 (Stuttgart, 1967), 284–303 and pl. VII. Bischoff calls the inscription a rhythmic hexameter, but misses the rebus. The hexameter is in fact incomplete unless we read "*Crux hec arma fides inlesos servat fideles.*"

17. Cf. Jacqueline de Romilly, *Magic and Rhetoric in Ancient Greece* (Cambridge, Mass.: Harvard University Press, 1975).

18. Cf. St. Gall, Stiftsbibliothek, Ms 221, p. 1, where the same basic form is maintained, except

that four separate interlace compositions replace the blocks of text in the Heidelberg miniature (J. Duft and P. Meyer, *Die irische Miniaturen der Stiftsbibliothek St. Gallen* [Olten, Bern, and Lausanne: Urs Graf, 1953], 82 and pl. XLII).

19. I would like to thank Professor Maggie Bickford of Brown University for elucidating the relation between language and symbolism in China.

20. Gerhart B. Ladner, "Medieval and Modern Understanding of Symbolism," *Speculum* 54.2 (1979): 222–56; reprinted in Ladner, *Images and Ideas in the Middle Ages*, vol. 1 (Rome: Edizioni di storia e letteratura, 1983), 241–82.

21. M. J. Green, *The Wheel as a Cult-Symbol in the Romano-Celtic World* (Brussels: Latomus, 1984); Patrik Reuterswärd, "The Forgotten Symbols of God," *Konsthistorisk Tidskrift*, 1982, 103–25; 1985, 47–63 and 99–121; reprinted in Reuterswärd, *The Visible and Invisible in Art*.

22. See John Onians, *Bearers of Meaning: The Classical Orders in Antiquity, the Middle Ages, and the Renaissance* (Princeton: Princeton University Press, 1988); on the shift to Ionic in Athens, 15.

23. George Hersey, *The Lost Meaning of Classical Architecture* (Cambridge, Mass.: MIT Press, 1988), 31.

24. Ruskin, *The Stones of Venice*, vol. 1, chap. 2, sec. 12.

25. Hersey, *Lost Meaning*, 1.

26. Arthur Watson, *The Early Iconography of the Tree of Jesse* (Oxford: Oxford University Press, 1934).

27. Ladner, "Medieval and Modern Understanding of Symbolism" (see note 20 above); Hermann Schadt, *Die Darstellungen der Arbores Consanguinitatis und der Arbores Affinitatis* (Tübingen, 1982).

28. Watson, *Early Iconography*, chap. 1.

29. Ladner, "Medieval and Modern Understanding of Symbolism," 244–46.

30. Franz Cumont, *After Life in Roman Paganism* (New Haven: Yale University Press, 1922), esp. 200 ff.; Frazer, *The Golden Bough*, pt. IV, "Dying and Reviving Gods," secs. 277–78.

31. C. R. Dodwell, *The Canterbury School of Illumination, 1066–1200* (Cambridge: University Press, 1954), 88–90.

32. "Tractatus de Psalmo LXXXIIII," *Corpus Christianorum*, vol. 78, pt. 2 (Turnhout, 1958), 107.

Notes to Preface to Part II

1. Marion J. Levy, Jr., *Modernization: Latecomers and Survivors* (New York: Basic Books, 1972).

2. On the significance of craft (including ornament) for a modernizing society, see Oscar Lovell Triggs, *Chapters in the History of the Arts and Crafts Movement* (Chicago, 1902). This work

occupies a unique position. On the one hand, it may be the first to approach the ornament question as a topic in cultural history, not just a current debate. On the other hand, Triggs wrote *before* the modernist rebellion, and his book has none of the partisan shrillness that characterizes later studies of the topic. *Chapters in the History of the Arts and Crafts Movement* was reprinted in 1971 by Benjamin Blom, Inc., of New York, a gesture requiring some courage, but premature: its recent influence has been negligible.

3. Rae Beth Gordon, *Ornament, Fantasy, and Desire in Nineteenth-Century French Literature* (Princeton: Princeton University Press, 1992).

Notes to Chapter 5

1. For an eloquent summary of these views, focusing on the utopian enterprise in modernism—and its failure—see Robert Hughes, *The Shock of the New* (New York: Knopf, 1981), chap. 4.

2. Herbert Read, *Art and Industry* (4th [rev.] ed., London: Faber and Faber, 1956), 23. The rose engine did not get its name from the patterns it made, but from the rosette-shaped cams that guided the mechanism. There is no obvious visual connection between the shape of the rosette and the engraved pattern, and the same rosette can produce a variety of patterns. See Martin Matthews, *Engine Turning, 1680–1980* (London: M. Martin, 1984); also more generally, Robert S. Woodbury, *History of the Lathe to 1850* (Cambridge, Mass.: MIT, 1961), and Joseph Conners, "Ars Tornandi: Baroque Architecture and the Lathe," *Journal of the Warburg and Courtauld Institutes* 53 (1990): 217–36.

3. Sometimes even the most lavishly decorated object is fully functional. The Cleveland Museum of Art has an eighteenth-century microscope whose "lavish gilt bronze housing . . . remained so appealing in its sweeping Rococo flourishes that even when the optics were outmoded in the nineteenth century, they were laboriously altered and updated so that the instrument could continue to be used" (Penelope Hunter-Stiebel, *Louis XV and Madame de Pompadour: A Love Affair with Style* [Rosenberg and Stiebel, Inc.,] New York: 1990, 35).

4. Matthews, *Engine Turning*, 73 (quotation), 9–10 (lathes).

5. David Watkin, *Morality and Architecture* (Oxford: Clarendon Press, 1977).

6. For a contrary view, in which the functional strain in nineteenth-century design *does* lead to modernism, see Herwin Schaefer, *Nineteenth Century Modern: The Functional Tradition in Victorian Design* (New York: Praeger, 1970).

7. Nikolaus Pevsner, *Pioneers of Modern Design* (1936; Harmondsworth: Penguin, 1974), 40.

8. Nikolaus Pevsner, "High Victorian Design," originally published separately by the Architectural Press, London, 1951; reprinted in Pevsner, *Studies in Art, Architecture and Design*, vol. 2: *Victorian and After* (New York: Walker, 1968) 38–95; 44.

9. *The Art-Journal Illustrated Catalogue: The Industry of All Nations 1851*, London, 1851; reprinted under the title *The Crystal Palace Exhibition* (New York: Dover, 1970).

10. *Pioneers of Modern Design*, 20–21; 42 and pl. 1; 43 and pl. 3.

11. "High Victorian Design," 40; *Pioneers of Modern Design*, 134, italics mine.

12. Levy, *Modernization: Latecomers and Survivors*, 3. For the historical limits of the Industrial Revolution (as distinct from its still-unfolding consequences), see Asa Briggs, *Iron Bridge to Crystal Palace: Impact and Images of the Industrial Revolution* (London: Thames and Hudson, 1979). Humphrey Jennings, ed., *Pandaemonium, 1660–1886: The Coming of the Machine as Seen by Contemporary Observers* (London: Deutsch, 1985), is a highly personal anthology of texts from 1660 to 1886 on a variety of social, technological, political, and artistic issues connected with industrialization.

13. Pevsner's fig. 115; *Catalogue*, 225; Wyatt, *The Industrial Arts of the Nineteenth Century* (London, 1851), pl. LIII. Both the *Catalogue* and Wyatt's publication include a silver vase or centerpiece by J. Wagner and Son, of Berlin (*Catalogue*, 149; Wyatt, pl. XXXV). Pevsner takes his illustration of it (fig. 51) from a different source, a drawing of slightly higher quality than the one in the *Catalogue*.

14. J. B. Waring, *Masterpieces of Industrial Art and Sculpture at the International Exhibition, 1862*, 3 vols. (London: Day and Son, 1863).

15. Cf. Simon Jervis, *High Victorian Design* (Ottawa: National Gallery of Canada, 1974). This interesting attempt to rehabilitate Victorian decorative art goes so far as to classify objects strictly according to the styles they imitate: Gothic, Renaissance, etc. "Bad taste" is thereby banished, and with it any suggestion that nineteenth-century designers loved to combine many styles in the same setting, even in the same object. Ridiculous as such combinations may seem now, they were the lifeblood of Victorian art. Without them, only an impeccable, bloodless shadow is left.

16. Mary Merrifield, "The Harmony of Colours as Exemplified in the Exhibition," one of the introductory essays in the *Art-Journal Catalogue*.

17. Whitney Walton, *France at the Crystal Palace: Bourgeois Taste and Artisan Manufacture in the Nineteenth Century* (Berkeley: University of California Press, 1992).

18. "Ornament und verbrechen" (*sic:* Loos rejected the German convention of capitalizing all nouns). For its early publication history see Kirk Varnedoe, *Vienna 1900: Art, Architecture, and Design* (New York: Museum of Modern Art, 1986), 229, n. 33. Contrary to some authorities, the essay was not *published* in 1908. Loos gave it as a lecture several times between 1908 and 1913; the first publication was in 1910 in the Berlin journal *Der Sturm*. For its background and impact, see Reyner Banham, "Ornament and Crime: The Decisive Contribution of Adolf Loos," *Architectural Review* 121 (February 1957): 85–88; Banham, *Theory and Design in the First Machine Age* (New York: Praeger, 1960), 88–97; Benedetto Gravagnuolo, *Adolf Loos: Theory and Works* (New York: Rizzoli, 1988), 66 ff. (originally published in Italian, Milan, 1982); Burkhard Rukschcio and Roland Schachel, *Adolf Loos: Leben und Werk* (Salzburg and Vienna: Residenz Verlag, 1982). "Ornament and Crime" appears in Loos's second volume of essays, *Trotzdem*

(Innsbruck, 1931; reprinted, Vienna, 1982, 1988). The exhibition catalogue, *The Architecture of Adolf Loos* (London: Arts Council of Great Britain, 1985, 1987), includes an English translation of the essay. A more recent version appears in Loos, *Ornament and Crime: Selected Essays*, ed. Adolf Opel, trans. Michael Mitchell (Riverside, Calif.: Ariadne Press, 1998). Mitchell's is the more accurate translation, but inexplicably omits portions of the original text. I have used my own translations, as literal as grammar and clarity permit.

19. Banham, "Ornament and Crime," 88.

20. Ibid.

21. Oskar Kokoschka, "In Memory of Adolf Loos," in Ludwig Münz and Gustav Kunstler, *Adolf Loos: Pioneer of Modern Architecture* (New York: Praeger, 1966), 11.

22. The analogy as such was understood at once in some quarters. Cf. an anonymous article of 1910, reprinted in Adolf Opel, ed., *Konfrontationen: Schriften von und über Adolf Loos* (Vienna: G. Prachner, c. 1988), 37–39.

23. Loos, "Ornament and Crime." Writers on Loos tend to get carried away by his reputation as an *artistic* revolutionary. Among the few who have read his work carefully enough to see how much economic factors mattered to him are Robert Hughes (*The Shock of the New*, 168–69) and Naomi Schor (*Reading in Detail* [New York: Methuen, 1987], 50–54).

24. Ludwig Münz, *Adolf Loos* (Milan: Il Balcone, 1956), 36.

Notes to Chapter 6

1. Helen North, *Sophrosyne: Self-Knowledge and Self-Restraint in Greek Literature* (Ithaca: Cornell University Press, 1966), esp. 197 ff. As Aristotle said: "both excessive and defective exercise destroys the strength, and similarly drink or food which is above or below a certain amount destroys the health, while that which is proportionate both produces and increases and preserves it. So is it, then, in the case of temperance and courage and the other virtues. For the man who flies from and fears everything and does not stand his ground against anything becomes a coward, and the man who fears nothing at all but goes to meet every danger becomes rash; and similarly the man who indulges in every pleasure and abstains from none becomes self-indulgent, while the man who shuns any pleasure . . . becomes in a way insensible; temperance and courage, then, are destroyed by excess and defect, and preserved by the mean" (Aristotle, *Nicomachean Ethics*, trans. W. D. Ross, 2.2).

2. Herodotus, *Histories* 7.36 ff.; Aeschylus, *Persians* 11.718–52.

3. Thucydides, *History of the Peloponnesian War* 1.6. Note that the Greeks did not necessarily practice what they preached. A large body of personal adornment in precious materials survives from classical times. Golden grasshoppers are the least of it.

4. Arthur O. Lovejoy and George Boas, *Primitivism and Related Ideas in Antiquity* (Baltimore: Johns Hopkins Press, 1935).

5. Ronald L. Meek, *Social Science and the Ignoble Savage* (Cambridge: University Press, 1976).

6. Turgot, *A Philosophical Review of the Successive Advances of the Human Mind*, in Ronald L. Meek, ed. and trans., *Turgot on Progress, Sociology and Economics* (Cambridge: University Press, 1973), 42.

7. For this background to modern anthropology, see George W. Stocking, Jr., *Victorian Anthropology* (London: Collier Macmillan; New York: Free Press, 1987). Most recently see the articles gathered under the heading "Uttermost Ends of the Earth," *Antiquity* 66.252 (1992): 710 ff.

8. *Turgot on Progress, Sociology and Economics*, 42.

9. *The Journal of Captain James Cook on His Voyages of Discovery*, vol. 2: *The Voyage of the Resolution and Adventure, 1772–1775*, ed. J. C. Beaglehole (Cambridge: University Press, for the Hakluyt Society, 1961), 255.

10. *Missions to the Niger*, vol. 3: *The Bornu Mission, 1822–25*, pt. II, ed. E. W. Bovill (Cambridge: University Press, for the Hakluyt Society, 1966), 532.

11. Ibid., 531.

12. Edward Burnett Tylor, *Primitive Culture*, 5th ed. (London: John Murray, 1913), 1:31.

13. Owen Jones, *The Grammar of Ornament* (London, 1856; reprint, New York: Van Nostrand Reinhold, 1972), 16.

14. Hoxie Neale Fairchild, *The Noble Savage: A Study in Romantic Naturalism* (1928; reprint, New York: Russell and Russell, 1961), esp. 120–39.

15. Jean-Jacques Rousseau, *The First and Second Discourses*, ed. Roger D. Masters, trans. Roger D. and Judith R. Masters (New York: St. Martin's Press, 1964); page references in the text are to this edition.

16. Plato, *Republic* 7.514 ff.; cf. 10.596 ff., *Sophist* 236 ff.

17. Liudprand of Cremona, *Antapodosis* 6.5, 8; see Cyril Mango, ed., *The Art of the Byzantine Empire, 312–1453* (Toronto: University of Toronto Press, 1986), 209. On the question of what such artifice meant to the Byzantines themselves, see J. Trilling, "Daedalus and the Nightingale: Art and Technology in the Myth of the Byzantine Court," in Henry Maguire, ed., *Byzantine Court Culture from 829 to 1204* (Washington, D.C.: Dumbarton Oaks; dist. Harvard University Press, 1997), 217–30.

18. Ben Jonson, *Timber: Or Discoveries* (1641; reprint, London, 1923), 25–26.

19. Ornament itself has been condemned as "feminine." For the background of this idea see Schor, *Reading in Detail*, and Paul Mattick, Jr., "Beautiful and Sublime: *Gender Totemism* in the Constitution of Art," *Journal of Aesthetics and Art Criticism* 48.4 (1990): 293–303. Despite the jargonish title, Mattick's article is to be recommended for its clarity. A related factor in the modern revolt against ornament was the association of ornament with unhealthy sexuality. As Rae Beth Gordon shows in her book *Ornament, Fantasy, and Desire in Nineteenth-Century French Literature*, the sexual symbolism of ornament was worked out on many levels, not just in literary descriptions of ornament but in the calculated use of "ornamental" language: many of the same terms and judgments applied to both visual and verbal art. Although Gordon is more con-

cerned with the meanings attached to ornament than with the reasons for its downfall, her book leaves no doubt that the two were inseparable. The claustrophobic sensuality of ornament could be eliminated only by eliminating ornament itself. Functionalism was not a direct response to the sexual connotations of ornament, any more than it was a direct response to its perceived femininity, but it appeared at the right time and offered a convincing aesthetic excuse for a puritanical reaction.

20. E. H. Gombrich, "The Debate on Primitivism in Ancient Rhetoric," *Journal of the Warburg and Courtauld Institutes* 29 (1966): 24–38.

21. Ruskin, *The Seven Lamps of Architecture* (1849), chap. 2, "The Lamp of Truth."

22. Andrew L. Drummond, *The Church Architecture of Protestantism* (Edinburgh, 1934), is a partial exception, as well as being the most thorough and thoughtful survey of Protestant architecture.

23. John Phillips, *The Reformation of Images: Destruction of Art in England, 1535–1660* (Berkeley: University of California Press, 1973), 60 ff.

24. Gerald Parsons, "Reform, Revival and Realignment: The Experience of Victorian Anglicanism," in Parsons, ed., *Religion in Victorian Britain*, vol. 1: *Traditions* (Manchester: University of Manchester Press, 1988), 14–66.

25. Alan D. Gilbert, *Religion and Society in Industrial England: Church, Chapel, and Social Change, 1740–1914* (London: Longman, 1976).

26. Remarks on the lecture by J. Forbes Royle, "The Arts and Manufactures of India," in *Lectures on the Results of the [Great] Exhibition*, no. 11 (London: Royal Society of Arts, 1852), 401.

27. James F. White, *The Cambridge Movement: The Ecclesiologists and the Gothic Revival* (Cambridge: Cambridge University Press, 1962).

28. Drummond, *Church Architecture of Protestantism*, 72–74.

29. P. M. C. Forbes Irving, *Metamorphosis in Greek Myths* (Oxford: Clarendon Press, 1990).

30. St. Augustine, *The City of God* bk. 18, chap. 18.

31. Addison, *The Spectator*, no. 413, June 24, 1712; reprinted in *The Spectator*, ed. Donald F. Bond, vol. 3 (Oxford, 1965), 546–47.

32. Sir Isaac Newton, *Opticks*, 4th ed. (London, 1730), bk. 1, proposition II, definition (color); bk. 3, pt. I, query 16 ("deceptive" light effects). For the philosophical background and implications of Newton's optical discoveries, see E. A. Burtt, *The Metaphysical Foundations of Modern Physical Science*, rev. ed. (Garden City, N.Y.: Doubleday, 1954), 233–39. Addison, in the essay quoted above, did not refer directly to Newton, but to the philosopher John Locke. For Locke's contribution to the debate on the validity of sense impressions, see Frederick Copleston, *A History of Philosophy*, vol. 5, pt. 1 (Garden City, N.Y.: Doubleday, 1964), 97 ff. On the cultural repercussions of Newtonian science see Marjorie Hope Nicolson, *Newton Demands the Muse: Newton's Opticks and the Eighteenth Century Poets* (Princeton: Princeton University Press, 1946), esp. chap. 6.

33. Vitruvius *On Architecture* 5.3–4. Cf. the most famous medieval denunciation of fantastic ornament, by St. Bernard of Clairvaux (*Apologia* 12.29; Rudolph, *The "Things of Greater Importance,"* 283, 334–36). Like Vitruvius, Bernard appealed to common sense at its most literal-minded: it is absurd to depict things that do not exist. Bernard worried far less about fantasy and monstrosity in themselves than about their power to distract. He wrote specifically for monks, who were supposed to isolate themselves from the temptations of the world.

34. J. Ward-Perkins, "Nero's Golden House," *Antiquity* 30 (1956): 209–19; Nicole Dacos, *La Découverte de la Domus Aurea et la Formation des Grotesques à la Renaissance* (London: Warburg Institute, 1969). Photographs of the Domus Aurea paintings convey only a shadow of the excitement that early visitors to the site must have felt. A set of colored drawings from the eighteenth century, though unreliable in matters of condition and detail, recreates the decoration in all its splendor. See Marie-Noëlle Pinot de Villechenon, *Domus Aurea* (Milan: Franco Maria Ricci, 1998). For the integration of the grotesque as a specific ornamental type and as a general aesthetic category, see Martin M. Winkler, "Satire and the Grotesque in Juvenal, Arcimboldo and Goya," *Antike und Abendland* 37 (1991): 22–42.

35. Francisco de Hollanda, *Four Dialogues on Painting*, trans. A. F. G. Bell (Oxford, 1928), 60–63; David Summers, *Michelangelo and the Language of Art* (Princeton: Princeton University Press, 1981), 129–43.

36. Francis J. Cole, *A History of Comparative Anatomy* (London: Macmillan, 1944), 427–60; A. M. Luyendijk-Elshout, "Death Enlightened: A Study of Frederik Ruysch," *Journal of the American Medical Association* 212.1 (1970): 121–26; K. B. Roberts and J. D. W. Tomlinson, *The Fabric of the Body: European Traditions of Anatomical Illustration* (Oxford: Clarendon Press, 1992), 290–99. The contemporary publication, with illustrations, is Ruysch, *Thesaurus Anatomicus* (Amsterdam, 1701–10, with later supplements).

37. *Thesaurus Anatomicus*, II, tab. IV. A deeply disturbing image.

38. *Oeuvre de Juste Aurèle Meissonnier* (Paris, n.d. [c. 1750]), f. 36; reprinted, with an introduction by Dorothea Nyberg (New York: Blom, 1969).

39. Marie-Hélène Huet, "Monstrous Imagination: Progeny as Art in French Classicism," *Critical Inquiry* 17 (1991): 718–37.

40. Today *Forbidden Planet* seems uncomfortably retrograde in its treatment of the one female character, although her passivity is largely built into the plot as a reworking of Shakespeare's *The Tempest*. We should note that here it is the *father's* imagination, with a little help from alien technology, which calls the invisible, polymorphous, invincibly destructive monster into being.

41. Arthur O. Lovejoy, *The Great Chain of Being* (Cambridge, Mass.: Harvard University Press, 1936); Bentley Glass, Owsei Temkin, and William L. Straus, Jr., eds., *Forerunners of Darwin, 1745–1859* (Baltimore: Johns Hopkins Press, 1959).

42. Carolus Linnaeus, *Systema Naturae*, facsimile of the first edition, with English translation by M. S. J. Engel-Ledeboer and H. Engel (Nieuwkoop: De Graaf, 1964), 19. Aram Var-

tanian, "Tremblay's Polyp, La Mettrie, and Eighteenth-Century French Materialism," *Journal of the History of Ideas* 11 (1950): 259–86.

43. Lovejoy, *Great Chain of Being*, chap. 9; Glass et al., *Forerunners of Darwin*, esp. chaps. 5, 12, and 13; Emile Guyenot, *Les sciences de la vie aux XVIIème et XVIIIème siècles: l'idée d'evolution* (Paris: A Michel, 1941), 337 ff.

44. Lamarck, *Philosophie Zoologique*, trans. Hugh Eliot (London: Macmillan, 1914). Basic works on Lamarckism include Richard W. Burkhardt, Jr., *The Spirit of System: Lamarck and Evolutionary Biology* (Cambridge, Mass.: Harvard University Press, 1977); Goulven Laurant, *Paléontologie et évolution en France de 1800 à 1860: une histoire des idées de Cuvier et Lamarck à Darwin* (Paris, 1987); and Pietro Corsi, *The Age of Lamarck: Evolutionary Theories in France, 1790–1830* (Berkeley: University of California Press, 1988).

45. John Farley, *The Spontaneous Generation Controversy from Descartes to Oparin* (Baltimore: Johns Hopkins Press, 1977).

46. Lamarck, *Zoological Philosophy*, 35.

47. *D'Alembert's Dream*, trans. L. W. Tancock (Harmondsworth: Penguin, 1966), esp. 154, 174.

48. W. Chilton, "Theory of Regular Gradation," *The Oracle of Reason* (1841), 21. On Chilton's place in the atheist movement, see Edward Royle, *Victorian Infidels: The Origins of the British Secularist Movement, 1791–1866* (Manchester: University of Manchester Press, 1974), 123 ff.

49. "Private Property and Communism," in *Karl Marx: The Early Texts*, ed. and trans. D. McLellan (Oxford, 1971), 155–56. It is not altogether clear (and does not in fact matter to my argument) whether spontaneous generation was for Marx the specifically biological concept or a more general evolution of the physical world by purely natural laws. Marx used the term *generatio aequivoca*, which in his time was a synonym for spontaneous generation (Farley, *Spontaneous Generation*, 193, n. 1).

50. For a revealing study of this mindset, see Stephen Jay Gould, "Does the Stoneless Plum Instruct the Thinking Reed?" *Natural History*, April 1992, 16–25. For another illustration of the political implications that accrued to Lamarckism, see Julian Huxley, *Heredity, East and West: Lysenko and World Science* (New York: H. Schuman, 1949), esp. 182 ff. Doubtless the Lysenko affair did much to reinforce the popular equation of Lamarck with discredited science.

51. Kenneth Clark, *The Gothic Revival* (London and New York, 1928), 54–56.

52. Gottfried Semper, *Science, Industry and Art: Proposals for the Development of a National Taste in Art at the Closing of the London Industrial Exhibition*, in Semper, *The Four Elements of Architecture and Other Writings*, trans. H. F. Mallgrave and W. Herrmann (Cambridge: University Press, 1989), 130–67 (here 135).

53. Redgrave quoted in Barbara Morris, *Inspiration for Design: The Influence of the Victoria and Albert Museum* (London: The Museum, 1986), 20. For a more modulated but still firm stand against naturalism in ornament, see Gilbert R. Redgrave, *Manual of Design, Compiled from the*

Writings and Addresses of Richard Redgrave (London: Charles Dickens and Evans, Crystal Palace Press, 1876), 18, 58–59.

54. Chilton, "Theory of Regular Gradation," *The Oracle of Reason* (1842), 165–67.

Notes to Chapter 7

1. Clark, *Gothic Revival*, 54, 56.

2. Semper, *Industry and Art*, 134.

3. "Das prinzip der bekleidung [*sic*]" (1898); Loos, *Spoken into the Void*, trans. Jane O. Newman and John H. Smith (Cambridge, Mass.: MIT Press, 1982), 66–69.

4. In addition to works already cited, especially those of Pevsner and Read, see Siegfried Giedion, *Mechanization Takes Command* (New York: Oxford: University Press, 1948); Alf Bøe, *From Gothic Revival to Functional Form* (Oslo: Oslo University Press, 1957); and E. R. de Zurko, *Origins of Functionalist Theory* (New York: Columbia University Press, 1957).

5. "The Lesser Arts" (1878), in Morris, *News from Nowhere and Other Writings*, esp. 239–41.

6. Paine, *Common Sense* (1776), appendix.

7. Bernard Yack, *The Longing for Total Revolution: Philosophic Sources of Social Discontent from Rousseau to Marx and Nietzsche* (Princeton: Princeton University Press, 1986).

8. English translation by Gary Brown in Nietzsche, *Unmodern Observations*, ed. William Arrowsmith (New Haven: Yale University Press, 1990), 89.

9. Comte, *Cours de philosophie positive* (1830–42); condensed translation by Harriet Martineau, under the title *The Positive Philosophy of Auguste Comte* (New York and London, 1853), 1 ff. Even in this condensed form, Comte's arguments are sometimes diffuse and hard to follow. The classic summary of his ideas is John Stuart Mill, *Auguste Comte and Positivism* (London, 1866). On the influence of positivism see W. M. Simon, *European Positivism in the Nineteenth Century* (Ithaca: Cornell University Press, 1963).

10. *Positive Philosophy of Auguste Comte*, esp. 2:173 (positive stage); 2:298, 369 ff. (industry and progress).

11. "There must certainly be an inexhaustible resource of poetic greatness in the positive conception of Man as the supreme head of the economy of Nature, which he modifies at will, in a spirit of boldness and freedom, within no other limits than those of natural law" (ibid., 2: 560). When "Comte" is eloquent we usually have his translator to thank. In the sentence just quoted, what Comte really said is more like this: "There is certainly, for those who know how to appreciate it, an inexhaustible source of new poetic greatness in the positive conception of man as the supreme head of the natural economy, which he modifies unceasingly to his benefit, with wise boldness, fully liberated from all pointless scruple and oppressive terror, recognizing no general limits but those relating to the totality of positive laws unveiled by our intelligence; whereas until now humanity remained, in contrast, passively subject, in all regards, to an arbitrary out-

side force, on which its undertakings of whatever sort were forced to rely" (*Cours de philosophie positive*, 2d ed. [Paris, 1864], 6:761). For Comte this is a fairly short sentence.

12. *Positive Philosophy of Auguste Comte*, 1: 20.

13. Ibid., 2:140–44 and 430–32.

14. *Historicism* is the more familiar term. Although *historical eclecticism* is ponderous, it has the advantage of greater precision, and precision is badly needed here, because historicism can mean very different things. In common academic usage, historicism is the recognition that a cultural product—idea, work of art, etc.—does not exist in a vacuum, but is the result of specific historical circumstances and cannot be understood apart from them. In the visual arts, especially architecture, it refers to the systematic use of past styles. This is more or less what I mean by historical eclecticism, although my term emphasizes freedom of choice, and a general awareness of the past as a source of models, while historicism emphasizes correct and consistent use of a past style. Unfortunately, even in this restricted context, historicism is a loaded term. Pevsner, who is largely responsible for making it a technical term in architectural history, used it in a thoroughly pejorative sense, to denote what was worst in nineteenth-century building (Watkin, *Morality and Architecture*, 104–11). The taint still lingers, and frustrates any attempt to use historicism in a neutral sense.

Karl Popper's use of the word in *The Poverty of Historicism* (London: Routledge and Kegan Paul, 1957) is also pejorative, but in a different way. There it means predicting the future from the evidence of history, a technique Popper argued is not only unsound but politically dangerous (cf. Lincoln Steffens on the Soviet Union: "I have seen the future and it works"). Popper considered his own use of the term idiosyncratic, but if we recognize that historicism can look to the future as easily as to the past, it is quite consistent with earlier (primarily architectural) usage.

15. Levy, *Modernization: Latecomers and Survivors*, 42–51.

16. Roger Shattuck, *The Banquet Years: The Origins of the Avant Garde in France, 1885 to World War I* (1958; New York: Vintage Books, 1968), 18.

17. *London Quarterly Review* 66 (1840): 176–74. These passages form part of a digression in an article entitled "The Fine Arts in Florence." The article is unsigned; for the attribution to Palgrave, see Briggs, *Iron Bridge to Crystal Palace*, 170.

18. Wyatt, *The Industrial Arts of the Nineteenth Century*, p. vii; William Whewell, *The General Bearing of the Great Exhibition on the Progress of Art and Science* (London, 1852). This point of view survives as an interpretation of the growth of industry: more and more people wanted *good* things, providing an incentive for large-scale manufacture. See John U. Nef, *Cultural Foundations of Industrial Civilization* (Cambridge: University Press, 1958), chap. 6; David A. Hounshell, *From the American System to Mass Production, 1800–1932* (Baltimore: Johns Hopkins Press, 1984), chap. 8. For the theoretical basis of the phenomenon, see Lloyd A. Fallers, "A Note on the 'Trickle Effect,'" *Public Opinion Quarterly* 18 (1954): 314–21.

19. Whewell, *General Bearing*, 14.

20. Ruskin, *The Stones of Venice*, vol. 2, chap. 6, secs. 19 and 20. As early as Plato (*Phaedrus* 260e), we find *technē* (skill, craft or method, with an emphasis on understanding) contrasted with *tribē* (literally "rubbing": in other words, patience and sandpaper).

21. Jeffrey M. Muller, "Measures of Authenticity: The Detection of Copies in the Early Literature on Connoisseurship," in *Retaining the Original: Multiple Originals*, *Copies, and Reproductions*. Washington, D.C.: National Gallery of Art; dist. University Press of New England, 1989), 1941–49.

22. Linda M. Austin, *The Practical Ruskin: Economics and Audience in the Late Work* (Baltimore: Johns Hopkins Press, 1991), 4–5, 187–88. On the more general implications of reproducibility for modern visual culture, see Walter Benjamin, "The Work of Art in the Age of Mechanical Reproduction," first published in 1936, reprinted in Benjamin, *Illuminations*, trans. Harry Zohn (New York: Harcourt, Brace and World, 1969).

23. *The Theory of the Leisure Class*, esp. chap. 6. Veblen's observations are still true on balance, but the nuances are more complex. Paisley shawls are now collectors' items. It is possible to rationalize this on the basis of their age and rarity, but that is not the point: they *are* machine-made. For a clear indication that status value is not always a matter of age or handwork, though it may be a function of relative (and deliberate) scarcity, see "Fueling a Frenzy: Swatch," *New York Times*, Sunday, May 10, 1992, sec. 9, p. 1. The print market, which has flourished since the Renaissance, is a less reliable gauge because the sense of handwork is never completely absent. The processes require direct intervention of a kind that is likely to affect the artistic result. The same is true of photography.

24. Ruskin, *The Stones of Venice*, vol. 1, appendix 17; Ruskin's italics.

25. Emil Lederer, "Labor," *Encyclopedia of the Social Sciences* (New York: Macmillan, 1932).

26. I follow Marion J. Levy, Jr., in using the term *modernization* rather than *industrialization* in this context. Levy defines modernization as the supplanting of animate by inanimate sources of power on a wide scale. Historically, modernization includes industrialization, but it is a more general term, denoting a complex of social and cultural phenomena inseparable from the growth of machine-based industry but not identical to it (Levy, *Modernization: Latecomers and Survivors*). For an early but still amazingly apt critique of modernized society, see Veblen, *The Instinct of Workmanship* (New York, 1914), chap. 7.

27. A highly readable introduction to the Industrial Revolution from a cultural as well as economic standpoint is Asa Briggs, *Iron Bridge to Crystal Palace* (with excellent bibliography). For the changes and conflicts in historical interpretation see R. M. Hartwell, "Interpretations of the Industrial Revolution in England: A Methodological Inquiry," *Journal of Economic History* 19 (1959): 229–49, and David Cannadine, "The Present and the Past in the English Industrial Revolution," *Past and Present* 103 (1984): 131–72. On the origins of the Industrial Revolution, and the reasons why it happened in England, see François Crouzet, *Britain Ascendant: Comparative Studies in Franco-British Economic History* (Cambridge: University Press, 1990). S. Lilley, *Men,*

Machines, and History (New York: International Publishers, 1966), gives a brief but clear account of the main technological developments.

28. Toshio Kusamitsu, "British Industrialization and Design Before the Great Exhibition," *Textile History* 12 (1981): 77–95 (here 82).

29. Adam Smith, *An Inquiry into the Nature and Causes of the Wealth of Nations* (1776), bk. 1; *The Positive Philosophy of Auguste Comte*, 2:140 ff; Emile Durkheim, *The Division of Labor in Society* (first published 1893), English translation by George Simpson (New York, 1933).

30. *The Positive Philosophy of Auguste Comte*, 2:144. The topos of the pinmaker goes back at least to Adam Smith, who considered the benefits of the division of labor to be self-evident. In his example it enables ten workers, with appropriate machinery, to produce forty-eight thousand pins in a day's work, the equivalent of 4,800 per worker, whereas a worker who was obliged to carry out the entire process alone would be hardpressed to make a single pin in the same time (*The Wealth of Nations*, bk. 1, chap. 1).

31. Karl Marx, *Capital* (*Das Kapital*), vol. 1, 1867, chaps 13–15. Page numbers refer to the translation by Ben Fowkes (London: Pelican Books, 1976; Penguin Classics, 1990).

32. Marx, "Alienated Labor," in Lloyd D. Easton and Kurt H. Guddat, eds. and trans., *Writings of the Young Marx on Philosophy and Society* (Garden City, N.Y.: Doubleday, 1967), 287–301. For the idea of alienation and its philosophical background, see Eugene Kamenka, *The Ethical Foundations of Marxism* (London and Boston: Routledge and Kegan Paul, 1962, 1972); and Isidor Wallimann, *Estrangement: Marx's Conception of Human Nature and the Division of Labor* (Westport, Conn.: Greenwood Press, 1981).

33. Hegel, *The Phenomenology of Mind*, trans. J. B. Baillie, with an introduction by George Lichtheim (New York, 1967), 229–40. For a brief explanation of this passage see Frederick Copleston, *A History of Philosophy*, vol. 7, pt. 1, 222.

34. Marx, "Alienated Labor," 289.

35. Ibid., 289–90, 291.

36. *Writings of the Young Marx*, 422–23. Cf. Wallimann, *Estrangement*, chap. 6.

37. Ruskin, "The Nature of Gothic," in *The Stones of Venice*, vol. 2, chap. 6, sec. 16.

38. For a survey of working conditions for the various crafts in late medieval England, see Heather Swanson, *Medieval Artisans: An Urban Class in Late Medieval England* (Oxford and New York: Basil Blackwell, 1989). For the increasingly regimented and systematic character of craftwork before the Industrial Revolution proper, see F. F. Mendels, "Proto-Industrialization: The First Phase of the Industrialization Process," *Journal of Economic History* 32 (1972): 241–61. For the hardships endured by the Kashmir shawl weavers, see Irwin, *The Kashmir Shawl*, 6–9.

39. Hartwell, "Interpretations of the Industrial Revolution in England," 245.

40. E. P. Thompson, *The Making of the English Working Class* (New York: Vintage Books, 1963), 306.

41. William H. Lazonick, "Industrial Relations and Technical Change: The Case of the Self-

Acting Mule," *Cambridge Journal of Economics* 3 (1979): 231–62; Lazonick, "Industrial Relations, Work Organization and Technological Change: U.S. and British Cotton Spinning," Harvard Institute of Economic Research, Discussion Paper 774 (1980); W. H. Chaloner, *The Skilled Artisans During the Industrial Revolution*, pamphlet of the Historical Association (London, 1969).

42. Patrick M. Malone, "Little Kinks and Devices at Springfield Armory, 1892–1918," *IA, Journal of the Society for Industrial Archeology* 14 (1988): 23–35 and 59–76.

43. "In a general way, the relation in which the skilled worker in the large industries stands to the machine process is analogous to that in which the primitive herdsman, shepherd or dairymaid stood to the domestic animals under their care, rather than to the relation of the craftsman to his tools. It is a work of attendance, furtherance and skilled interference rather than a forceful and dexterous use of an implement" (*Instinct of Workmanship*, 307 n.).

44. Joseph Gutteridge, *Lights and Shadows in the Life of an Artisan* (Coventry, 1893); reprinted in Valerie E. Chancellor, *Master and Artisan in Victorian England* (New York: A. M. Kelley, 1969), 101–2.

45. For a radically different interpretation of the British economy in the nineteenth century, in which handwork continued to play a central role, see Raphael Samuel, "Mechanization and Hand Labour in Industrializing Britain," *History Workshop* 3 (1977): 6–72.

46. *The Stones of Venice*, vol. 2, chap. 6, sec. 16.

47. R. G. Collingwood, *The Principles of Art* (Oxford: Clarendon Press, 1938), v; see also Christopher Janaway, "Arts and Crafts in Plato and Collingwood," *Journal of Aesthetics and Art Criticism* 50 (1992): 45–54.

Notes to Chapter 8

1. For some examples of the "new" tattooing, see Chris Wroblewski, *Skin Shows: The Art of Tattoo* (London: W. H. Allen, 1990); and William DeMichele, *The Illustrated Woman* (Albany, N.Y.: Proteus Press, 1992).

2. Richard Dorment, *Alfred Gilbert: Sculptor and Goldsmith*, catalogue of an exhibition at the Royal Academy of Arts (London, 1986). Gilbert is best known for the Shaftesbury Fountain in Piccadilly Circus, with its landmark statue of Eros. Students of ornament would do well to look more closely at the fountain itself.

3. Linda Merrill, *A Pot of Paint: Aesthetics on Trial in "Whistler v. Ruskin"* (Washington, D.C.: Smithsonian Institution Press with the Freer Gallery of Art, 1992).

4. For an example of this principle in action long after it had lost its revolutionary force, see James F. O'Brien, *How to Design by Accident* (New York: Dover, 1968).

5. For the Chinese background of this convention of spontaneity, see Charles Lachman, "'The Image Made by Chance' in China and the West: Ink Wang Meets *Jackson Pollock's Mother*," *Art Bulletin* 74:3 (September 1992): 499–510.

6. Ryoichi Fujioka, *Tea Ceremony Utensils* (New York: Weatherhill, 1973).

7. Widar Halén, *Christopher Dresser* (Oxford: Phaidon/Christie's, 1990), 17.

8. Ibid., 142.

9. Christopher Dresser, *Japan: Its Architecture, Art, and Art Manufactures* (London, 1882; reprinted under the title *Traditional Arts and Crafts of Japan* [New York: Dover, 1994]), 157 ff. (tea ceremony); 371 (*raku*).

10. Ibid., 159.

11. Wilhelm Worringer, *Abstraktion und Einfühlung* (Munich, 1908); English translation by Michael Bullock as *Abstraction and Empathy* (New York: International Universities Press, 1953). On Worringer's concept of abstraction, see J. Trilling, "Medieval Art Without Style? Plato's Loophole and a Modern Detour," *Gesta* 34.1 (1995): 57–62; and "The Tyranny of Style," *Common Knowledge* 4.2 (Fall 1995): 108–14.

12. The term "Damascus steel" refers to two quite different techniques. "Oriental" or "true" Damascus displays a light-and-dark crystalline pattern on its surface, while in "mechanical" or "pattern-welded" Damascus the pattern is formed by two separate alloys which turn different colors when etched. Both techniques are controllable within limits: the overall effects remain indeterminate, but a skillful smith can decide whether the major elements will be large or small, tight or loose, predictable or unpredictable. Of the two types, only pattern-welded Damascus has a long (if somewhat sporadic) history in Western craft. See Leo S. Figiel, *On Damascus Steel* (Atlantis, Fla.: Atlantis Arts Press, 1991). The last quarter of the twentieth century saw a revival of interest in pattern-welded knives for both display and use. Most makers follow the principle of controlled indeterminacy, but a few, notably Daryl Meier, Stephen Schwarzer, and Hank Knickmeyer in the United States, Pierre Reverdy in France, and Conny Persson in Sweden, have managed, with extraordinary effort, to create fully controlled patterns and even representational images in the two-colored steel. Once again, artists and patrons have a choice: to go "with" or "against" what are popularly seen as the intrinsic demands of the material.

On marbled paper, see Richard J. Wolfe, *Marbled Paper: Its History, Techniques, and Patterns* (Philadelphia: University of Pennsylvania Press, 1990).

13. Benedetto Gravagnuolo, *Adolf Loos* (New York: Rizzoli, 1988 [first published in Italian, Milan, 1982]), 125–33.

14. Abbott Thayer wrote only a few brief articles on camouflage. The definitive account of his ideas is a book by his son, Gerald H. Thayer, *Concealing-Coloration in the Animal Kingdom* (New York, 1909). The second edition, 1918, includes an account of the military uses of camouflage in the First World War.

In light of what we have learned about indeterminacy, Rudyard Kipling's well-known fable about the origin of camouflage, "How the Leopard Got His Spots" (1901) strikes a distinctly "modern" note:

So they waited till dark, and then the Leopard heard something breathing sniffily in the starlight that fell all stripy through the branches, and he jumped at the noise, and it smelt like Zebra, and it felt like Zebra, and when he knocked it down it kicked like Zebra, but he couldn't see it. So he said, "Be quiet, O you person without any form. I am going to sit on your head till morning, because there is something about you I don't understand."

Presently he heard a grunt and a crash and a scramble, and the Ethiopian called out, "I've caught a thing I can't see. It smells like Giraffe, and it kicks like Giraffe, but it hasn't any form."

"Don't you trust it," said the Leopard. "Sit on its head till the morning—same as me. They haven't any form—any of 'em."

—Just So Stories (New York, 1903), 56.

15. Cf. D'Arcy Wentworth Thompson, *On Growth and Form* (Cambridge: University Press, 1917), chap. 16; Lancelot Law Whyte, ed., *Aspects of Form* (London: Pellegrini and Cudahy, 1951), especially the essay by C. H. Waddington.

16. Jack Cowart, Jack D. Flam, Dominique Fourcade, and John Hallmark Neff, *Henri Matisse: Paper Cut-Outs* (St. Louis: St. Louis Art Museum, 1977).

17. Karl Jettmar, *Art of the Steppes* (New York: Crown, 1967); Sergei I. Rudenko, *Frozen Tombs of Siberia* (Berkeley: University of California Press, 1970).

Notes to Epilogue

1. Clarence John Laughlin, *The Personal Eye* (Philadelphia: n.p., 1973), Group U: American Victorian Architecture.

2. Peter White, "Between a Rescuing Coast and a Drifting Boat," notes written in collaboration with Barbara Todd, to accompany the installation *A Bed Is a Boat*, of which *Adam's Boat* was a part, at the Museum for Textiles, Toronto, 1997.

Bibliography of Ornament

E. H. Gombrich's *The Sense of Order* (Ithaca: Cornell University Press, 1979) is the best-known recent book on ornament, and the most widely misunderstood. Readers have flocked to it, drawn by the magnificent illustrations and the author's deserved reputation for clarity and insight. Most are looking for an introduction to the subject. They will not find it there. The book's subtitle, *A Study in the Psychology of Decorative Art*, should be fair warning. Anyone who approaches it with the wrong expectations will emerge exhilarated but bewildered. *The Sense of Order* is a book to read *after* one has learned something about the mechanics and history of ornament.

The same is true of Oleg Grabar's *The Mediation of Ornament* (Princeton: Princeton University Press, 1992). For the general reader, the focus on Islamic art may limit the book's accessibility and applicability. Eva Wilson's *8000 Years of Ornament* (London: British Museum Press, 1994) represents a very different approach. It belongs to the tradition of pattern books, anthologies of ornament intended more for the use of artists than historians. By a quirk of fate, many such books are available today, the only genre of ornament book to survive the modernist purge. Since late twentieth-century taste in ornament is almost an oxymoron, most are reprints of nineteenth-century works. Wilson's book is the exception, a truly up-to-date pattern book. It shows, if I may put it so, what people of our time might like if they liked ornament, and the difference from earlier books is illuminating. Unfortunately the choice of patterns is weakened by the decision to use line drawings throughout. This is very much in the pattern-book tradition, and the drawings, all by Wilson herself, are a tour de force. Nevertheless, line drawings inevitably give a one-sided impression of "pure" patterns divorced from the materials, colors, and ultimately the styles of the original objects.

For anything like a general introduction to ornament in the earlier literature, we must turn to A. H. Christie's *Pattern Design* (1929; reprint, New York: Dover, 1969). As the title suggests, the focus is the classification and analysis of patterns. The treatment is clear and wide-ranging, but we miss any sense of the historical development or cultural meaning of ornament. Also, many interesting styles are unrepresented. A comparison with Wilson's book reminds us how dramatically tastes can change.

The best guide to "reading" ornamental patterns is still *Primitive Art* by Franz Boas (1929; reprint, New York: Dover, 1955; feel free to disregard the title). The section on the art of the Northwest Coast Indians is especially good. Its lessons on how representational art, ornament, and functional design are related can be applied to virtually any style.

Several recent books deal with ornament in specific cultures. *Ornament: A Social History Since 1450* by Michael Snodin and Maurice Howard (New Haven: Yale University Press, 1996), and *Form and Decoration: Innovation in the Decorative Arts, 1470-1870* by Peter Thornton (London: Weidenfeld, 1998), focus on postmedieval western Europe. The two books complement each other. Taking a formal approach, Thornton has produced an authoritative, contemporary history of his material. In contrast, Snodin and Howard concentrate on the meanings and applications of ornament in a broader sense of the term than I have chosen to use, comprising not just patterns but jewelry and other forms of adornment.

Approximately the same period and territory are covered in two lavish volumes edited by Alain Gruber: *The Renaissance and Mannerism in Europe* (New York, London, and Paris: Abbeville Press, 1994), and *Classicism and the Baroque in Europe* (New York, London, and Paris: Abbeville Press, 1996). Unequaled as visual anthologies, they also give a clear account of the major trends in European ornament.

For non-Western ornamental traditions, see Jessica Rawson, *Chinese Ornament: The Lotus and the Dragon* (London: British Museum Publication, 1984), and Eva Baer, *Islamic Ornament* (New York: New York University Press, 1998). Neither is definitive, but they differ from other studies of Chinese and Islamic art in being *about* ornament instead of just including it.

Two classic works on ornament have been translated from the German. Alois Riegl's *Problems of Style* (*Stilfragen*, 1893; translation by Evelyn Kain, with an introduction and notes by David Castriota [Princeton: Princeton University Press, 1992]) is the most famous. Despite its reputation as the cornerstone of the art-historical study of ornament, for a whole century it remained unavailable in English. Although deeply embedded in old debates, it is still the standard account of continuity and change in the history of ornament. Josef Strzygowski's *Origin of Christian Church Art* (*Ursprung der christlichen Kirchenkunst*, 1919; translation by O. M. Dalton and H. J. Braunholtz, 1923; reprint New York: Hacker Art Books, 1973) offers a very different perspective. Dealing with the aesthetic and symbolic—above all, religious—significance of ornament on a supranational scale across virtually all of ancient Eurasia, it is in many ways the most important book ever written on ornament as cultural expression. It is also one of the most controversial, and unquestionably the hardest because it presumes familiarity, not just with the history of ornament but with Strzygowski's earlier interpretations of that history. Strzygowski was a controversial thinker in his own time, but even then few scholars had the breadth of learning to judge his work. The situation is much worse today. Not only is ornament in disrepute, but scholarly specialization has eclipsed the cross-cultural and cross-disciplinary studies that Strzygowski pioneered. Worse still, his arguments have a racial cast, making them hard to read dispassionately.

If I mention him here, it is to set a goal. Strzygowski confronted some of the central questions in the large-scale history of ornament: What is the significance of subject matter? How can we balance similarities and differences in defining the relation between styles? And to what extent do cognate styles imply other cultural affinities? We too must confront these questions, and though we may postpone our answer, sooner or later the future of ornament studies will turn on whether we decide Strzygowski was mostly right or mostly wrong. We shall know that the field is reborn when a new generation of scholars is able to defend or refute him in something like his own terms.

Ornament never exists in a vacuum. It is rooted in society, and its strongest roots are craftsmanship and taste. Through them, society calls ornament into being, gives it physical form, launches it into the world and determines its subsequent fate. Although craftsmanship in its social setting is widely if sporadically studied, the nature of craft itself is far more elusive. *The Art of the Maker* by Peter Dormer (London: Thames and Hudson, 1994) is a fascinating inquiry into the intuitive, nonverbal character of craft, addressing such questions as what the skills of the maker consist of, how they are acquired, and how they differ from other kinds of knowledge.

No one interested in the meaning of taste can ignore Thorstein Veblen's *The The-*

ory of the Leisure Class (1899). It is eccentric, tendentious, and satirical, the only classic of social science that is also a classic of humorous writing. *Taste Today*, by Peter Lloyd Jones (Oxford: Pergamon, 1991), is a far more balanced and systematic study, though restricted, as the title implies, to the modern world (actually the modern West). Together, these books provide an introduction to the human context of ornament, from the double perspective of its creators and its consumers.

Most recently, James Trilling's *The Language of Ornament* (London and New York: Thames and Hudson, 2001) is a profusely illustrated, less technical companion to the present volume, emphasizing the worldwide evolution and variety of ornamental styles over problems of meaning and cultural implications.

Index